'Leaders and consultants in organisational change across the world continue to work diligently with the best intentions, only to encounter one or more of disillusionment, disengagement and business failure. Deeper understanding of the dynamics at work and more effective approaches to facilitate change are urgently needed. This book delivers both, with practical insight based on rich experience and a deep grasp of theory and method. For any leader or change practitioner involved in the apparently intractable mess and anxiety of organisational change, this book could be the fresh breeze of sanity you crave.'

— *Tom Kenward, Programme Director, Roffey Park Institute, UK*

'Andrew Day has done a superb, perhaps unique, job of integrating various fields of knowledge – psychology, sociology, social psychology, anthropology, philosophy, applied behaviour science – to expand his readers' understanding of the disruptive effect change has on people's psychological state. Each chapter offers clear exposition of theories and concepts, backed up by illustrative stories which increase his readers' desire to do things differently. Time has come for all of us to do our part to support not just organisations, but social networks and communities, in re-establishing a more connected, compassionate way of relating – to rebuild a stronger social fabric for human beings to thrive in this constantly changing world. No doubt that is Andrew's purpose in writing this book.'

— *L. Mee-Yan Cheung-Judge, BSc, MA, Ph.D.,*
Fellow of Roffey Park Institute, UK

'The time is right for this wonderful book. Never before has disruption been such a part of our lives, and never before has there been such a need for human connection and collaboration. This book points the way towards a place where that connection and collaboration might be truly possible. Not only is this needed at an organisational level to encourage generative work and commercial success but perhaps more importantly it is needed at an individual level to give us all a way of dealing with the alienation and anxiety disconnection brings.'

— *Brian Marshall, Organisation and Change Discipline Lead,*
Hult Ashridge Executive Education, UK

'*Disruption, Change and Transformation in Organisations: A Human Relations Perspective* is a deeply thoughtful synthesis of social psychology, leadership, organization theory and philosophy from someone who has been on the front lines of guiding significant organizational change. Issues of human identity and sense-making are the key ingredients that weave together both an understanding of why planned change is so difficult, and the many recommendations for how to do a better job of it. It is appropriate for use both in university courses, and by managers and consultants who want more than simplistic formulas.'

— *Gervase R. Bushe, Ph.D., Beedie School of Business,*
Simon Fraser University, Canada

D1590926

Disruption, Change and Transformation in Organisations

This book explores the psychological and social dynamics of continuous, disruptive and discontinuous change. It examines the emotional strain and challenges of disruption, studies the nature of organisation transformation and examines what can be done to develop an organisation's capacity to adapt and thrive in turbulent environments.

An organisation's long-term survival increasingly rests on its adaptive capacity, its ability to continuously change and transform itself. Yet, people experience ongoing and fundamental change as disorientating and unsettling because it challenges accepted assumptions and identities. This book assists leaders and change practitioners to understand these dynamics, help people to make sense of change and to create the conditions that enable people to self-organise and creatively adapt.

With case studies and personal accounts from individuals and companies, this is an ideal resource for practitioners and managers dealing with organisational change, as well as students, academics and researchers.

Andrew Day is an Organisation Development Consultant and Executive Coach who works with individuals, teams and organisations to support their development and growth. He is a partner with Metalogue Consulting.

Disruption, Change and Transformation in Organisations

A Human Relations Perspective

Andrew Day

Routledge
Taylor & Francis Group

LONDON AND NEW YORK

First published 2020
by Routledge
2 Park Square, Milton Park, Abingdon, Oxon OX14 4RN

and by Routledge
52 Vanderbilt Avenue, New York, NY 10017

Routledge is an imprint of the Taylor & Francis Group, an informa business

British Library Cataloguing-in-Publication Data
A catalogue record for this book is available from the British Library

Library of Congress Cataloging-in-Publication Data
A catalog record has been requested for this book

ISBN: 978-0-367-25302-8 (hbk)
ISBN: 978-0-367-25305-9 (pbk)
ISBN: 978-0-429-28708-4 (ebk)

Typeset in Bembo
by Newgen Publishing UK

Πάντα ῥεῖ
'Everything Flows'
Heraclitus
500 BC

Contents

PART 3
Transformation, learning and adaptation   145

Acknowledgements

I would like to thank both Kathleen King and Liz Wiggins for their support and critique when I was developing my thinking for the book. I am also grateful to my fellow partners at Metalogue, Kevin, Sophy, Sarah, Dev and Simon, for their valuable contributions to my thinking about organisations and their practical insights about organisational change and development. I am particularly indebted to Simon Martin who provided his comments, feedback and reactions to the draft manuscript for the book. Much of my thinking in this book has been influenced by other writers and practitioners in the field of organisation development and the social sciences and by my ex-colleagues from Ashridge Business School. They are too many to single out. I have not been able to acknowledge all the sources or influences on my writing. I apologise in advance if I have not given due credit to others' ideas or perspectives.

Finally, and most importantly, I am eternally grateful to my wife, Georgia, for her love, patience and support throughout the years of researching and writing this book.

1   Introduction

We are currently experiencing a period of ongoing and disruptive change as we move from the industrial into the digital age, and globalisation continues unabated. We stand on the edge of another breakthrough in technology which the World Economic Forum has called the Fourth Industrial Revolution. This involves the application of digital technology, artificial intelligence, machine learning and quantum computing to transform society and how work is done. We are only starting to see the impact of these new technologies and the possibilities of disruption and transformation they will bring. In this context, the central challenge facing contemporary organisations is how to adapt quickly enough to respond to these profound shifts.

In stark contrast to today, if we look back over the history of humanity, for most of the time, whilst life was unpredictable, the dominant social order remained relatively stable. For the first 70,000 years of human life we existed in small groupings of hunter gathers. Approximately 30,000 years ago, small agricultural settlements started to emerge. It has only been in the past 300–400 years that we have witnessed more dramatic periods of social upheaval with the formation of cities, the industrialisation of society, the acceleration of technological developments and globalisation. This exponential shift in the rate of change is unambiguously clear if we examine how the speed of travel has changed for mankind over the millennia. For most of our existence, this was limited to walking and running speeds; this changed when humans mastered the horse, increasing in both speed and range of travel. This situation remained static until the discovery of the wheel and the design of the chariot, which led to an incremental increase in travel speed. It was not until the invention of the steam engine at the start of 18th century that the speed of change started to increase dramatically. Talking of the rate of change in this way presents it in absolute terms. Our experience of change, however, is relative to our concept of stability. Nevertheless, I think it is safe to argue that our lived experience of change is that it is accelerating and that our lives and organisations are becoming increasingly unstable and unpredictable.

It is human nature to desire continuity and order. We have a need for coherence in our lives and to understand our place in the social order. Change disrupts familiarity and challenges our sense of self. Our first response is often to attempt to re-establish order. When this is not possible, we are thrown into a paradoxical struggle to find continuity in the face of change as we grieve the loss of the familiar and have to acknowledge and adapt to the reality of what is emerging and unfolding. In the early 1970s, the sociologist and futurologist Alvin Toffler (Toffler, 1970) coined the term 'future shock' to reflect the stress and disorientation that we experience when we are subjected to too much change in too short a time. He described this as a feeling of impermanence that arises with the premature arrival of the future. We each therefore experience an inherent tension between the dynamic nature of modern life and our capacity to adapt. This represents a fundamental conflict between holding onto the past and moving on. At an individual, organisational and societal level, we are at risk of exceeding our capacity to adapt to change.

We already know a great deal about the difficulties people faced in adapting to disruptions to the social order brought about during previous periods of social upheaval. Karl Marx (1844 [1964]) wrote about how the early period of industrialisation brought about alienation for many workers. The French sociologist Emile Durkheim (1893 [1933]) documented how the process of industrialisation of European societies in the early 20th century led to disorientation, alienation and a sense of up-rootedness, which he called 'anomie'. He observed that:

> Whenever serious readjustments take place in the social order, whether or not due to a sudden growth or to an unexpected catastrophe, men are more inclined to self-destruction.
>
> (Durkheim, 1893 [1933], p. 246)

Unfortunately, his observations proved to be prophetic for the coming century. The sociologist Robert Merton (1938) made similar observations of the breakdown of the social structure and cultural chaos of American society in the period between the World Wars. In the post-war era, Fred Emery and Eric Trist at the Tavistock Institute studied how the introduction of new technologies often disrupted the existing social system, which led to the alienation of workers and the failure to fully utilise the potential of new technology.

Similar social and political dynamics can be seen today. Technological developments, such as artificial intelligence and machine learning, are fundamentally changing organisations and disrupting existing organisational forms. We are witnessing a disintegration and reconfiguration of both society and organisations. The social is breaking down. This generates uncertainty and a sense of chaos which people find destabilising and anxiety provoking. A sense of loss prevails as social bonds are broken, norms are lost and identities fragment. These conditions are the antithesis of those that are required to foster the vibrant, creative and dynamic organisations that are necessary in turbulent environments.

In contrast to the above, when seen across a longer time horizon we can observe the success of humankind's capacity to adapt to different environments and changes in those environments. Our behaviour does change over time and in different contexts. When I read Toffler's (1970) book, two themes stood out to me. Firstly, he described changes that were fundamental and disruptive 40 years ago but are now simply accepted or even seen as dated; and secondly, it is evident how dramatically society has changed in reaction to the technological developments he describes. Human systems are nothing if not adaptive, yet this is often a painful and difficult experience.

The need for a different map of the world

Change is difficult because it questions how we make sense of and interpret our world. Thomas Kuhn (1970), in his ground-breaking book, *The Structure of Scientific Revolutions*, observed that different scientific communities develop shared ways of understanding and seeing phenomena. He called these 'paradigms', which he defined as: 'the entire constellation of beliefs, values, techniques, and so on shared by members of a given community' (Kuhn, 1970, p. 175). If we extend Kuhn's ideas beyond science, we can observe that paradigms exist across different social communities, including organisations. These paradigms influence the problems that we perceive and the solutions that we enact. In organisations, they influence how people organise, their measures of effectiveness and how they make sense of and engage in organisational change and development. Paradigms also influence organisational theory and the praxis of practitioners, including managers and consultants. How people understand, react and respond to disruptive change thus reflects the paradigms they hold. At the same time, disruption often emerges from different ways of thinking which challenges and threatens the established paradigms.

Many organisations are still based on the bureaucratic model that has its roots in the Industrial Revolution. This paradigm is underpinned by metaphors of machinery and engineering (Morgan, 2006) which reflected the need for organisations to be efficient producers of standardised products. This way of thinking about organisations reifies them, assuming they are 'things' that can be engineered, taken apart and put back together or controlled by those in charge. In this paradigm, control is valued and change becomes a matter of social engineering. Since the 1980s, we have also seen the emergence and dominance of the neo-liberal economic paradigm, which has influenced how we think about organisations. This paradigm sees an organisation as existing primarily for economic reasons whose purpose is to maximise profits and returns to shareholders. The underlying metaphor is that the organisation is an 'economic' entity in a competitive world. Economic value is privileged over other forms of value. At its heart is a belief that human beings act on the basis of self-interest and strive to maximise financial rewards. Competition rather than collaboration is the basis of survival and success.

Both of these paradigms discount the role of social connections, emotional attachments and a deeper sense of purpose to the development and growth of organisations. This has profound consequences for how organisations respond to ongoing and disruptive change. The drive to change and control organisations without due involvement of those affected is creating a crisis in the psychological well-being of employees. In part, I believe that the denial of the importance of human relations has become a defence against the pain of constant and unresolved loss that is inherent to organisational and social change. If organisations are to adapt to a constantly changing world, we need to think differently about them and how they change. We cannot create new forms of organisations whilst we continue to think in old ways (Morgan, 2006). We live in a non-linear world but pretend it is linear (Wheatley, 2006). We need to change our world view – our maps of the world – yet this does not come easily to us.

Over the past 50 years, science has undergone a paradigm shift. Chaos theory (Gleick, 1987) and complexity science (Capra, 1996; Prigogine, 1987) have encouraged us to understand phenomena as patterns of relationships, connections and interdependencies between phenomena rather than as independent and separate parts. The world is an integrated whole, in which there exists a fundamental interdependence of all phenomena, rather than a collection of dissociated parts (Capra, 1996). In other words, everything is related to everything else. This challenges the fundamental premise of traditional science that assumed order to be determined by hidden forces that if understood can be manipulated to produce a desired order. We need to accept that our world is fundamentally uncertain: we cannot fully predict the future.

To understand organisations in an unstable and uncertain world, we therefore need to study patterns and focus our attention on relationships, connections and interdependencies between different processes. This paradigm encourages us to see organisations as communities of interactive processes, or 'living systems' (Capra, 1996; Wheatley, 2006). This does not mean to say that we should discount technology and economic dynamics, but rather see them as shaping and being shaped by social processes. If we pay attention to the full complexity of the social patterns of organisational life, we can see that organisations are not ordered and structured phenomena but messy and dynamic social processes. These give meaning to organisational life and come into being through the complex process of collaboration that emerges as people work together to achieve the organisation's aims.

This frame for understanding the world encourages us to see change and transformation as natural processes that are necessarily messy, unpredictable and uncertain. Organisational change cannot, hence, be controlled or managed. Leaders and change practitioners can only help create the conditions that support the processes of creative adaptation, learning and transformation. This paradigm draws attention to the role of social relations and networks, revealing their importance not just to the effectiveness of organisations but also to their resilience and capacity to adapt to change.

This book is an attempt to understand how people respond to, cope with and adapt to sudden, dramatic and disruptive organisational change. As a psychologist and organisation development consultant my interest is to try to understand what is happening and to find ways to help employees and organisations to adapt, function and perform in dynamic and turbulent environments.

I have three hopes in writing this book.

Firstly, that it will help the reader understand the complexity of social, psychological and emotional responses to ongoing, disruptive and discontinuous change. We need to go beyond simple prescriptions or facile methodologies that promise much in their simplicity but overlook the complexities and uniqueness of social contexts. Secondly, that leaders and change practitioners will be more able to act in a manner that recognises the needs of employees during periods of disruption. Finally, I hope that my writing will demonstrate that it is through developing relationships, connection and social cohesion that new flexible and adaptable organisational forms can emerge which create a collective sense of meaning and purpose.

I believe it is possible to mobilise people and communities to take charge of changes in organisations rather than change requiring those at the top to impose new organisational forms whether for benign or more coercive motives. All the evidence, and my personal observations, suggests that the latter is a flawed change strategy, yet it is the most commonly deployed approach for bringing about change.

Throughout this book, I have drawn on findings from research, observations and direct experience from internal and external consulting assignments and my managerial roles. I have included direct references to these experiences to illustrate arguments in the text. These references are based on *my* experiences, observations and interactions with clients and colleagues. I offer them as a perspective on the social processes that I am describing in my writing. I have attempted to be considered and descriptive in my accounts, coming from the perspective of an enquirer into change and disruption in organisations. I am in no doubt that others who were involved in the situations that I describe would have contrasting experiences and viewpoints to my own. My account is reflective of my own position at the time, and my assumptions and prejudices.

Works cited

Capra, F. (1996). *The web of life*. New York, NY: Anchor.

Durkheim, E. (1893 [1933]). *The division of labour in society*. Translated by George Simpson. New York, NY: Macmillan.

Gleick, J. (1987). *Chaos: Making a new science*. London, England: Vintage.

Kuhn, T. (1970). *The structure of scientific revolutions*. Chicago, IL: University of Chicago Press.

Marx, K. (1844 [1964]). *Economic and philosophic manuscripts of 1844*. New York, NY: International Publishers.

Merton, R. K. (1938). Social structure and anomie. *American Sociological Review*, 3, 672–682.

Morgan, G. (2006). *Images of organisation*. Thousand Oaks, CA: Sage Publications.

Prigogine, I. (1987). *The end of certainty: Time, chaos, and the new laws of nature*. New York, NY: Free Press.

Toffler, A. (1970). *Future shock*. New York, NY: Random House.

Trist, E., Emery, F., & Murray, H. (1997). *The social engagement of social science: A Tavistock anthology. Vol III: The socio-ecological perspective*. Philadelphia, PA: University of Pennsylvania.

Wheatley, M. J. (2006). *Leadership and the new science: Discovering order in a chaotic world*. San Francisco, CA: Berrett-Koehler.

Part 1

Turbulent fields and organisation dynamics

2   Dynamic complexity and disruption

On 15 September 2008, the world's press reported the collapse of the US bank Lehman Brothers. The bank had become, in the words of *The Guardian*: 'the biggest victim so far of the credit crunch and sub-prime crisis' (Wearden, Teather, & Treanor, 2008). The news brought about a system-wide collapse in confidence in the financial sector, which triggered the fall of the stock markets around the world. The bank's UK staff arrived at work that morning not knowing anything about what was happening. Emblematic images of the collapse show employees carrying boxes of their belongings out of the building, looking bemused and sombre.

The collapse of Lehman Brothers is an illustration of how abruptly contexts can change. Admittedly, the collapse of large global financial institutions remains an exception and a rare event. Nevertheless, rather than being seen as a one-off event, the financial crisis needs to be considered to be part of an underlying process of change. Modern life is becoming more complex, unpredictable and uncertain. The start of the 21st century has been one of unprecedented social turbulence. Societies and economies are changing at a rate not seen since the Great Depression.

If I reflect on the past few years of my working life, I have experienced disruption and unexpected change that has altered the direction of my working life in ways I could not have predicted. I was a director of a consultancy that was part of a leading business school. With little planning or advanced notice, we were merged with the executive education department of the school, which in effect meant the closure of the consultancy. As part of this change, I took on the leadership of a new department that was responsible for organisation development and change services. In less than 12 months, the business school was acquired by another larger business school. A year later, the organisation development and change department was closed down and merged with several other departments. I left the organisation shortly afterwards and, together with five colleagues, founded Metalogue Consulting. This period of my career has been an emotional rollercoaster, imbued with uncertainty, change and loss; in which my colleagues and I found ourselves still in the process of making sense of one change whilst encountering and embarking on another. None of these changes I predicted or anticipated before they happened. Even looking back, it is not entirely clear to me how they came about and what, if anything, I might have done to influence the course of events.

Liquid modernity

We are living through a major period of historical transition (Giddens, 2002). The post-industrial information age economy of the postmodern world is one of dynamic complexity characterised by constant change, permanent flux and uncertainty. Society is changing in a manner that is not planned and this generates continual turbulence (Beck, 1992). New social forms and configurations are emerging, whilst traditional institutions are collapsing. According to the sociologist Zygmunt Bauman (Bauman, 2000, p. 1), we have moved from a time of 'solid' modernity to a 'liquid' phase:

> …in which social forms (structures that limit individual choices, institutions that guard repetitions of routines, patterns of acceptable behaviour) can no longer (and are not expected) to keep their shape for long, because they decompose and melt faster than the time it takes to cast them, and once they are cast for them to set. Forms, whether already present or only adumbrated, are unlikely to be given enough time to solidify, and cannot serve as frames of reference for human actions and long-term life strategies because of their short life expectation.

For Bauman, the conditions under which individuals act are changing faster than it takes the new ways of acting to consolidate into habits and routines (Bauman, 2005). We now live in a world of transformations. Dramatic social and economic change are rupturing the existing social order. The familiar patterns of everyday life are unravelling, confronting us with ambiguity and the unfamiliar. A senior UK civil servant captured this experience beautifully, 10 months after the UK's referendum to leave the EU, when she said to me:

> Some things stay the same. I get up in the morning, I go to work, I take the train home. Everything else at work feels like it's changing. The ship is changing shape whilst we are sailing in it. It's like being in a Terry Gilliam movie. I feel existentially challenged.

Globalisation – the free flow of trade, people and capital around the world – is creating a more complex, connected and tightly coupled global economy. At the same time, it is undermining, disembedding and challenging the taken-for-granted assumptions that form the local social order at an accelerating rate (Giddens, 2002). As part of this process, economic power is shifting from Western to the Eastern economies.[1] Whilst bringing about clear economic and social benefits, globalisation has a darker side. It is generating widespread economic uncertainties and insecurities for many communities. This effect is not trivial. To give one example: I joined Ford Motor Company in 1996, where I took up a role in its European Head Office in Essex in the UK. At the time, Ford was by far the biggest automotive manufacturer in the UK with production plants at Southampton, Leamington, Liverpool, Bridgend, Dagenham, Enfield and Basildon. Over the past 20 years, virtually all of these plants have been closed or been divested. Engine plants remain at Dagenham and Bridgend; however, Ford no longer assembles cars in the UK. Production has been either consolidated across European plants or moved to lower-wage countries in Eastern Europe and Turkey. At the time of finalising this book, Ford announced the closure of what had been its head office in Essex and its engine plant in Bridgend.

As Giddens (2002) observes, globalisation transforms social transactions, stretching them across time–space. Local happenings are increasingly shaped by events occurring many miles away and vice versa. The movement of people across regional and national borders is creating a global cosmopolitan society. As a consequence of these processes, culturally, public institutions and everyday life are being opened up from the hold of tradition. In almost every country, beliefs and practices around the family, marriage and sexuality are changing. A revolution is taking place in how we form social ties and connections. Where historically our identity was pretty much defined by our place in a stable social structure, we now need to be far more active in how we create our self-identity.

Climate change

The earth's climate is also increasingly unstable as the result of human behaviour. Climate change scientists estimate that we exceeded the biosphere's regenerative capacity in the 1980s; this takes us past the point of return. Our economic systems are however deeply rooted in the assumption that growth can be unlimited and unending – yet the planet has finite resources. This is a crisis that threatens the future of the entire planet. As Gregory Bateson (2000) warned: 'If the creature destroys its environment, it destroys itself'. Organisations are central to both the problem of climate change and any potential solution.

Climate change is affecting socio-economic patterns and will increasingly do so. Government policies and consumer behaviour are (slowly) changing and the greening of economies is starting to accelerate. These developments are the source of potential disruption for several global sectors and industries. For instance, the British and French governments have announced that cars running on diesel and gasoline will be banned within 25 years. The electrification of the car industry threatens to disrupt the global car manufacturers, oil producers and infrastructure around the refuelling of cars. Other sectors and industries, such as energy and utilities, will experience similar reconfigurations that will require incumbent firms to innovate and adapt.

Disruptive innovation and technology

New technologies are emerging at a speed and reach that only a few decades ago could not be imagined. Both the rate of technological innovation and the diffusion of innovation across society are accelerating at an exponential rate (Brynjolfsson & Mcafee, 2016). The radio took 40 years to reach 40 million users in the US. The personal computer took 15 years to achieve 40 million users in the US. However, the internet reached 50 million users in just four years.

In 2016, the World Economic Forum argued that we have started a Fourth Industrial Revolution, which 'is fundamentally changing the way we live, work, and relate to one another' (Schwab, 2017, p. 1). They anticipate that this will be unlike anything that we have experienced in the history of civilisation. Technological innovations include quantum computing, a much more mobile internet, smaller and more powerful sensors and the capacity of machines to learn and be intelligent. The 'Internet of Things' is starting to emerge and enter our lives. This promises to connect many of our everyday appliances, such as fridges, heating systems or cars, to the internet. It is reconfiguring practically every aspect of our lives: how we make things; how we communicate and interact with each other as humans; and the way we do business.[2]

Technology promises to revolutionise and transform the workplace. Artificial intelligence (AI), machine learning and robots are starting to be introduced for the completion of a wider range of routine jobs in the manufacturing and service industries. Manufacturing, public sector and financial services businesses are starting to use AI and advanced computerised decision-making systems to automate administrative and even complex analytical roles.[3,4] Whilst the long-term impact of new technologies is far from certain, what is clear is the anxiety and sense of threat that it generates for employees.

Digital technologies are transforming entire economic systems that span countries and industries. Joseph Schumpeter's (1942) process of 'creative destruction' is being played out at a global level rather than a national or regional level. The disruptive side of innovation is fundamentally changing industries as new entrants break the existing rules of the market (Bower & Christensen, 1995). We are seeing the emergence of businesses that are leveraging technology to create new business models, products and services. Digital platforms are creating digitally driven organisations that are, in effect, networks that match buyers and sellers of products or services. Almost overnight, the introduction of these new technological platforms, such as Uber or Airbnb, is reconfiguring and disrupting markets and sectors.

Firms such as Amazon, Uber and Google have grown at exponential rates to become global brands. At the same time, we have also seen the decline of many traditional businesses and industries as they struggle to compete with new entrants or find that their markets are disappearing or becoming obsolete. Over the past 20 years, Nokia grew at an unrivalled rate and then at the height of its powers, competitor products such as the BlackBerry and then the iPhone led to an unrivalled decline. The next wave of innovation triggered the collapse of BlackBerry. In 2016, BlackBerry announced it would no longer manufacture phones. Other examples of disruptive entrants include Spotify in the music industry, Netflix in the entertainment industry or Amazon and ASOS in the retail sector. Scientific breakthroughs are also disrupting different sectors.

In medicine, for instance, the field of genomics will revolutionise health care, which will require changes to health services and how patients are engaged with and treated by the medical profession.

In sum, we are experiencing a dramatic acceleration in the levels of inter-dependence between social, political, economic, climate and technological dynamics. Economies and sectors are now tightly coupled and connected with each other. Events in one region, sector or system impact others. Social change has become constant, changing the fundamental characteristics of many societies, and threatening traditional identities and values.

Dynamic complexity and its effects

Change used to be incremental, gradual and evolving from the past, or there was a period of change against a backdrop of relative stability. However, the post-war era of the stable state has come to an end (Schon, 1971). Most organisations are now in a continual process of transformation. Organisations are now operating in what Fred Emery and Eric Trist (1965) described as 'turbulent fields', socio-economic environments associated with a gross increase in the area of *relevant uncertainty*.[5] As illustrated in Figure 2.1, this arises because of an increase in both the levels of instability and complexity in a given environment. In turbulent environments, a number of events start to be connected with each other in a way that leads to irreversible general changes. Under these conditions, organisational effectiveness and survival is a function of an organisation's capacity to continually adapt, change and innovate. This is analogous to Charles Darwin's

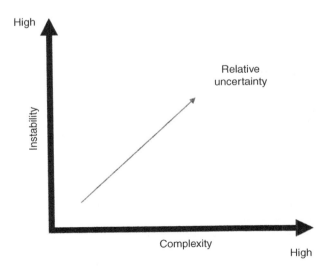

Figure 2.1 Typical organisational environment

observations that those species that survive are those that are most adaptable, rather than the strongest or most intelligent.

Developments in complexity science can help us to understand the dynamics and behaviour of highly complex, connected and interdependent systems, such as societies and economies. More complex, tightly coupled and densely connected systems tend to be more dynamic, unstable and vulnerable to reconfigurations (Perrow, 1984). Warren Weaver, the former Chief Scientific Officer at the Rockefeller Foundation, in a ground-breaking paper in 1948, identified the phenomenon of 'organized complexity' (Weaver, 1948). This arises when a large number of mutually interacting parts or agents self-organise to generate properties that are novel, emergent and systemic. As a system becomes increasingly complex, predictions about how it will behave in the future become increasingly uncertain. For instance, who can predict what the UK's society will look like in 30 years?

Complexity science (Capra & Luisi, 2014; Prigogine, 1987) observes that complex systems exhibit the capacity for sudden and dramatic change. Very few people anticipated the global economic crisis and fewer still anticipated that Lehman Brothers would collapse. When complex systems become unstable, even small changes can reconfigure the system in unexpected and unpredictable ways. Events in one part of the system can affect other parts, in ways we cannot easily understand. They exhibit greater non-linearity and emergent surprises (Homer-Dixon, 2011). In complex systems, abrupt discontinuities define the rhythm of the unfolding future (Buchanan, 2004). This is equivalent to the discovery of palaeontologists Stephen Jay Gould and Niles Eldredge (Gould & Eldredge, 1977) that evolution is not a gradual process but characterised by what they called periods of 'punctuated equilibrium' whereby major environmental disturbances triggered the proliferation of new species and the acceleration of changes within species.

Complexity science has helped us understand how in systems that are highly interconnected and tightly coupled, we find small, frequently occurring outcomes mixed with rare, hard-to-predict extreme ones. In other words, such systems are more prone to unexpected shocks or systemic failures (Clearfield & Tilcsik, 2018). This phenomenon is known as 'power laws' (Ramalingam, 2013). We also find what are known as 'cascade effects' (Homer-Dixon, 2011) where the failure in one part of the system ripple out across the system, causing other parts of the system to fail or collapse. In the global economy, chains of economic interdependence reach across the world. Changes reverberate with speed, creating 'interdependence risk' (Homer-Dixon, 2011). As we witnessed, with the financial crisis of 2008 and the subsequent financial problems in the eurozone, a shock or significant event in one part of the system cascades throughout the entire system creating a domino effect.

Weaver contrasted organised complexity with 'complicated systems'. The latter are problems that can be solved by understanding the fundamental principles or laws of how the system operates, such as a car engine. These systems can be designed, predicted and controlled. When problems arise in complicated systems, they can be solved by applying technical knowledge and solutions that have worked in the past. As societies and economies become more complex and interconnected, they start to take on the properties of 'organized complexity', becoming more dynamic, unstable and unpredictable. This generates challenges that are novel, unknown and have no obvious solutions. The complexity of many of the challenges we now face, such as climate change or managing a global financial system, has exceeded our capacity to comprehend them. In other words, we simply do not understand and cannot solve many of the challenges that are emerging.

In turbulent fields, organisations are thus more likely to experience discontinuous and disruptive changes in their environments. Such changes are likely to:

- Be sudden and rapid;
- Be unexpected and unanticipated;
- Involve the emergence of new patterns and dynamics;
- Lead to the collapse of familiar patterns or structures;
- Create a disjuncture between the past and the future;
- Present organisations with novel and unknown challenges; and
- Generate new and unknown risks.

Such challenges could include a firm's markets disappearing, new entrants radically changing the dynamics of a market or political and economic shocks creating new and unforeseen pressures on the organisation. The fundamental changes that are happening to the UK high street retail sector is one example of discontinuous and disruptive change. Over a relatively short period of time, a number of changes, such as a movement in consumer behaviour towards online shopping, have precipitated the decline and collapse of a number of household names. Ron Heifetz has called such events 'adaptive challenges' (Heifetz, 1994). These are complex, novel and interconnected problems that are difficult to identify and understand, and do not lend themselves to simple solutions. Attempts to solve the problem often produces unforeseeable or unintended consequences that can compound the problem. In other words, unlike technical problems, past knowledge and solutions do not solve the problem.

Discontinuous change is likely to feel overwhelming or incomprehensible to those affected. When change is a discrete and incremental event, it has a beginning, a middle and an end. This allows change to be conceived as a movement from steady state A to steady state B. This gives us a feeling of control over change. In contrast, socio-economic, technical and organisational changes increasingly are experienced as if they are impingements from our environment, something that is inflicted on us. This fundamentally challenges our deeply held desire to exercise control over our environments. More than ever, we are aware that the future cannot be known or predicted in advance. This inability to predict the future causes anxiety, feelings of insecurity and paranoid fears in organisations and more broadly across societies.

Implications for organisations

In turbulent fields, an organisation's long-term survival and success has less to do with efficiency and productivity and far more to do with its capacity to adapt to change, to innovate. Environmental scanning (Day & Power, 2009) becomes crucial as organisations need to be attuned to emerging trends and potential developments both within and outside of their established markets. In dynamic environments, it becomes necessary to look beyond the immediate horizon and the established boundaries of a market or sector. However, human systems tend to have confirmation biases, looking for information that supports their world view whilst excluding information that might be contradictory or unsettling. The capacity to adapt requires therefore not just an ability to notice emerging trends but also a willingness to do so.

The basic organising logic of organisations needs to change from maximising productivity, which privileges control, stability and order, to valuing generative innovation and adaptability. Organisations need adaptive capacity. This is the ability of a system to modify itself in response to changes in its environment. Organisations that were successful in the Industrial Age are increasingly having to reinvent themselves. Markets are no longer clearly bounded and stable, defined by a business's products and services. Many are having to ask themselves what business or market they are in. Take the car industry: for over a century, the market was clearly defined. Many car companies, however, are now redefining themselves as selling mobility rather than simply producing and selling cars. Those organisations that are unable to adapt fast enough will experience decline and ultimately go out of business.

Organisations are having to transform themselves (or face being disrupted) to stay ahead of their competitors, to catch up with them or just to survive. Actual or anticipated disruption requires them to change fundamentally both their purpose and form. Anthony, Gilbert, and Johnson (2017) argue that transformation involves the dual challenge of creating a new business whilst simultaneously protecting the existing one that is faced with new competitors or declining markets. Take the case of Philips, which was founded in 1891 by Gerard Philips and his father Frederik. The company was the first producer of lighting in the world. Over the next hundred years, Philips pioneered a range of technological innovations in consumer electronics, from TVs, radios to CD and DVD players, creating a multi-divisional structure of different operating units. In June 2016, Philips spun off its lighting division and licenced off its consumer electronics division. This changed the company into a health technology business. Its company website[6] now describes Philips as:

> …a leading health technology company focused on improving people's health and enabling better outcomes across the health continuum from healthy living and prevention, to diagnosis, treatment and home care. Philips leverages advanced technology and deep clinical and consumer insights to deliver integrated solutions. The company is a leader in diagnostic imaging,

image-guided therapy, patient monitoring and health informatics, as well as in consumer health and home care.

Such transformations require a radical change to the identity and core purpose of the organisation. The connection to history is altered or lost. In practice, however, transformation of a business is incredibly difficult, and despite the rhetoric, the success rate is low, particular for organisations in turbulent competitive environments or who have experienced significant downturns in financial performance (Reeves, Fæste, Whitaker, & Hassan, 2018). More tangential evidence from the turnover and survival rate of the list of S&P 500 companies suggests that organisations are increasingly struggling to adapt. In 1964, the average tenure of a company on the list was 34 years, but this had fallen to 20 years by 2016 (Anthony, Viguerie, Schwartz, & Landeghem, 2018). Anthony et al. forecast that this will fall to 16 years by 2027.

Conclusion

Few people would argue that we can expect the world to settle down in the foreseeable future. We can expect hyper-competitive, dynamic and turbulent environments to continue and, possibly, even increase. Where in the past, change tended to be incremental, linear or episodic, now it is often ongoing and punctuated by periods of exponential change. Such changes are unpredictable and uncontrollable. Predicting or anticipating the future is becoming an increasingly challenging, if not impossible, task. No longer can we assume that we can determine the future by understanding the past. We need to start thinking about the world and organisations in a different way because it has changed fundamentally. No longer can we rely on mechanistic or linear accounts of the world.

The long-term survival of organisations will increasingly be influenced by their capacity to adapt and to transform themselves both in terms of what they do and how they do it. We can also expect the decline and death rate of organisations to increase as organisations embracing new technologies replace the traditionally established ones.

We need to discover how to humanely navigate discontinuous and disruptive change, and to help people to step into new realities and let go of the past, the familiar and what is known. This is going to be increasingly important if organisations are going to transition to more adaptive and flexible forms. At a more personal level, we are all having to learn to cope in a more fluid, ambiguous world in which we have to adapt in both our professional and personal lives.

Notes

1 In 1991, China's share of global manufacturing exports was 2%. By 2013 this had risen to 20% of worldwide exports [Source: *The Economist*, October 2016, www.economist.com/finance-and-economics/2016/10/27/the-greatest-moderation]. Over a similar period, 1999–2011, the US lost almost 6 million manufacturing jobs.

2 World Economic Forum, 'The world is changing: Here's how companies must adapt', www.weforum.org/agenda/2018/01/the-world-is-changing-here-s-how-companies-must-adapt

3 Predictions of job losses due to robotics and automation vary considerable from 35% in a study by the University of Oxford (www.oxfordmartin.ox.ac.uk/publications/technology-at-work-v2-0-the-future-is-not-what-it-used-to-be/) to 5% in a McKinsey 2017 study (www.mckinsey.com/featured-insights/digital-disruption/harnessing-automation-for-a-future-that-works).

4 The OECD is predicting that 65% of today's children will have jobs that have not yet been invented (http://reports.weforum.org/future-of-jobs-2016/chapter-1-the-future-of-jobs-and-skills/#view/fn-1).

5 Today's business schools have popularised the term 'VUCA' – Volatility, Uncertainty, Complexity and Ambiguity – as a way of describing the economic and social environment.

6 Philips, 'Company – about', www.philips.com/a-w/about/company.html

Works cited

Anthony, S. D., Gilbert, C. G., & Johnson, M. W. (2017). *Dual transformation: How to reposition today's business while creating the future.* Boston, MA: Harvard Business Review Press.

Anthony, S. D., Viguerie, S. P., Schwartz, E. I., & Landeghem, J.V. (2018, February). *2018 corporate longevity forecast: Creative destruction is accelerating. S&P 500 lifespans continue to shrink, requiring new strategies for navigating disruption.* Retrieved from www.innosight.com/wp-content/uploads/2017/11/Innosight-Corporate-Longevity-2018.pdf

Bateson, G. (2000). *Steps to an ecology of mind: Collected essays in anthropology, psychiatry, evolution, and epistemology.* San Francisco, CA: University of Chicago Press.

Bauman, Z. (2000). *Liquid modernity.* Cambridge, England: Polity Press.

Bauman, Z. (2005). *Liquid life.* Cambridge, England: Polity Press.

Beck, U. (1992). *Risk society.* New York, NY: Sage.

Bower, J. L., & Christensen, C. M. (1995). Disruptive technologies: Catching the wave. Harvard Business Review, January–February.

Brynjolfsson, E., & Mcafee, A. (2016). *The second machine age: Work, progress, and prosperity in a time of brilliant technologies.* New York, NY: W. W. Norton & Company.

Buchanan, M. (2004, Spring). Power laws & the new science of complexity management. *Strategy & leadership.* Retrieved from www.strategy-business.com/article/04107?gko=b2303

Clearfield, C., & Tilcsik, A. (2018). *Meltdown: Why our systems fail and what can we do about it.* London, England: Atlantic Books.

Day, A., & Power, K. (2009). Developing leaders for a world of uncertainty, complexity and ambiguity. *The Ashridge Journal*, Winter 2009–2010. Retrieved from https://bit.ly/2mbdiyp

Emery, E. F., & Trist, E. L. (1965, February). The causal texture of organizational environments. *Human Relations, 18*, 21–32.

Giddens, A. (2002). *Runaway world: How globalisation is reshaping our lives* (2nd ed.). London, England: Profile Books.

Gould, S. J., & Eldredge, N. (1977). Punctuated equilibria: The tempo and mode of evolution reconsidered. *Paleobiology, 3*(2), 115–151.

Heifetz, R. (1994). *Leadership without easy answers.* Cambridge, MA: The Belknap Press.

Homer-Dixon, T. (2011, January). Complexity science. *Oxford Leadership Journal, 2*(1), 1–15.

Perrow, C. (1984). *Normal accidents.* New York, NY: Basic Books.

Prigogine, I. (1987). *The end of certainty: Time, chaos, and the new laws of nature.* New York, NY: Free Press.

Ramalingam, B. (2013). *Aid on the edge of chaos.* Oxford, England: Oxford University Press.

Reeves, M., Fæste, L., Whitaker, K., & Hassan, F. (2018, January). The truth about corporate transformation. Retrieved from https://sloanreview.mit.edu/article/the-truth-about-corporate-transformation

Schon, D. (1971). *Beyond the stable state.* New York, NY: Random House.

Schumpeter, J. (1942). *Capitalism, socialism and democracy.* London, England: Harper & Brothers.

Schwab, K. (2017). *The Fourth Industrial Revolution.* Geneva, Switzerland: Portfolio Penguin.

Trist, E. L., & Emery, F. E. (1965). The Causal Texture of Organizational Environments. *Human Relations, 18,* 21–32.

Trist, E., Emery, F., & Murray, H. (1997). *The social engagement of social science: A Tavistock anthology. Vol III: The socio-ecological perspective.* Philadelphia, PA: University of Pennsylvania.

Wearden, G., Teather, D., & Treanor, J. (2008). Banking crisis: Lehman Brothers files for bankruptcy protection. *The Guardian,* 15 September. Retrieved from www.theguardian.com/business/2008/sep/15/lehmanbrothers.creditcrunch

Weaver, W. (1948). Science and complexity. *American Scientist, 36*(4), 536–544.

3 The transformation of organisational form

We are witnessing a crisis of the traditional bureaucratic model of organising and the birth of a new organisational form (Castells, 2000), which has been variously described as the 'post-modern', the 'networked' (Castells, 2000) or the 'self-organising' organisation. This crisis arises because of the difficulties experienced by bureaucracies in operating in environments of dynamic complexity and the deep contradiction this creates between their existing form and the demands of their environments. Many organisations are therefore in transition between two competing paradigms of organising – each with its own organising logic. This feels ambiguous, contradictory and confusing to those involved as they are pulled between the past, the demands of the present and the needs of the future.

Competing paradigms of organising

The German sociologist Max Weber (1947) recognised how bureaucracy is ideally suited to the solving of routine problems in stable environments. He observed how the bureaucratic form is characterised by management hierarchies, the division of labour to perform specialised tasks and rules around how individuals should perform their roles. Core to bureaucracy are the twin beliefs of efficiency and the need for control. The informing metaphor is that of the 'machine' that can be controlled, designed and engineered (Morgan, 2006). The bureaucratic form came to symbolise the Industrial Age and formed the basis of state institutions, the church, the army and corporations. A number of variants of the bureaucratic model have evolved, including simple, professional and divisional bureaucracy (Mintzberg, 1981). Common to each of these is the organising logic of hierarchy and management control.

Weber saw bureaucracy as a form of social domination whereby power and authority is concentrated in the hands of a small number of top managers and given legitimacy through rational laws, rules and regulations. He argued that bureaucracy achieves social regulation through the application of impersonal and de-humanising regulation and rules. As such, the bureaucratic form is an attempt to produce order and stability through prediction, planning and

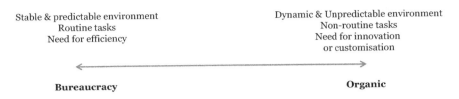

Stable & predictable environment
Routine tasks
Need for efficiency

Dynamic & Unpredictable environment
Non-routine tasks
Need for innovation
or customisation

Bureaucracy

Organic

Figure 3.1 Continuum of organisational form
(Adapted from Burnes, 2009)

control. Under such conditions, employees tend to conform to the wishes of those in authority (Milgram, 1974).

However, when demand becomes unpredictable and difficult to control, bureaucracy is too rigid and unable to adapt (Burns, 1963; Emery & Trist, 1965; Lawrence & Lorsch, 1967). Hierarchies become problematic in situations of dynamic complexity because centralised authority and control hinder quick decision making and flexibility. Furthermore, functional structures start to become 'silos' that limit information sharing and hinder collaboration between disciplines and different parts. Under more dynamic conditions, organisations tend to be more networked, flexible and decentralised (Lawrence & Lorsch, 1967). Figure 3.1 summarises the different forms of organising that we find under different environmental conditions.

Technology is also shaping organisational form. Digital technology enables tasks to be completed asynchronously and non-linearly, rather than through standardised, sequential processes. Artificial intelligence and analytics enables routine, low-value administrative or complex analytical tasks to be automated. This reduces the need for management control, standardised processes and task specialisation.

Organic, networked structures organise work around semi-permanent projects rather than stable and fixed tasks. This requires boundaries to be more ambiguous, permeable and temporary. Roles are more flexible and fluid with broader responsibilities. Employees are often multi-skilled and able to perform a range of tasks. Work is undertaken through a process of internal regulation by the work group, cooperation and mutual adjustment between individuals rather than through rules, prescribed roles or external management. Coordination and decision making are decentralised and distributed rather than centrally controlled, which facilitates the solving of non-routine work and innovation.

Hierarchies tend to be tightly coupled (Weick, 1976) with high interdependence between different parts. Change in one part of the system therefore affects the performance of the rest of the system. This means that local changes can only be supported if changes are made more broadly across the system. This reduces their adaptability and responsiveness to change. In contrast, organic forms tend to be more loosely coupled (Weick, 1976). The different parts or

Table 3.1 Comparison of bureaucratic and organic forms

	Bureaucratic form	*Organic form*
Characteristics	Hierarchical control, established rules and controls, division of labour, work specialisation and standardisation of tasks, clear and stable work units	Flat structures, cross-disciplinary project teams, flexible roles, boundaries and multi-skilling
Unit of production	Stable and fixed tasks and functions	Short and longer-term projects
Measures of effectiveness	Productivity, efficiency and quality	Innovation, flexibility and responsiveness
Leadership and authority	Legal-rational authority based on position in hierarchy	Negotiated and fluid authority based on competence and personal authority
Coordination of activities	Achieved through rules, processes and management control systems	Achieved through shared values, mutual adjustment and self-organisation
Strengths	Ability to produce standardised output efficiently	Innovation, flexibility and adaptability to change
Limitations	Difficulty to respond to and adapt to non-routine and unpredictable demands	Struggles with standardisation and efficiency
Organising principles	Control, order and standardisation	Local flexibility, collaboration and adaptability
Informing metaphor	Machine	Living self-organising system

elements of the organisation retain a separateness and independence of identity, affecting each other only occasionally, negligibly or suddenly (rather than continuously) (Weick, 1976). This, combined with distributed decision making, enables them to more adaptable to environmental changes, and therefore more resilient, because they permit high levels of local discretion. Loose coupling means the failure of one part of the system has less effect on other parts (Orton & Weick, 1990). Organic network structures also tend to exhibit greater variety, internal differentiation and diversity. This gives a system a greater diversity of responses in complex environments (Ashby, 1956), which increases its adaptive capacity.

Self-organising structures tend to be made up of relatively small units that transact and collaborate together (Laloux, 2014). These tend to be based on the principle of redundancy of function (Emery, 1993), whereby employees and teams have multiple skills, some of which they will not be using at any point in time. This gives a work system flexibility because teams are able to self-organise according to the immediate local demands or problems. This reduces reliance on external interventions from specialists or managers because they have the capacity to solve problems for themselves.

Self-organising structures emerge out of social processes rather than being a fixed, static structure. The informing metaphor of such organisations is that of 'the living system' (Morgan, 2006) which continually adapts to its environment. W.L. Gore's lattice structure is an often-cited example of a networked, self-organising organisation.[1] It has no hierarchy or job titles but a 'latticework' of connections between individuals. Everyone is referred to as an associate and individuals organise around projects and customers. To facilitate mutual adjustment and self-organisation, the organisation limits the size of a plant to 150 employees. This enables everyone to know each other and for decisions to be made without the need for fixed hierarchies. Other innovative variants of the self-organising structure include matrix structures, holographic organisations (Morgan, 1993; Robertson, 2016), agile organisations (Holbeche, 2015) and teal organisations (Laloux, 2014).

Organisations are also forming networks with other organisations to help them to adapt to growing complexity, to leverage new technologies and to respond to the disruption to traditional markets. The growth in alliances, partnerships, joint ventures and complex supply chains is blurring the boundaries of traditional hierarchies and shifting the focus from competition towards collaboration and partnership.

A summary of the comparisons between the bureaucratic and organic forms is given in Table 3.1.

In his book, Reinventing Organizations, *Frederic Laloux* (Laloux, 2014) *describes a Dutch nursing organisation called Buurtzorg (which means 'neighbourhood care') that functions as a self-organising network. Laloux reports how Buurtzorg has been phenomenally successful since it was founded in 2006. In its first seven years, it grew from ten nurses to 7,000. It manages to deliver 40% fewer hours care than other nursing organisations whilst healing patients faster and giving them greater autonomy. Employee job satisfaction is high and turnover is 33% lower than comparable organisations.*

Laloux attributes the success of Buurtzorg to its unique structure and clear sense of purpose, which is 'to help patients lead lives that are as rich and autonomous as possible'. Teams of 10–12 nurses serve small neighbourhoods of around 50 patients. Each team has full responsibility for serving these patients and for organising themselves. The teams are effectively self-governing, having no leaders and making important decisions collectively. Regional coaches provide support to the teams to make their own decisions. Staff functions and the headquarters are kept to the bare minimum of about 30 staff. Their role is again to support the teams in their decision making and planning.

Gary Hamel and Michele Zanini (Hamel & Zanini, 2018) describe a comparable case of a Chinese appliance manufacturer, Haier, that is run as a self-organising network. Like Buurtzorg it has been highly successful and is currently the world's largest appliance maker with revenues of $35 billion and a worldwide workforce of around 100,000. Hamel attributes Haier's success to a transformation of its traditional bureaucracy which started in 2010. The firm is organised around 4,000 'microenterprises' (MEs) of between 10 and 15 employees that are free to form and evolve. These take three forms: customer-centric market-facing units; 'incubating' MEs, or entirely new businesses and 'node' MEs which sell component products and services such as design, manufacturing, and human resource support to the market-facing MEs. The microenterprises are grouped into platforms of approximately 50 MEs around different industries.

Transforming form: becoming a self-organising network

The shift from a hierarchical structure to a self-organising network is by no means a straightforward path. At its heart is a paradigm shift. This requires that the basic assumptions which lie behind the current organisational logic are understood, alternative assumptions agreed and used to create alternative forms and practices. In practice, this process involves ongoing dialogue, disagreement and conflict as people surface, question and revise their implicit assumptions and beliefs about how to effectively organise to achieve the organisation's aims. Typically, the following activities have to be accomplished:

1. The de-coupling and flattening of hierarchies;
2. A change in authority relations;
3. Changes to roles, boundaries and identities; and
4. Deep change in the culture and values.

This process of transition rarely, if ever, happens in a single event. In practice, it requires a series of adaptations and adjustments over time. This is typically slow – consuming energy, time and resources.

The de-coupling and flattening of hierarchies

Self-organising networks require only minimal structures and simple rules and specifications for how work is to be conducted. The concept can be simply put as: no more should be specified than is absolutely essential and that what is specified is essential (Cherns, 1976). This creates internal flexibility and space for work units to self-organise (Morgan, 1993). To create these conditions, hierarchies first need to be de-coupled.

This is a challenging and difficult transition, given that most (almost all) social systems organise around social hierarchies (Laumann, Siegel, & Hodge,

1970). The dissolution of hierarchies disrupts this natural pattern. This tends to be disturbing and disorienting for employees who are used to operating in hierarchical relationships. Such structures meet employees' primitive needs for security and dependency (Miller, 1993) and are used by people as a defence against anxieties (Jaques, 1955; Menzies-Lyth, 1990). The loss of such stable and familiar structures stimulates high levels of anxiety and mobilises people's psychological defences (Krantz, 1998). These defences need to be worked through during the process of change.

The flattening of hierarchies removes of layers of middle management. Knowing this, middle managers tend to oppose the changes by resisting letting go of control. This is simply to protect their interests. They equally tend to find themselves literally caught in the 'middle', under pressure from the executive to implement new structures whilst, at the same time, experiencing resistance from those they manage. In other words, whilst flatter decentralised structures are often presented as exciting and innovative, to those affected they can feel threatening and as not operating in their interests.

A change in authority relations

The transition to self-management requires a different form of relatedness between leaders and followers. Authority that tended to run in clear lines becomes more diffuse, negotiated and based on the demands of the immediate task. Rather than exercising control, the role of managers is more about creating the conditions that enable self-organisation. This requires managers to give up control and to trust in the willingness and abilities of others to take responsibility (Miller, 1993). Equally, employees have to exercise greater personal authority, creativity and initiative (Miller, 1993). This exposes them to the psychological risks of failure as they invest and show more of themselves rather than simply following rules (Krantz, 1998).

Changing the paradigm of management–employee relationships tends to be extremely difficult (Emery, 1993). The shift from dependency cultures to self-management and independence is experienced by many as a threat (Miller, 1993). Most managers in hierarchical structures experience a sense of vulnerability in letting go of control, whilst employees experience authority and the institution as failing to meet their expectations and needs for dependency. As the authority relations become less controlling, employees typically experience frustration when their managers no longer step in to take responsibility for problems or difficulties, as happened in the past.

In hierarchical organisations that are attempting to move away from a dependency culture to one of greater decentralisation and self-management, we find a confused and ambivalent relationship to authority. Employees expect and experience power and authority to be exercised by those at the top of the hierarchy. They equally experience an underlying anger and resistance to such authority when it is experienced as inconsistent and contradictory. On the one hand, employees are told they need to exercise initiative and discretion, whilst attempts to do so are judged as being risky or as challenges to authority.

Employees are equally contradictory in their expectations of their managers. They want to be able to exercise discretion and yet they equally find comfort and security in dependency, particularly given the increasing uncertainties and ambiguities of their work environment. Such contradictory messages and expectations are par for the course as leaders and followers adjust their expectations of each other and reformulate their relationships. They do however undermine employees' trust and confidence in both hierarchical authority and their institution (Brunning, 2012).

Changes to roles, boundaries and identities

The role of the small bounded group as a unit of organisation within a stable and established hierarchy disappears in the networked structures. Employees are less contained by temporal and spatial boundaries. These are increasingly permeable and ambiguous, whilst roles are becoming fluid and negotiated. This changes team boundaries and the relationship between work units. Traditional identities that reflect the historical division of labour are altered and eroded. The process of change often necessitates departments merging or disbanding altogether. More often than not, this occurs without sufficient time to mourn the end of the group and allow a new group to form.

Deep change in the culture and values

The move to self-organising forms requires widespread and deep change at the levels of values and culture. Shared social values (rather than rules) are required to support consistent responses to uncertainty (Emery & Trist, 1965). The move from hierarchy to self-management therefore requires the creation of cultures that encourage teamwork, openness and cooperation. Members of the organisation also need to acquire 'a kind of self-questioning ability that underpins the activities of systems that are able to learn to learn and self-organize' (Morgan, 1997, p. 86).

Such a change in culture requires fundamental changes to the reward system, the status system, identities, norms and values. Deep cultural change of this form takes many years as hierarchical cultures are highly resistant to change. The pace tends to be slower than the speed of environmental change in many sectors. This generates significant internal pressures to adapt at speed, yet change can only move at a pace that employees are able to accommodate. For these reasons, perhaps the most significant obstacle in transforming the organising logic of an organisation is culture.

In sum, the transformation of an established hierarchical system to a flexible, network structure based on the principles of self-organisation requires a paradigm shift. This requires an unlearning of existing assumptions and values, the letting go of the familiar patterns of organising, which reconfigures relationships and alters identities. Such a process of change is far from straightforward because it unleashes considerable anxieties and fears amongst both managers and employees.

> *For my doctoral research (Day, 2000), I studied the introduction of self-managed teams in two UK plants of a global automotive company. In the early stages of the change, both managers and the teams experienced considerable confusion around their mutual expectations of each other. The teams lacked confidence in their ability to make decisions whilst the managers found it hard to trust them. The result of which was a reversion back to managers exercising control and direction during crises on the production line. This further exacerbated the sense of confusion around authority and undermined the confidence of the teams.*
>
> *I recall one day asking a team about their experience of self-management. One member of the team pointed to a row of cabinets next to their work area. In a frustrated tone, he told me how the team had decided to move them because they interfered with their movement between areas. A few days later, the area manager, seeing the change, instructed the team to put the cabinets back, without any clear explanation. The individual explained to me that this event led them to conclude they were not trusted to make decisions. This resulted in the team disengaging and becoming disillusioned.*
>
> *Over several years, as expectations became clear and as the teams and managers developed and matured, the teams started to exercise more responsibility and the managers were more willing to see their roles as coaches and support for the teams. At the same time, a significant proportion of individuals and managers were still opposed to the changes and found it hard to adapt to the new system. These individuals were often long-serving employees who had either grown used to being told what to do or lacked the confidence to exercise initiative or engage in team decision making. The areas that were most successful in making the changes had managed to engage the teams to take ownership, creating a spirit of collective responsibility for their task. The style of direct management for the area and the extent to which the teams felt involved in the introduction of the work group concept played a critical role in whether the teams felt ownership over their work.*

An alternative strategy for adapting to uncertainty and risk

Many, or arguably most, organisations are pursuing an alternative strategy that gives them economic and operational flexibility to respond to uncertainty. This involves:

- Outsourcing risk to customers, suppliers, employees and other parties;
- Separating core from non-core activities;

- Creating a system of flexible employment relationships; and
- The application of technology to replace and control employees.

The underlying paradigm remains one of management control. Indeed, there is some evidence that organisations appear to be adding to, rather than taking away, hierarchy. Hamel and Zanini (2018), for instance, report that the number of managers, supervisors and administrators in the US workforce has increased significantly in comparison to other occupations over the last two decades.

This perhaps should not surprise us, since most of us desire control when confronted with the unknown and unfamiliar, particularly if we are feeling scared and anxious.

Differentiating what is core and non–core

Over the past 20–30 years, organisations have increasingly made distinctions between activities that are core, or critical, to the organisation and those that are considered non-core. Those judged to be non-critical are either outsourced, moved off-shore or moved onto flexible employment contracts. The relationship with the non-core activities becomes contractual. This enables the organisation to increase or decrease the size of such activities in accordance with changes in market demand, thus protecting the organisation against economic uncertainties and risk.

Organisations are off-shoring services and production, moving them from high-wage to lower-wage countries. Outsourcing equally involves moving services and work performed within the boundaries of an organisation to an external supplier. These changes necessitate the closure of departments and a redrawing of the boundaries of the organisation.

For several years, I was part of a consulting team that was helping a European telecommunications company to transform itself from a hierarchical, functional bureaucracy to an agile, customer-centric and digital business. The economic pressures on the business required it to halve the size of its workforce from 30,000 to just under 15,000 employees over a period of five years. The organisation was struggling to change quickly enough to adapt to its markets and keep up with much smaller and more agile entrants. The economics of the survival required the organisation to dramatically cut costs to survive and at the same time to reinvent itself. Individuals would suddenly disappear as part of another round of redundancies without an opportunity to say farewell. The organisation's executives had concerns about the speed of change being too slow, with the middle managers and longer-serving employees seen to be the primary block against change. Such dramatic changes, unsurprisingly, generated strong emotional undercurrents of fear and anxiety, which meant that individuals were reluctant to take risk and tended to protect their interests.

Flexible employment relations

In the 1980s, the concept of the flexible firm (Atkinson, 1984) emerged, which argued for a differentiation between 'core' and 'peripheral' employees. The 'core' are fully employed and highly skilled employees whilst the 'peripheral' were assessed as non-vital to the organisation, meaning that their employment becomes temporary and flexible. This gives the organisation the capacity to reduce the size of the workforce in response to changes in demand.

This model of organisation has become widely adopted, particularly in the US and UK economies where employment rights are weaker than in many countries in Europe.[2] In these countries, the flexible labour market has become the norm for low-skilled jobs or non-core jobs. New technologies are also shifting employment relationships increasingly towards temporary and freelancing arrangements (World Economic Forum, 2018).

For flexible workers, organisation membership is transient, transactional and temporary. The psychological contract between them and the organisation is dissolved. Gone is the exchange of loyalty and conformity for security, stability and a job for life. Any sense of mutual obligation and commitment has been replaced with a 'What's in it for me?' mentality. 'Zero-hours contracts' are the ultimate in 'zero commitment'. Under such conditions, a relationship lasts only as long as it is necessary to perform a task or complete an exchange. The individual is now left to cope with the uncertainty generated by the rapid pace of change. This leaves each person feeling that he or she has to fend for him/herself and cannot rely on others in times of vulnerability or threat. Such an environment amplifies an individual's sense of insecurity, vulnerability and anxiety, particularly if they have low skills and little power in the relationship. Once again, to protect themselves, they are likely to look after their interests and avoid taking risks.

The application of technology to replace and control employees

Technology is being used by many organisations as a mechanism to manage risk whilst maintaining management control. Uber, for instance, is using computer algorithms to replace managers in coordinating and controlling employees (Rosenblat, 2018). This enables the company to change policies, pay rates and incentives for drivers in accordance with fluctuations in market conditions. Unlike traditional forms of management, however, the drivers have little or no opportunity to discuss or negotiate the changes (Rosenblat, 2018).

Research suggests that many organisations have started to use new technologies to replace administrative and analytical roles with automated processes and computer algorithms. A survey by Deloitte in 2017, for example, found that 53% of companies had started to use automation to replace work done by people.[3] I am aware of at least one large pharmaceutical firm using digital processes to replace jobs in its R&D function to achieve efficiencies and to speed up the research process. As you can imagine, the changes are provoking widespread anxiety as people fear for the future of their jobs.

Conclusion

Many organisations are now engaged in a constant process of reorganisation and adaptation of their structures as they respond to environmental turbulence and dynamic complexity. The effect of this is that structures are becoming temporary, are not keeping their shape or are not lasting for long. No sooner has one reorganisation finished than another one begins. This leaves many employees in a constant state of confusion, unsure of the rules of engagement and of what is happening and why. For many people, organisational life now feels chaotic, disorienting and overwhelming with few clear boundaries and little order, continuity or predictability. In part, this is because the organisation is betwixt and between two different forms, neither a hierarchy nor a network. Yet despite the rhetoric and exciting models of self-organising and networked organisations, the reality is that most organisations still operate with and will continue to operate with some form of hierarchy.

At the heart of the transformation of organisational form is a paradox. Complexity, turbulence and uncertainty call for greater cooperation, interdependence and personal risk-taking. This requires individuals to show more vulnerability to each other, which relies on individuals trusting each other. However, the actions that are often necessary to become more flexible and adaptable often undermine mutual trust, commitment and engagement. The process of transformation itself generates considerable tensions, strain and anxiety. Employees find themselves stretched between traditional and familiar practices and new emergent structures, approaches and roles. This creates change fatigue, cynicism and alienation. Likewise, the move to short-term, transient and transactional relationships impedes mutual trust and collaboration. These address the immediate economic challenges faced by many organisations yet undermine employee commitment, engagement and relatedness to the organisation. Ultimately, this undermines the organisation's adaptive capacity.

Organisations have considerable choice (Trist, Higgins, Murray, & Pollock, 1963) as to how they respond to turbulence and uncertainty. One choice is to shift risk to employees through contractual relationships that give the organisation economic flexibility and minimise economic risk. The other choice is to invest in creating a high-trust, connected and high-commitment culture which encourages innovation, flexibility and adaptability. Equally, in using new technologies to transform how work is performed, a choice exists as to whether new technology is designed and implemented with or without taking the needs of the existing social system in account (Miller & Rice, 1970; Trist & Bamforth, 1951). This means in practice designing and introducing new work systems with people, rather than imposing them without consultation or involvement.

Notes

1 'At W.L. Gore, 57 years of authentic culture', http://fortune.com/2015/03/05/w-l-gore-culture
2 In the UK there are now close to 2 million people employed on zero-hours contracts whilst almost 5 million are self-employed (Dellot & WS, 2018).
3 Deloitte Global Robotic Process Automation (RPA) Survey, www2.deloitte.com/bg/en/pages/technology/articles/deloitte-global-rpa-survey-2018.html

Works cited

Ashby, W. R. (1956). *Introduction to cybernetics*. London, England: Chapman & Hall.
Atkinson, J. (1984, August). Manpower strategies for flexible organisations. *Personnel Management*, 28–31.
Brunning, H. (2012). *Psychoanalytic reflections on a changing world*. London, England: Karnac.
Burnes, B. (2009). *Managing change* (5th ed.). London, England: FT Prentice Hall.
Burns, T. (1963, January). Mechanistic and organismic structures. *New Society*, 17–20.
Castells, M. (2000). *The rise of the network society*. Cambridge, MA: Blackwell Publishers, Inc.
Cherns, A. (1976). Principles of socio-technical systems design. *Human Relations, 29*, 783–792.
Day, A. (2000). *Part A: An investigation into the impact of the introduction of multiskilled semi-autonomous work groups in two 'brownfield' manufacturing sites*. Unpublished Professional Doctorate in Occupational Psychology, University of East London.
Dellot, B., & WS, F. (2018, July). *Good work in an age of radical technologies*. Retrieved from https://medium.com/@thersa/good-work-in-an-age-of-radical-technologies-52c7bc6b8cc2
Emery, F. E., & Trist, E. L. (1965, February). The causal texture of organizational environments. *Human Relations, 18*, 21–32.
Emery, F. E. (1993). Characteristics of sociotechnical systems. In E. L. Trist & H. Murray (Ed.), *The social engagement of social science: A Tavistock anthology. Volume II: The socio-technical perspective*. Philadephia, PA: University of Pennsylvania Press.
Hamel, G., & Zanini, M. (2018, November – December). The end of bureaucracy. *Harvard Business Review*. Retrieved from https://hbr.org/2018/11/the-end-of-bureaucracy
Holbeche, L. (2015). *The agile organization: How to build an innovative, sustainable and resilient business*. London, England: Kogan Page.
Jaques, E. (1955). Social systems as a defence against persecutory and depressive anxiety. In M. Klein, P. Heimann, & R. E. Money-Kyrle, *New directions in psychoanalysis* (pp. 478–498). London, England: Tavistock Publications.
Krantz, J. (1998). Anxiety and the new order. In E. B. Klein, F. Gabelnick, & P. Herr (Eds.), *The psychodynamics of leadership* (pp. 77–107). Madison, CT: Psychosocial Press.
Laloux, F. (2014). *Reinventing organizations: A guide to creating organizations inspired by the next generation of human consciousness*. Brussels, Belgium: Nelson Parker.
Laumann, E. O., Siegel, P. M., & Hodge, R. W. (1970). *The logic of social hierarchies*. Chicago, IL: Markham Publishing Company.

Lawrence, P. R., & Lorsch, W. J. (Eds.) (1967). High-performing organizations in three environments. In *Organization and environment* (Chapter 6). Boston, MA: Harvard University Press.

Menzies-Lyth, I. (1990). A psychoanalytic perspective on social institutions. In E. Trist, & H. Murray (Eds.), *The social engagement of social science. Vol. 1: The socio-psychological perspective* (pp. 463–475). London, England: Free Association Books.

Milgram, S. (1974). *Obedience to authority.* London, England: Tavistock.

Miller, E. (1993). *From dependency to autonomy: Studies in organization and change.* Oxford, England: Free Association Books.

Miller, E., & Rice, A. K. (1970). *Systems of organization: Control of task and sentient boundaries.* London, England: Tavistock Publications.

Mintzberg, H. (1981). Organizational design: Fashion or fit? *Harvard Business Review, 59*(1), 103–116.

Morgan, G. (1993). Organizational choice and the new technology. In E. Trist & H. Murray (Ed.), *The social engagement of social science: A Tavistock anthology. Volume II: The socio-technical perspective* (pp. 354–368). Philadelphia, PA: University of Pennsylvania Press.

Morgan, G. (1997). *Images of organization* (2nd ed.). Thousand Oaks, CA: Sage Publications.

Morgan, G. (2006). *Images of organization* (Updated ed.). Thousand Oaks, CA: Sage Publications.

Orton, J. D., & Weick, K. (1990). Loosely Coupled Systems: A Reconceptualization. *Academy of Management Review, 15*(2), 203–223.

Robertson, B. J. (2016). *Holacracy: The revolutionary management system that abolishes hierarchy.* London, England: Penguin Business.

Rosenblat, A. (2018). *Uberland: How algorithms are rewriting the rules of work.* Oakland, CA: University of California Press.

Trist, E. L., Higgins, G. W., Murray, H., & Pollock, A. B. (1963). *Organizational choice.* London: Tavistock.

Trist, E., & Bamforth, K. W. (1951). Some social and psychological consequences of the long wall method of coal getting. *Human Relations, 4*, 3–38.

Weber, M. (1947). *The theory of social and economic organization.* New York, NY: Free Press.

Weick, K. (1976). Educational organizations as loosely coupled systems. *Administrative Science Quarterly, 21*, 1–9.

World Economic Forum. (2018). *The future of jobs report.* Retrieved from www3.weforum.org/docs/WEF_Future_of_Jobs_2018.pdf

4 Complexity, order and transformation

Organisations are complex social processes that form through ongoing, everyday interactions between people (Stacey, 2003a). They have an unfolding order that is simultaneously stable and continuously engaged in a process of transformation (ibid.). A constant tension therefore exists between change and continuity; and organisational change is therefore an ongoing process and not a discrete event or episode. In my experience, what receives attention in organisations are the deliberate and intentional attempts to bring about change, whilst the ongoing process of adaptation, innovation and local adjustments get overlooked. In this chapter, I explore how complexity theory, social psychology and sociology can help us understand how change and transformation happen in organisations.

Social order: an emergent phenomenon

Complexity theory argues that order emerges from the interactions of many agents or, in a social system, people. Local interactions spontaneously give rise to system-wide patterns. In an organisation, the ordered behaviour that we observe is a result of a vast number of local self-organising interactions that take place between people. These patterns are paradoxically both stable and unstable, ordered and disordered (Stacey, 2003a). Order therefore emerges out of chaos. That is to say, what happens one moment will not necessarily happen in the next. Patterns cannot be predicted from understanding the individual agents of the system. Nor can order be imposed from outside of the system as control is distributed across everyone and no one is in complete control.

In a complex system, 'the whole is greater than the sum of its parts'. In other words, the behaviour of the system is qualitatively different from the behaviour of the properties of the individual agents. To give an example, we cannot understand the dynamics of a crowd from knowing the psychology of each individual in the crowd. Examples of complex systems include the ecosystem of a rainforest, the weather system, the stock market, the spread of a virus or crowds at Victoria train station. The remarkable characteristic of all these phenomena is that they arise without the need for a central coordinator or designer. If we observe a flock of starlings, we can see that each bird is coordinating its movements in response to the birds that are closest to it. As the flock moves back and forth across the sky, we can see that patterns emerge and disappear but the overall characteristics of the flock is recognisable. This process is called 'emergence' and is one of the hallmarks of life (Capra & Luisi, 2014).

Stable, relatively consistent and repetitive patterns give an organisation its defining form and characteristics. These patterns become predictable in qualitative terms; however, at a micro level they are predictable only for relative short-term, local occurrences (Stacey, 2003b). Complex systems tend to gravitate and remain in these stable states or dynamics, called attractors, unless they are perturbed or disturbed. We might find, for instance, that a global corporation takes a particular form characterised by patterns of behaviour between the centre and the country business units that are recognisable and relatively predictable. These patterns are relatively stable states that tend to re-emerge if they are perturbed. Attractors represent the system's long-term dynamics and characteristics. As information or energy levels increase then these stable patterns start to disintegrate and we start to observe greater novelty and more chaotic and unpredictable events.

> *The medical director of a UK hospital wanted to involve the junior nurses in the hospital more directly in making quality improvements. He met directly with groups of junior nurses who responded positively to his invitation to get involved. What surprised him was the reaction of the senior nurses in the hospital who were critical of his actions, reacted angrily and resisted getting involved. He later understood that his gesture to involve the junior nurses in making changes had to the senior nurses felt as if he was undermining their role in managing the junior nurses. Unwittingly, he had changed the relationship between the junior and senior nurses by changing his relationship with the junior nurses. His intervention revealed the patterns of interdependence between himself, the junior nurses and the senior nurses.*

A few simple rules can generate complex patterns

Computer models of complex systems developed by the Santa Fe Institute have demonstrated that a few simple rules can generate highly complex patterns of behaviour (Kauffman, 1993). The same principle seems to apply to social systems where we can deduce that a few basic rules inform how individuals interact with each other. For instance, if we study a crowd moving through Victoria station at 'rush hour' we are likely to observe that people are taking the least congested path they can see towards where they wish to go, whilst at the same time trying to avoid bumping into the people coming towards them. People mutually regulate each other's speed, so we tend not to see people running and we do not observe people pushing others out of their way. We can think of everyone simultaneously collaborating and competing with each other as they try to get through the station as quickly and safely as possible. If we stood at one of the vantage points in the station and looked down, then we would observe flows of people moving through the station concourse and as bottlenecks emerged people changing their direction of travel to avoid the busier spaces. Those managing the station can affect these patterns by trying to regulate the flow of people into the station, by changing the design and layout of the station, by deploying staff to influence the behaviour of people in specific areas, or by using signs and symbols to communicate rules to individuals.

A sociological and anthropological perspective on social order

Human relating is a dynamic process that has a fractal quality. Every interaction is to some degree novel whilst at the same time has a similarity to many other interactions. We find patterns within patterns at many levels of scale within a complex system. Or as the philosopher Alfred North Whitehead observed (1929), we find 'the general in the particular and the eternal in the transitory'. If we walked into an organisation that we did not know and observed the social milieu around us, at first, we would probably be confused and any patterns we noticed would probably be relatively superficial. Social interactions may seem rather messy and unpredictable. Over time and as we learn more, we might gradually discern patterns in terms of who interacted with whom and how individuals interacted with each other. We might also see differences between individuals both in terms of their appearance but also the level of importance they seemed to have for others. Whilst every interaction is different and unique, we might see some typical pattern that we would label in a particular way – such as hierarchical behaviour. We might notice for instance that managers and their reports related to each other by ascribing higher status to the manager. The reports may defer judgement to those they consider above them in the hierarchy and comply with their wishes or expectations. If we spent more time in the system, we might then notice that different parts of the region have a hierarchical relationship with the regional centre; and that the region has a hierarchical relationship with the global centre. This fractal quality of complex systems enables us to understand wider patterns by studying or paying attention to the patterns that emerge at a local level. Local patterns are a microcosm of the whole. This is reminiscent of the English poet William Blake's encouragement to 'see a world in a grain of sand'.

What makes human action distinctive is the capacity of people to understand the world symbolically. The meaning of events or objects arises out of social interactions and changes through our encounters with others (Mead, 1967). We act towards things on the basis of the meanings that things have for us. We also imagine how the future will be and could be, which informs how we act in the present. Our gestures are based on our interpretations of the social rules at play in the situation and how we imagine others will respond to our gestures. We act therefore with intent towards others and their responses are influenced by their interpretation of our gestures (Blumer, 1969). Gesture and response together constitute a social act through which meaning arises (Stacey, 2012). We are constantly therefore mutually regulating, enabling and constraining each other's behaviour and in doing so creating and recreating social patterns.

Social rules are reflected in an organisation's norms, conventions, ideologies,[1] rituals, ceremonies and customs. These shape what we can, must not, should or ought to do – for instance, how open or closed individuals should be with each other, how much discretion individuals have to express their individuality or how much an individual can challenge authority. We habitually enact these rules in our everyday behaviour. Each of us feels an 'involvement obligation' (Smith & Berg, 1997) in our interactions with others to follow these rules so that we do not lose face (Goffman, 1967).

For the most part, social rules operate outside of our everyday awareness. We reproduce them in our normal and ordinary encounters with each other. They evolve naturally over time as people adapt to changing demands upon them. However, disruptive change brings the social rules into question and challenges them. Once we start to question them, the social patterns they give rise to become vulnerable.

When norms, rituals and customs are disturbed, people tend to experience disorientation, confusion and maybe even alarm. We tend to revert to familiar responses to situations in the absence of alternative principles of behaving to make life more tolerably predictable. One day whilst I was writing this book, I was walking along a street on my way to a meeting. A smartly dressed young man walking towards me stopped in front of me, smiled and then shook my hand. My immediate response was to assume I must have known him and I recall trying to place him and work out if I had met him before. He then proceeded to ask me, in a friendly tone with a foreign accent, how he looked. I was immediately confused and wondered what he meant. Not wanting to cause any offence, I responded that he looked very presentable and smiled. He then said to me: 'what about my face?'. To which, I asked: 'why are you asking me?'. He responded to say he had been in an accident and was worried about how his face looked to others. I replied that it looked fine, as I could see nothing unusual about his appearance. I then shook his hand, smiled and wished him a good day. As I wandered off, I felt somewhat bemused and confused about the interaction. My immediate thought was that he must have been mad. I also noticed that at some point I felt anxious and worried, but his smile indicated to me that he was not being aggressive.

Most of our interactions, however, are not out of the ordinary and we learn to navigate our relationships with others in such a way that they maintain an element of predictability and 'normality'. Whenever we try to change a pattern in our relationships, we can therefore expect people to react to the disturbance. For instance, many of my clients over the years have told me that when they try to do something different at work, their behaviour is met with bemused reactions from their colleagues and attempts to restore the original pattern.

Our need for order and continuity

Anthropologists and sociologists argue that norms, ideologies and social rules are mechanisms for maintaining society. Indeed, the sociologist Emile Durkheim

(1897 [1951]) observed that social order is so deep rooted and pervasive that we cannot escape it because even our thinking is shaped by it. We participate in maintaining it because we have a desire for some level of certainty and predictability in our lives. We create an illusion of a stable state as a bulwark against uncertainty and the threat of change (Schon, 1971). We attempt to maintain the status quo through our conformity to social norms. We cling to tradition, convention and habit.

Conformity is at the heart of social interaction. We comply with social norms because of our need for belonging and our fears of rejection from social groupings. Most of us become adept at interpreting the gestures of others and responding in a manner that conforms with the expected norms. If individuals violate or transgress social norms then groups will typically sanction the individual or pressurise them to change. Failure to comply or conform typically leads to the individual being vilified, ignored, ridiculed or alienated. At the heart of this process is shame. It brings about powerful feelings of inferiority, insecurity and a sense of rejection. Instinctively, we conform to protect ourselves from experiencing shame. Conformity both helps us to feel safe yet equally frustrates our ability to express our difference and individual identity. In this way, shame acts as a dampener of change and serves to maintain conformity with social norms. Conformity is however a poor guide to the future, particularly when our environment is changing or unfamiliar. Yet, individuals who seek to bring about social change by not conforming often do so at considerable personal risk of being rejected or excluded by the in-group.

When social patterns are disrupted, no set template exists for guiding social interactions. This creates a form of social vacuum in which people are unsure of their expectations of each other. This uncertainty around how to interact more often than not creates social anxiety. The higher the stakes and the higher the ambiguity, the higher the levels of anxiety. In the absence of alternative agreements around how to relate and interact, we tend to revert to what is known and familiar. The outcome of social transformation therefore rests upon how, during the disintegration of the existing social order, alternative, attractive and realisable alternatives for behaving are offered to people (Marris, 1982).

I consulted to a large global corporate that has established a new business unit to develop a range of digital products and services. The unit was deliberately set up as an incubator, outside of the boundaries of the core business. The senior management's reasoning was that they did not want the dominant and established culture to hinder the creativity and entrepreneurial spirit of the new unit. About six months after the unit was established, I had a coaching session with one of the experts they had hired into the unit. Within a few minutes, his frustration and disillusionment were all too apparent. He explained how he was expected to report to eight different boards on the progress of his projects. Senior management would ask for analyses of different markets and want to see worked-through business cases of all of the unit's projects. He estimated that over half his time was spend drafting reports and attending reviews. When I asked whether he or others had questioned the need for such extensive reporting, he described how the management above him were all reluctant to say 'no' or express their concerns. He had decided to enact quiet acts of rebellion by reporting back as little information as possible and investing his energies in creating small wins. Despite his frustrations, when I asked him where he felt he was making progress, he was able to describe how a network of digital experts and enthusiasts was developing at a grass-roots level. This was virtually unknown to the senior management team. This emerging network felt like it had potential to grow and develop if nurtured and given space to evolve. Several months later, however, he left the organisation frustrated with his inability to effect change. Other members of the new unit were also experiencing symptoms of stress and distress, feeling under pressure to deliver results by the senior management whilst experiencing resistance to change from the business.

This story reveals the power of the existing social order to constrain the emergence of attempts to innovate and change. Established patterns of hierarchical control, decision making and risk aversion limited attempts to introduce changes. Yet, at the same time, new patterns were emerging that had the potential to develop, which were less visible to senior managers. Rather than understanding the difficulties the unit faced in the context of the established social patterns and norms, the leadership of the organisation decided that those recruited into the unit were not sufficiently competent. This suggests that they could not see their role in maintaining the status quo.

The dynamics of transformation

A complex system is characterised by 'non-linear dynamics'. In a linear system, more or less of one variable will result in a proportional change in another. So, if we press our foot down on the accelerator, our car goes faster. In a non-linear system, this is not the case. Positive feedback loops amplify a behaviour within the system, whilst negative feedback dampens behaviour. Dynamics act back on the agents themselves to affect local interactions and yet at the same time local interactions are altering the system-wide patterns. There is therefore a complex interplay between the macro patterns of the system and the micro moment-by-moment interactions between agents. Because of this, every action will have both intended and unintended consequences. Change cannot be controlled or managed, as it is an emergent phenomenon. This perhaps helps us understand why only around 30% of change programmes are judged to have achieved their intended outcomes.[2]

When the general environment is relatively stable, patterns emerge and sustain over time. As the rate of flow of energy and information increases in a complex system, it becomes less stable. We see greater disruption to established patterns and the emergence of new patterns. Small changes can have large effects and large changes can have no effect. This is the famous 'butterfly effect' or Malcolm Gladwell's 'tipping point' (Gladwell, 2015). Complexity science refers to such changes as 'phase transitions'. An abrupt qualitative change in the system's overall state is triggered by a small change in one element of the system. The transition of water into steam is one example. At a critical temperature, a small change in temperature results in a systemic change in the properties and form of the substance. In complexity theory, this phenomenon is commonly referred to as 'the edge of chaos' (Kauffman, 1993) or 'bounded instability' (Stacey, 2003b). This is a transitional space between order and stability and dis-order and chaos. It represents a state in which patterns are changing and novelty is emerging, creating the potential for a qualitative shift in the system as a whole. In such a state, a potentiality exists for the system to reconfigure. Critical points of instability arise, called 'bifurcation points' (Prigogine, 1987), when the system changes abruptly and new forms of order suddenly appear. We cannot therefore have transformation without disruption.

The 'edge of chaos' describes the instability, uncertainty and discontinuous change that arises in complex systems. Established patterns start to collapse as new patterns emerge and co-exist with uncertainty and chaos. We start to see qualitatively different forms of behaviour and interactions between people, groups and organisations. As new possibilities start to emerge, so the behaviour of firms, investors, governments and consumers starts to shift as they anticipate new patterns and changes in behaviour. For instance, if we look at the auto-motive market, we are starting to see the emergence of new platforms, such as Uber, new entrants, such as Tesla and Google, different technologies, including electric vehicles and driverless cars, and new sources of energy. The market, which has historically been relatively stable and ordered, is becoming more disordered. The process of electrification of vehicles appears to be accelerating, amplified by technological breakthroughs, developing concerns about climate change and the sudden shift in public and governmental attitudes to diesel engines and air pollution. At some point, a tipping point might be reached in which the behaviour of consumers, manufacturers and public authorities shifts dramatically. When and whether this point will be reached is highly unpredictable.

Organisational change is therefore ongoing, continuous and necessarily messy, contradictory and unpredictable and intertwined with wider socio-economic patterns and trends. Small acts of change may have a dramatic impact on the behaviour of others, whilst large-scale change initiatives may simply reinforce established patterns. We may have periods of apparently little change that are dramatically interrupted by sudden shifts and cascade effects that start a process of transformation. These moments have been variously termed as 'dis-continuous', 'revolutionary' or 'transformational' change.

When Nokia missed the abrupt shift in the mobile market, they were forced to take radical action. Their share of the smartphone market had fallen from 49.4% in 2007 to just 3% at the start of 2012. By now the company was haemorrhaging cash, with an operating loss of close to 2 billion euros. As a result, they were having to let go of large numbers of staff. At the same time, they had a partnership with Microsoft to produce smartphones. When Microsoft announced that they were about to bring out their own tablet, moving them into the device market, this was perceived to be a significant threat by Nokia. Their chairman at the time, Risto Siilasmaa, later recounted that this: '...was a real shot across the bow, since they were moving for the first time into the device business'.[3] Microsoft then reached out to see if Nokia was interested in selling their handset business. This led to a decision to get out of the mobile handset business by selling it to Microsoft in 2013. At the same time, Nokia had to decide whether it wanted to continue to be an investor in NSN (Nokia Siemens Networks), a networking joint venture that had been spun off at the height of Nokia's mobile dominance. NSN had gone from a struggling business to a healthy business. Nokia decided to buy out Siemens and take on full ownership of the business. From these two decisions, a new focus and identity started to emerge for Nokia of being a provider of network infrastructure. They could not however provide an end-to-end experience to their customers and this led to the decision to purchase their competitor in networking, Alcatel-Lucent. Their move into networks enabled them to capitalise on the emergence of a rapid and dramatic expansion of connectivity brought about by mobile sensors feeding data into cloud networks and enabling intelligent analysis and machine learning. They called this emerging opportunity 'the programmable world'.

The success of Nokia's transformation has been dramatic with their market capitalisation growing from $5 billion to $40 billion. The turnover in personnel is equally dramatic. Only 1% of employees in 2016 were Nokia employees in 2013. The transformation of Nokia has been something of a metamorphosis, which Risto Siilasmaa described as being like 'a complete renewal of the engines, cabin and the wings of the airplane and reassembling the plane to look very different'.[4]

The story of Nokia (Siilasmaa, 2018) reveals how transformative change is less about planning and managing into the future than about responding and reacting to crises and emerging opportunities. The decision to get out of the mobile handset business was partly a response to Microsoft's decision to get into the device market. Having bought back into the network business, the decision to buy Alcatel-Lucent emerged because Nokia was able to imagine how connectivity and networks were going to rapidly develop as a market. Out of crisis came a new opportunity, which led to the reinvention of Nokia. Whilst the transformation has been dramatic, continuity can be found. At the heart of Nokia's success as a manufacturer of mobile phones was a purpose around connecting people with each other. We can see a similar purpose being expressed in a different form through its new focus on network services.

The tension and conflict of transformation

In organisations that are experiencing disruption to their markets and business models, a tension arises between people's desire to preserve order and the need to adapt. We find people investing in business as usual and others trying to initiate change. In these contexts, the old rules have been discredited whilst the new order is yet to emerge (Bauman, 2010). This tension gives rise to the experience of fragmentation, contradiction and confusion as established structures, forms and patterns dissolve. This unleashes conflicting emotions and anxiety as those affected grapple with feelings of loss mixed with hope and expectation, and primitive concerns around one's ability to cope and survive.

Conflict arises when the existing social order is disrupted. Individuals and groups take positions based on their interests and frames of reference. These positions often form out of anxiety around 'real' and 'imagined' losses and plans around how to protect their needs and identities. They may also relate to different assessments about whether change is necessary and the form that this must take. These differences can be the source of novelty, energy and creative tensions, out of which new ideas and adaptive responses can emerge. They can also be the source of considerable distress, anxiety and frustration when conflicts become polarised and entrenched. When the latter arises, each group will consciously experience one aspect of a conflict or dilemma whilst denying its opposite. For instance, one group invests in maintaining tradition and order whilst the other focuses on innovation and changing the organisation. As the dynamic develops, two opposing sub-groups form that experience themselves as being in opposition to each other. This sets up recursive, self-referential and paradoxical dynamics (Smith and Berg, 1997), with each group defining itself in opposition to the other group. We can think of the emergence of the split between the 'Remain' and 'Leave' groups in the UK following the EU referendum as a manifestation of polarisation. The acknowledgement, recognition and expression of such different perspectives can be creative. As the exploration of difference can enable a system to move from a simple to more complex understandings of itself, which allows it to adapt to changes in its environment. The process can equally be destructive and degenerative in nature when each group becomes overly invested in protecting its position and invested in denying the complexities of the situation.

Our capacity to reflect

Humans demonstrate the capacity to reflect on and change their behaviour. Social groups are also able to adapt their norms. If the stock market starts to fall, investors rapidly adapt their behaviour in responses to the behaviour of other investors. If I find that Victoria station is becoming more and more congested, I may change my route and go via a different station. In social systems, people can therefore change the rules they are choosing to follow. This capacity of each person or group to adjust their behaviour gives a social system adaptive capacity.

The European telecommunications business (referenced in the previous chapter) was historically a state-run bureaucracy that operated the national telephone network, which had been privatised and its markets opened up for competition. In recent years, the speed of change in the technology markets, and the advent of digitalisation and cloud computing meant that its traditional markets were disappearing. The firm was struggling to adapt fast enough to the changing environment. The traditional hierarchical culture, process orientation and fear of risk-taking meant that innovation and product development was slow. Whilst the instability and turbulence of the situation was highly uncomfortable and challenging for most, it also created opportunities for change as many of the existing practices, services and products were being questioned. The business was having to radically rethink how it serviced its customers.

My colleagues and I faciliated a leadership programme that was a deliberate attempt to help senior leaders to disrupt and reinvent their own business. The participants engaged in a range of exercises to raise their awareness of the existing social patterns and rules, and support them to experiment with breaking or disturbing them. They formed into cross-disciplinary teams that were challenged with collaborating across organisational boundaries to experiment with rapid prototyping to deliver improved services to customers. These teams were encouraged to work in short cycles of experimentation with customers and employees to make improvements to services or design new ones.

The intent of the programme was to create a transformative space in which the participants could learn about change by trying to change the organisation. Executive sponsorship gave permission to participants to take risks and encourage them to focus on learning by doing rather than worrying about achieving a short-term objective or result. Participants also formed into action learning sets to help them reflect together on their experiments and what they were learning about change and disruption.

The experiments required leaders to engage directly with customers and front-line staff to address problems that were being experienced. This gave them insight into how the external market was changing and challenged them to help teams to find innovative solutions to emerging challenges. Some teams were successful whilst others had little tangible impact. When we brought the teams together to reflect on what they had learnt, deeper insights emerged into the challenges the business was facing, the need to engage local teams in finding solutions and the value of connecting across functional and hierarchical boundaries.

Implications for practice

The complexity paradigm challenges traditional change frameworks (Beckhard & Pritchard, 1992; Conner, 1993; Kotter, 1996; Nadler, 1992) that are underpinned by linear and deterministic assumptions. Table 4.1 provides a comparison

Table 4.1 Comparison of traditional, linear and deterministic frameworks of organisational change and a complexity paradigm

Linear frameworks of organisational change	*Complexity perspective on organisational change*
Change is a linear, ordered process that can be planned, managed and controlled	Change is a non-linear, emergent and unpredictable process
Organisational change involves the movement from one stable state to another	Order arises from local interactions between people and change happens when these shift
Unitarist view of organisations, i.e. a single common purpose and set of interests exists	Pluralist view of organisations, i.e. divergent, competing interests and contested world views
The future can be predicted and determined	Change is an ongoing, dynamic and continuous process
The current state can be measured to identify what needs to change	Acts to change the organisation will have both intended and unintended consequences
Change results from the manipulation of variables such as structure, culture, processes etc.	Change arises as people interact and relate to each other differently, disturbing norms, habits and social expectations

of traditional, linear models of change and a complexity paradigm. Traditional frameworks emphasise the role of leaders in designing and planning how the organisation needs to change, communicating a vision and leading the process of change to overcome employee resistance. Complexity theory challenges these assumptions and suggests that to facilitate change we need to:

Accept that we can never see the full picture. We are all immersed in patterns of interaction, some of which we can make sense of and others that we are unaware of or are yet to comprehend. This means that no person or group is able to stand outside of the system to see it as it is. We can only respond to patterns that we are experiencing at a local level and the information that we are receiving through our interactions with others. If this is the case, then change and adaptation is an unfolding process that we are working out with others in response to anticipated and unanticipated events. We all need to act into the unknown, putting our best foot forward and learning what happens next. Making sense of change and the planning of change are therefore necessarily ongoing, iterative and imperfect processes.

Recognise that organisational change is necessarily emergent, messy and unpredictable (and not ordered and sequential in nature). We cannot fully anticipate or know in advance what will happen or, indeed, what will be the consequences of different actions. If the future is unknowable, we cannot choose a desired state for the organisation and plan a route for achieving it. There is nothing wrong with having visions and plans to inform our actions; we cannot, however, know or predict what will happen when we implement them. Interventions intended to effect change will have both intended and unintended consequences. Change processes are therefore characterised by the dynamic interplay between attempts to effect change and responses to these actions.

Embrace disturbance, disruption and uncertainty. Organisations have the propensity to change when they are disrupted, disturbed and become unstable. Innovations emerge not from seeking to maintain order but from moving towards uncertainty and novelty. Changes are unknown until they start to take shape and are made sense of retrospectively.

Facilitate the expression of difference and non-conformity. Change emerges through the expression of difference and the disturbance of social norms. Valuing difference and creating inclusive environments encourages people to express their opinions and ideas and to challenge each other. Likewise, processes that bring people together from different parts of the organisation and outside of it create spaces in which novelty and difference can be recognised, expressed and explored.

Be aware that change can and does arise from anywhere in the system. Traditional theories argue that change needs to be led from the top. If we accept that change emerges from local interactions, then small actions and changes can trigger system-wide patterns. This is not to say that senior leaders do not have influence but that we can relax our assumptions about who needs to be involved and what is necessary. Small groups of innovators working informally and at the margins can generate new ideas, products or services that can be suddenly adopted and applied by others. Indeed, imitation and adaptation of others' ideas appears to be central to the process of change in organisations.

See the process of changes as involving learning, improvisation and muddling through. In practice, organisational change is more a participative process of improvisation, learning and muddling through rather than a rationally planned technocratic project. Involving people in the process of change is necessary if people are going to recognise how they act together to maintain patterns and to learn together how to adapt. Complexity theory also suggests that by increasing the flow of information and feedback in a system, new and different patterns are likely to emerge. This can be facilitated by making information freely available and by bringing people together to share perspectives on what they are experiencing, doing and observing.

Conclusion

Organisations are characterised by relatively stable and enduring social patterns which are continually reproduced through the interactions of people as they engage in their work. Human nature is such that we attempt to maintain social order through our compliance with norms and social expectations. If, however, an organisation only has order and stability, then it is in stasis and decline. Instability, difference and novelty are therefore necessary and become critical for adaptation as the environment becomes more turbulent and uncertain. We can expect that as instability and disorder emerge, the levels of conflict, disagreement and anxiety will increase. Whilst this is uncomfortable for people, it does generate a creative potential in which novelty, new patterns and different forms of organising can also emerge. If people are able to tolerate this discomfort and reflect on their behaviour, then they are more able to co-create new ways of working, collaborating or performing their work.

Notes

1 Ideologies are: 'the ruling ideas in a particular society [or group] at a particular time. They are the ideas that express the naturalness of any existing social order and help to maintain it' (Dalal, 1998, p. 116).
2 McKinsey & Co (2008) survey of 3,199 executives, http://gsme.sharif.edu/~change/McKinsey%20Global%20Survey%20Results.pdf
3 'Nokia's next chapter', www.mckinsey.com/industries/high-tech/our-insights/nokias-next-chapter
4 'The rebirth of Nokia: An interview with chairman Risto Siilasmaa', www.bcg.com/en-gb/publications/2016/corporate-development-finance-telecommunications-risto-siilasmaa-rebirth-nokia.aspx

Works cited

Bauman, Z. (2010). *Letters from the liquid modern world*. Cambridge, England: Polity Press.
Beckhard, R., & Pritchard, W. (1992). *Changing the essence: The art of creating and leading environmental change in organizations*. San Francisco, CA: Jossey-Bass.
Blumer, H. (1969). *Symbolic interactionism: Perspective and method*. Englewood Cliffs, NJ: Prentice-Hall.
Capra, F., & Luisi, P. L. (2014). *The systems view of life: A unifying vision*. Cambridge, England: Cambridge University Press.
Conner, D. R. (1993). *Managing at the speed of change: how resilient managers succeed and prosper where others fail*. New York, NY: Villard Books.
Dalal, F. (1998). *Taking the group seriously: towards a post-foulkesian group analytic theory*. London, England: Jessica Kingsley.
Durkheim, E. (1897 [1951]). *Suicide: A study in sociology*. Glencoe, IL: The Free Press.
Gladwell, M. (2015). *The tipping point: How little things can make a big difference*. London, England: Abacus.
Goffman, E. (1967). *Interaction ritual: Essays on face-to-face behaviour*. New York, NY: Pantheon Books.
Kauffman, S. (1993). *The origins of order: Self-organization and selection in evolution*. Oxford, England: Oxford University Press.
Kotter, J. (1996). *Leading change*. Boston, MA: Harvard Business Review Press.

Marris, P. (1982). *Meaning and action: Community planning and conceptions of change.* London, England: Routledge and Kegan Paul.

Mead, G. H. (1967). *Mind, self and society from the standpoint of a behaviorist.* Chicago, IL: University of Chicago.

Nadler, D. (1992). *Organizational architecture: Designs for changing organizations.* San Francisco, CA: Jossey-Bass.

Prigogine, I. (1987). *The end of certainty: Time, chaos, and the new laws of nature.* New York, NY: Free Press.

Schon, D. (1971). *Beyond the stable state.* New York, NY: Random House.

Siilasmaa, R. (2018). *Transforming NOKIA: The power of paranoid optimism to lead through colossal change.* New York, NY: McGraw-Hill Education.

Smith, K., & Berg, D. N. (1997). *Paradoxes of group life: Understanding conflict, paralysis and movement in group dynamics.* San Francisco, CA: Jossey-Bass.

Stacey, R. (2003a). *Strategic management and organisational dynamics: the challenge of complexity.* Harlow, England: FT/Prentice-Hall.

Stacey, R. (2003b). *Complexity and group processes: A radical social understanding of individuals.* London, England: Routledge.

Stacey, R. (2012). *Tools and techniques of leadership and management: Meeting the challenge of complexity.* London, England; New York, NY: Routledge.

Whitehead, A. N. (1929). *The aims of education & other essays.* New York, NY: Macmillan Co.

5 Networks, social capital and lost connections

Organising arises as people coordinate their activities to accomplish particular economic and social purposes. By collaborating with others, we can achieve more than we can on our own; the achievements of modern civilisation have come about through this complex process of organising. Frederic Laloux (2014) illustrates this point wonderfully in his book *Reinventing Organizations*. He observes how the dramatic improvements in health over the last century added nearly 20 years' life expectancy to the average person in the United States. This was achieved by a vast and dense network of organisations – research centres, pharmaceutical companies, hospitals, medical schools, health insurance companies – meshed together into a highly sophisticated medical system.

Organising gives rise to complex patterns of dense, enduring and complex relationships. These social networks play a critical role, not just in creating a capacity for coordinated action, but also in how an organisation adapts to external changes. Networks are therefore the basic fractal of organisation of life (Capra & Luisi, 2014). In a world of uncertainty and turbulence, the quality of networks, relationships and connections between people become critical for competitiveness and survival.

The nature of social networks

Social networks are characterised by clustering between people with a few critical links and connections between different clusters (see Figure 5.1). This is a universal phenomenon of social networks. Nodes, which are hubs in a network that have large numbers of connections, help to connect different parts of the network together. These might be departments that play an important coordinating role or individuals who act as brokers between different populations or specialisms. The size of a network is reflective of the number and breadth of interactions within it. Much like Russian dolls, networks tend to be embedded in other networks. Organisations likewise are embedded in wider networks of communities, suppliers, partners, customers and competitors.

Social networks are dynamic and evolving patterns of ongoing communication. They are continually being constructed as people interact, formally and informally. These patterns of communication have an inherent circularity,

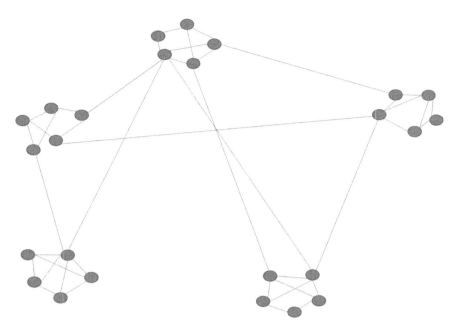

Figure 5.1 Representation of a network

generating the pattern of the network (Luhmann, 1990) and maintaining shared beliefs and assumptions. Through this process, social interactions reproduce the identity of the social network. In this regard, an organisation is 'autopoietic' – continually reproducing itself to maintain a coherent identity (Maturana & Varela, 1980).

The network paradigm draws attention to the connectivity within a system. This enables the exchange of information that would be difficult or not possible in its absence. Social connectivity supports the emergences of clusters of interconnected communities of practice (Capra & Luisi, 2014) within organisations. These are groups of people bound together by shared expertise and aims (Wenger, 1998). These informal communities create, maintain and share tacit knowledge, know-how and expertise (ibid.). We therefore need to see the connections between people and parts of the organisation. Generally, as the level of connections increases across a social system, it becomes more dynamic and fluid in its form. An organisation with low connectivity behaves very differently to one with a high level of connectivity.

Adaptability and resilience of social networks

The performance and resilience of a network is dependent on the level and quality of connectedness and the extent to which shared interests and goals exist across the network. Hubs and links foster communication between disparate elements of a network. Only a small number of redundant bridging relationships are required across a network to give it high levels of resilience to external disturbance, as it allows information to travel across alternative paths if a connection is lost. This basic principle can be found across a whole range of networks in society, such as energy networks or the internet (Buchanan, 2004).

Decentralisation also helps networks to be resilient to external shocks and more adaptable to change. This is because a network has distributed capabilities and redundancy (Homer-Dixon, 2011). A failure in one part of the network does not cause failure in other parts because of loose coupling across the system. Equally, if one part of the network is unable to function, other parts of the network can take on its role. This is one of the reasons why decentralised terrorist networks, such as Al-Qaeda, have proved to be so resilient and difficult for larger and far more powerful states to destroy. This is not the case with hierarchies, where centralised decision making and tight coupling between different parts means that the failure of one part can trigger failure in other parts of the system. Hierarchies are therefore less adaptable to shocks, unanticipated events or discontinuous change.

High connectivity however does not necessarily give a network resilience. Where centralisation is high (i.e. there are a few hubs with a high percentage of connections with the rest of the network) and overall connectivity is high, a complex system is more vulnerable to systemic risks and cascade effects. A shock in one part of the system can spread out across the whole system. This is what happened during the financial crisis of 2008. A study by researchers at the International Monetary Fund into the 2008 economic crisis found that high interconnectivity combined with high levels of centralisation led to the destabilisation of the global banking system. A shock to the central hub of the network destabilised the entire network (Minoiu & Reyes, 2010).

Social capital

The capacity for an organisation to develop integrated, vibrant and genuine human relations is a competitive advantage in turbulent environments. Social networks, connections and high-trust relationships facilitate the flow of information and ideas. This fosters innovation in organisations (Aalbers & Dolfsma, 2015). Equally, stable and enduring relationships enable tacit knowledge to develop and to be shared between individuals and groups. Such practical know-how resides in the relationships. Shared obligations, mutual expectations and reciprocity facilitate collaboration and enable individuals to act together effectively in the pursuit of shared objectives. Shared values equally create a moral and ethical framework that guides people's behaviour. Such *intangible value and resources* have been called 'social capital' (Lin, 1999).

The sociologist Robert Putnam first coined the concept of social capital when, through his research, he discovered that the health, educational and economic strength of North American communities were dependent on the quality of relationships and social cohesion between citizens. Putnam (2000) argued that the evidence is clear that social capital is positively linked to well-being and health because of the psycho-social support it offers. Evidence also suggests that it helps maintain identities that reinforce well-being and mental health (Lin, 1999). Putnam defined social capital as 'features of social organization, such as trust, norms and networks, that can improve the efficiency of society by facilitating coordinated actions' (Putnam, 1993, p. 196). In his book, aptly titled *Bowling Alone*, he argued that social capital has collapsed in the United States as communities 'have withered' and that such changes have 'very real costs'. His argument was very simple: if communities and governments invest in social relations, they get returns. We can apply these basic ideas to organisations. This would imply that investment in social networks develops intangible resources and relational assets that are fundamental to the health and resilience of the organisation. Social norms, such as trust and reciprocity, enable resources and capabilities to be combined in different ways. This gives an organisation the ability to do things or perform to standards that other organisations cannot replicate. This makes sense intuitively; however, my observations and experiences suggest that much of what organisations are doing to adapt to changes is destroying rather than developing social capital.

A poignant illustration of social capital is described by the business anthropologist Ann Jordan (Jordan, 2013). In her book, she describes an ethnographic study conducted by Miriam Kaprow (Kaprow, 1999) into the culture of the New York City fire service prior to the terrorist attack on the World Trade Center. Her study helps us to understand the heroics of the firefighters during the disaster. Firefighters would come to work early, stay late and bring their families in on days off. Almost 30% of the police force would transfer to the fire service, yet the transfer rate in the other direction was negligible. Kaprow wanted to understand what was behind these patterns. Her study revealed how firefighters felt a sense of autonomy and control over how they planned and undertook their work (in contrast to police officers). She observed that a shared professional culture existed which centred around some core rituals. Firefighters would have a communal dinner together at the fire station, and a code of behaviour was shared across the firefighters. This 'tribal' cohesion created a strong sense of belonging, camaraderie and investment in the community. This no doubt played out in the courage and teamwork the New York firefighters displayed during the disaster.

In a somewhat perverse way, social capital was demonstrated to me one day, some 15 years ago, in a conversation with an area manager at an automotive plant. He was frustrated and equally a little impressed that in response to the planned volumes for the plant being dropped, the productivity for the plant had fallen to a level that was required to maintain the existing levels of overtime in the plant. Given the workforce was organised into three shifts and composed of some 700-odd people, this is a fairly significant demonstration of collaboration and shared understanding of how to manage the productivity of the plant. If workers had publicly organised to work towards this achievement, their behaviour would, in all likelihood, have been judged as highly subversive. This collective achievement was done with little explicit communication or coordination.

Many large consultancies have developed costly knowledge management systems in attempts to systematise the recording of and sharing of knowledge between consultants. These systems record both data and information from consulting projects and create databases of individuals' expertise. Such systems are intended to help consultants find information on past projects that are similar to the one they are engaged with and to support the resourcing of projects. In practice, however, consultants resource projects through their informal networks, inviting individuals into projects on the basis of their trust of the individual or they recruit colleagues based on recommendations from colleagues they trust. Consultants also do not keep the systems up to date because this tends not to be rewarded. They also have to invest time in keeping entries updated when they often have billable hours targets. A system cannot replace or represent the quality and nature of the relationship that exists between individuals. For this reason, knowledge management and resourcing systems tend to be resisted in consultancies and consultants find ways of working around them.

Bridging and connecting relationship

Robert Putnam (2000) divided social capital into bonding and bridging relationships. Bonding reinforces exclusive identities, creates close social ties and maintains homogeneity, whilst bridging relationships or more distant social ties bring people together across social boundaries (see Figure 5.2). Bonding social capital supports the development of strong identities, solidarity and reciprocity. Bridging relationships between people in complex social networks facilitate the exchange and diffusion of new ideas and information. These connections bind together the social fabric. Mark Granovetter (1973) made similar observations about the importance of 'weak' ties in a social network. He found compelling evidence that we gain access to new ideas and opportunities through our more distant social relationships that are outside of our network of 'strong' ties. *Strong ties* are similar to bonding relationships. They are characterised by higher quantity, higher quality and frequency of interactions. Strong ties facilitate intense and rich communications between individuals, which enable assimilation and the combining of knowledge and expertise. In comparison, *weak ties* enable

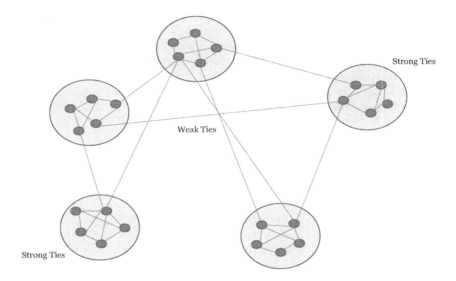

Figure 5.2 Strong and weak ties within a social network

exchange amongst diverse stakeholders that have limited or no contact with each other. This facilitates the emergence of novelty. Relationships with other groups and individuals also enable the leveraging and mobilising of resources and capabilities to which an individual or group do not have access. One study, for instance, found that in a major consultancy more innovative consultants had a greater number of bridging ties (Gray, Parise, & Iyer, 2011). High levels of local cohesion with few connections to other clusters are likely to reduce adaptive capacity because the group does not have access to alternative information, ideas or perspectives. Social capital therefore should not be confused with local cohesion. Weak ties are critical in helping local clusters feel connected to a wider, larger community or social entity.

Communications technology, including the internet and social media, has dramatically accelerated and amplified both the numbers of and reach of connections across societies and organisations. This increases bridges between networks and accelerates the flow of information and data across organisations. It therefore has the potential to bring about a revolutionary rise in social capital. For instance, one of my clients, a global construction business, is utilising digital platforms to help create global communities of practice in different specialisms to enable knowledge sharing and collaboration across regions. It is worth noting, however, that all the evidence suggests that online interaction complements and supplements face-to-face communication (Field, 2008), rather than replacing it.

I consulted to an automotive company that had historically experienced ongoing problems and difficulties with the launch of new vehicles. The launch process involves the transition of responsibility from a large product development team to a team in manufacturing. This transition takes place over many months as the product development programme comes to an end and the manufacturing department prepares plants to produce the new model. A series of launches had experienced delays and poor quality. To try and effect change, together with a colleague I designed and facilitated a process that brought together representatives from across all the major functions who had been involved in the most recent programmes, the current one and the one that was planned to start in the coming months. Over a period of three days, we explored the critical events for the past and present programmes to understand the complex dynamics that would play out during a launch. Through the process we were able to see connections between programmes and events. We also took time to invite individuals to join the conversation who had worked in other automotive companies to hear their experiences. Over an intense three days, insights emerged around how the early organisation and management of launches triggered patterns that started to amplify as the programme grew in size. These dynamics would appear as significant problems as the programme moved into production. They were causing delays, raising costs and affecting the quality of production. What is more, we were able to see how the patterns would absorb resources and time, which triggered the same initial problems at the start of the next programmes. Managers who were involved in current and future launches were able to take these insights and apply them to their programmes. Following the workshop, a group of those involved also engaged the executive team and senior leaders in the product development in a conversation around the dynamics that were affecting the launch process and what actions could be taken to effect change.

This process brought together individuals with both strong and weak connections with each other. The process of dialogue and collaborative exchange of perspectives helped a richer understanding of the current reality to emerge and facilitated the imagining of an alternative future. The intervention also facilitated the emergence of a community of practice.

Difference, variety and variation

Social patterns start to shift when they are disturbed by differences such as new information, deviance from the norm or new ideas. Change needs a 'mix of difference (diversity), connections between people, energy or information and ongoing interaction between people' (Shaw, 2006, p. 101). New patterns and novelty emerge not from individual parts but rather from the connections across the system. The diffusion of ideas across social systems is fostered by information that is shared across connections and networks. Complexity allows for ideas, resources or people to be brought together and combined in unexpected ways, increasing a system's capacity to adapt to change. For instance, as cities grow in complexity they facilitate innovation because they enable people, ideas, cultures and resources to combine in novel and unexpected ways (Florida, 2002).Variation and diversity give a system resilience and the capacity to adapt. If we turn to biology for lessons, we know that species adaptation to environmental change is brought about through mutations and deviation from the norm (Capra & Luisi, 2014). Difference and diversity are necessary therefore for a complex system or organisation to be able to adapt to environmental change.

The possibility for change to emerge is enabled when connections are made with outliers, those at the margins or 'positive deviances' (Richard Pascale, 2010) in a social system. Individuals or groups who are outside of or deviate from the norm tend to have unusual or different ways of solving problems than their peers. Listening to them can generate new information, different ways of thinking and/or solving problems. The theory of positive deviance (Richard Pascale, 2010), for instance, was developed on the back of insights from projects by Save the Children to help the people of Vietnam reduce childhood malnutrition in their rural villages. Their programmes had a profound impact on the lives of millions of people. Jerry and Monique Sternin (Sterin & Choo, 2000, p. 274), working closely with the residents of several villages in Thanh Hoa province, discovered very poor families who were not malnourished. These families had somehow found enough food to keep their children healthy. The mothers in these families were discovered to be collecting tiny shrimps and crabs from local rice paddies, which they were adding, along with sweet-potato greens, to their children's meals. Traditionally these foods were considered inappropriate for young children. These families also fed their children three or four times a day rather than the customary twice a day. The researchers were able to help other families to learn from these 'positive deviants' and, through mimicry and imitation, the behaviour of village communities changed. Because the solutions were local in origin, levels of resistance to change were lower than if they were designed and imposed from outside.

Mark Granovetter's observations on the strength of weak ties highlight that it is not just difference that is important but also the form of social connections that helps gives rise to innovation (Granovetter, 1973). Both 'strong' and 'weak' social ties play a role in the creation and spread of new ideas. Within networks, individuals with dense and rich connections, hubs and nodes in the network have the potential to act as brokers in connecting people and groups. These individuals become increasingly important during disruptive change when rapid and novel responses are required. They support the flow of information and ideas across parts of the organisation. Whether these ideas are taken up by others is, however, influenced by the quality of connections and relationships more widely across the organisation. A few influential and trusted 'brokers' can act as hubs in a social network, helping to disseminate new ideas or practices, as they tend to have links into other networks or groupings.

During the 2008 financial crisis, my colleague Kevin Power and I interviewed executives in European organisations to understand their experience of leading during a period of disruption and uncertainty. We discovered that many were relying on their networks to help them to make sense of the rapidly changing landscape (Power & Day, 2010). Senior executives increasingly contacted 'weak' ties in their networks to gain information and perspectives on economic developments. They were reaching out beyond their usual horizons to talk to customers, suppliers, competitors and government representatives with whom they had rare or no contact. These contacts became a source of information about change and novelty.

Mutual trust: 'the magic ingredient'

The quality of relationships, trust and 'goodwill' act as a form of social glue and lubricant that enables the potential of a social network to be realised. Trust is a willingness to show vulnerability to others based on the mutual assumptions that the other person has the best of intentions. This capacity to be vulnerable with others encourages open and candid exchanges that are rich in information. This increases the probability that people are making judgements based on a range of perspectives and supports creative adaptation because people are sharing ideas with each other. Trust enables people to influence each other and it provides different individuals or parts of the organisation with access to resources or capabilities. When trust is high between groupings within a network then people tend to be more willing to interact across boundaries, share information and collaborate. Trust therefore facilitates connections between groups, creating bridges for the flow of information and ideas across an organisation.

In contrast, when distrust is high, group relations tend to become defensive and boundaries close. The interactions between groups then become limited. As contact between groups is reduced, opportunities for reality testing decrease and groups start to form assumptions about the motives and agendas of others. This can create a cycle of distrust, whereby paranoid anxieties and projections lead to hostile or defensive behaviour which further erodes trust, and so forth. In low-trust environments, social media tends to amplify paranoid dynamics. Ambiguous messages tend to be interpreted through a lens of suspicion, causing people to see hostility where and when it was not intended. If they respond with hostility, then dynamics escalate and spread across social networks.

Several years ago, a colleague, Guy Lubitsh, and I were working together on different organisation development projects in the UK's National Health Service (Day & Lubitsh, 2012). We noticed that in some organisations, change seemed to be very challenging and difficult, whilst in others people were much more willing

> to work together to make improvements. To understand what was happening, we interviewed leaders in different NHS Trusts to explore their experience of initiating change projects in their organisations. We discovered that the level of mutual trust that existed between different professional groups and between staff and managers featured strongly in the accounts of the leaders. They described how trust shaped how their behaviour and decisions were interpreted by different stakeholders and, likewise, shaped how they interpreted the behaviour and motives of others. In those organisations where mutual trust appeared high, individuals generally assumed the best of intent in their colleagues. In contexts of low trust, anxiety and fear associated with organisational change was high. Different stakeholders perceived other actors in the system as possible threats whose motives may lead them to act in a manner that is in opposition to their interests. Individuals were suspicious of the intention of those leading changes and more likely to act to protect their interests. Hostility provoked further hostility and individuals reported significant difficulties in collaborating with people outside their departments. Managers reported that it was difficult to gain support for changes and that staff were unwilling to take risks or adopt new practices.
>
> We concluded, unsurprisingly, that trust is a necessary condition for change where there is uncertainty and a level of risk.

Social capital is particularly vulnerable during periods of discontinuous or rapid change. Social networks can be torn apart, fragmented or destroyed altogether. For instance, reorganisations break up teams and local networks, which creates anxieties and damages bonding relationships. This makes it more difficult for information and ideas to flow locally. It also makes bridging relationships less effective because information might be communicated between parts of the organisation but the absence of local connectivity means this does not get shared. Reorganisations can also damage bridging relationships, particularly when hubs are removed or brokers moved out of influential roles. If not understood, these changes can reduce the connectivity between teams or parts of an organisation.

Dramatic change can reduce social integration by undermining trust, shared norms and values, particularly when planned changes do not convey respect and consideration to those affected or leave people feeling that they do not matter and are expendable. Poorly managed change can therefore destroy social capital. An estimated 75% of mergers (Burke & Biggart, 1997), for instance, damage economic value in the long term. One explanation for this finding is that social capital and the uniqueness of each party's culture is rarely recognised and appreciated in the process of integration. The dominant party tends to impose its cultural beliefs and values on the other's. This dampens or destroys the uniqueness of the culture of the weaker party.

As part of our research into the financial crisis, Kevin Power and I studied a business unit of a German pharmaceutical multinational that had experienced a dramatic fall in demand for one of its specialist products that was used in the production of cars. Because of the abrupt decline in global car production, their customers had cut their orders. The plant itself had produced more product that it had orders for, meaning the plant could meet demand for several months by running down its stocks. This resulted in the plant having no work. Rather than lay people off, the plant's management expressed their commitment to their employees and engaged in a process of consultation with staff and the works council about how to handle the crisis. The result was a decision by the staff to take their holiday early and the management to invest in both training and maintenance during a plant slowdown. The regional government also contributed through funding and investment for training. The consequence of such an enlightened response was a deep sense of trust and loyalty between employees and management. The plant was also able to retain highly skilled employees who would have been difficult to replace in the future.

To support the process of change at the European telecommunications business, I was part of a consulting team that facilitated a leadership development process that was designed to develop strong ties and bridging connections across the middle and senior management population. Participants were drawn from across divisions, hierarchical levels and functions. These individuals were encouraged to think of themselves as 'disruptors' of the business. As part of the programme, they self-organised into cross-disciplinary teams that worked with a pair of business sponsors on a change project. These projects required them to work with customers and operational teams in the business. The executive team were involved in different parts of the programme to participate in dialogue sessions with the participants. A final one-day conference event was run at the end of the process in which the executive team, participants, sponsors and alumni from past programmes engaged in exploring what had been learnt about the organisation from trying to change it. This process facilitated intense and rich interactions between individuals from different networks, helped to develop a network of leaders who were invested in supporting change and developed links across different levels of the hierarchy.

Implications for practice

According to network theory, change spreads through formal and informal connections, not through hierarchies. There is evidence to suggest that organisations that successfully implement change make greater use of organisation-wide and local learning networks (Mohram, Tenkasi, & Mohrman, 2009). For instance, Rowland and Higgs (2008) found that changes that tended to be unsuccessful relied on hierarchies to implement changes. This suggests that to create change we need to worry less about implementing plans, and invest our energies in developing social networks and communities of practice (Capra & Luisi, 2014). The process of change needs therefore to encourage new patterns of communication and interactions across social networks. As people converse with people who fall outside of their typical, everyday interactions, new meanings and understandings arise. From this perspective, change is more like a virus that spreads through connections than an outcome to be engineered or produced.

The following principles are likely to help facilitate change:

Pay attention to the patterns of relationships and connections within and between networks. For leaders, consultants and change agents who are trying to effect change in organisations, it is important to understand the patterns of connections and relationships within the organisation. One helpful intervention is to bring individuals from across the organisation together to explore and map the central social networks and critical communities of practice. Important questions to explore include:

- Who is connected to whom?
- How densely clustered are networks?
- How are these clusters distributed?
- How connected are these clusters?
- Where are the critical hubs and critical links?
- Who are the brokers who connect people in the network?

Understanding these properties offers insights as to how information and ideas flow around the organisation. This enables people to understand how social networks enable collaboration and to plan changes that develop, and do not damage, social capital.

Foster and facilitate connectivity within and between networks. Developing the number and quality of connections within and between networks amplifies the flow of information and ideas, whilst the establishment of bridging relationships across networks and with external networks provides access to environment trends, technological developments, new ideas and diverse communities. By amplifying the exchanges between those at the margins, edges and boundaries and those in the 'mainstream' or 'centre', we facilitate the cross-pollination of ideas and the generation of new perspectives. Large-group events, such as Future Search, World Café and Open Space, create an intense and structured process for facilitating within group and intergroup connections and relationships.

Creation of cross-boundary task forces. One strategy that helps to develop connections between different parts of an organisation is the creation of task forces that are given responsibility for finding solutions, creating new products or leading changes. The task force itself becomes a crucible for establishing relationships, sharing ideas and establishing bridges between different networks. The focus on a shared task – so long as it is perceived to be relevant and meaningful – creates a need for collaboration, which itself helps to develop cooperative relationships.

Nurturing trust within and between groupings. Establishing trust is paradoxical. Both parties have to be willing to make themselves vulnerable to others, which individuals tend to be reluctant to do when they mistrust the other. To develop trust requires people to put time aside to reflect on and develop their relationship (and not just focus on the performance of tasks). Trust develops slowly and requires both parties to progressively take greater risks with each other in order to demonstrate that they trust the other party. This requires small steps that are low risk, rather than giant leaps of faith that involve significant risks. Open and transparent communication and sharing of information, even if it is about difficult and challenging topics, helps people to understand others' intentions, expectations and concerns.

Cultivating communities of practice. As communities of practice are informal, self-organising and maintained through the active participation of their members, they do not lend themselves to being designed and formally managed. They can however be cultivated, encouraged and supported by creating the conditions that enable them to take hold and grow. This might be as simple as leaders acknowledging their importance, legitimising them and providing space, time and resources for them to meet and function. Where employees have to account for their time and demonstrate productivity, they are unlikely to prioritise activities that involve the sharing of practice, ideas and knowledge with others.

Designing physical and virtual spaces to support social interaction. Physical space influences the nature and intensity of social interaction. Many companies have recognised how the design of workspaces and offices can encourage human interaction and networking. Virtual communications technology and social media, if used thoughtfully, can equally facilitate and support the connection across social and geographic boundaries. IBM, Apple and Google have designed workspaces to facilitate interpersonal interaction (Schawbel, 2017). For instance, Apple's new workspace is designed to promote relationships, idea sharing and collaboration, whilst Google Cafes are designed to encourage interactions between employees across departments and teams. The converse is equally true. Impersonal hotdesking spaces, walls between departments, an absence of meeting rooms or an absence of shared social spaces all hinder the ability of people to connect and network beyond their existing boundaries.

Conclusion

As we cannot see or observe social networks, we risk overlooking their value and importance in the functioning and development of an organisation. Relationships and social connections are however the essence of an organisation. We often see their tangible effects without appreciating the hidden interactions that made such effects possible. To a large degree, investing in developing social networks is an act of faith during periods of change, as the returns are not immediate and often not directly linked in time or space. Change itself either ruptures these networks, destroying social capital, or develops and strengthens them. As social networks emerge and self-organise, we cannot engineer them. We can only cultivate and support their development and help facilitate connections between people. This is, however, often invisible work that is not easily measured or possible to link to tangible outcomes.

Works cited

Aalbers, R., & Dolfsma, W. (2015). *Innovation networks: Managing the networked organization*. London, England: Routledge.

Buchanan, M. (2004, Spring). Power laws & the new science of complexity management. *Strategy & Leadership*, Issue 34.

Burke, W. W., & Biggart, N. W. (1997). Interorganizational relations. In D. Druckman, J. E. Singer, & H. V. Cott (Eds.), *Enhancing organizational performance* (pp. 120–149). Washington, DC: National Academy Press.

Capra, F., & Luisi, P. L. (2014). *The systems view of life: A unifying vision*. Cambridge, England: Cambridge University Press.

Day, A., & Lubitsh, G. (2012). Mutual trust is essential for successful change: Lessons from implementing NHS reforms. *360° The Ashridge Journal*, Autumn, 13–21.

Field, J. (2008). *Social capital* (2nd ed). London, England: Routledge.

Florida, R. (2002). *The rise of the creative class: And how it's transforming work, leisure and everyday life*. New York, NY: Basic Books.

Fukayama, F. (1995). *Trust*. New York, NY: Free Press Paperbacks.

Gleick, J. (1987). *Chaos: Making a new science*. New York, NY: Penguin Books.

Goffman, E. (1967). *Interaction ritual: Essays on face-to-face behaviour*. New York, NY: Pantheon Books,.

Granovetter, M. S. (1973). The strength of weak ties. *American Journal of Sociology*, 78(6), 1360–1380.

Gray, P. H., Parise, S., & Iyer, B. (2011). Innovation impacts of using social bookmarking systems. *Management Informations Systems Quarterly*, 3, 629–643.

Hendry, J. (2016). *An introduction to social anthropology* (3rd ed.). London, England: Palgrave.

Homer-Dixon, T. (2011, January). Complexity science. *Oxford Leadership Journal*, 2(1), 1–13.

Jordan, A. T. (2013). *Business anthropology* (2nd ed.). Grove, IL: Waveland Press, Inc.

Kaprow, M. L. (1999). Magical work: Firefighters in New York. *Anthropology of Work Review*, 19(2), 5–25.

Kramer, R. M., & Tyler, T. R. (1996). *Trust in organisations: Frontiers of theory and research.* Thousand Oaks, CA: Sage.

Krantz, J. (1998). Anxiety and the new order. In E. B. Klein, F. Gabelnick, & P. Herr (Eds.), *The psychodynamics of leadership* (pp. 77–108). Madison, CT: Psychosocial Press.

Laloux, F. (2014). *Reinventing organizations: A guide to creating organizations inspired by the next generation of human consciousness.* Brussels, Belgium: Nelson Parker.

Lin, N. (1999). Building a network theory of social capital. *Connections, 22*(1), 28–51.

Luhmann, N. (1990). *Essays on self-reference.* New York. NY: Columbia University Press.

Maturana, H., & Varela, F. (1980). *Autopoiesis and cognition: The realization of the living* (2nd ed.). Boston, MA: D. Reidel.

Minoiu, C., & Reyes, J. A. (2010). *A network analysis of global banking: 1978–2009.* Working Paper 11/74. Washington, DC: IMF.

Mohram, S. A., Tenkasi, R. V., & Mohrman, A. M. (2009). The role of networks in fundamental organizational change: A grounded analysis. *Journal of Applied Behavioural Science, 39*(3), 301–323.

Power, K., & Day, A. (2010). Developing leaders for a world of uncertainty. Rotman School of Management, *Rotman Magazine,* Autumn.

Putnam, R. D. (1993). *Making democracy work: Civic traditions in modern Italy.* Princeton, NJ: Princeton University Press.

Putnam, R. D. (2000). *Bowling alone: The collapse and revival of American Community.* New York, NY: Simon & Schuster.

Richard Pascale, J. S. (2010). *The power of positive deviance: How unlikely innovators solve the world's toughest problems.* Boston, MA: Harvard Business Review Press.

Rowland, D., & Higgs, M. (2008). *Sustaining change: Leadership that works.* Chichester, England: John Wiley & Sons.

Schawbel, D. (2017, November). 10 workplace trends you'll see in 2018. *Forbes Magazine.* Retrieved from www.forbes.com/sites/danschawbel/2017/11/01/10-workplace-trends-youll-see-in-2018/#5e50cd0b4bf2

Shaw, P. (2006). *Changing conversations in organizations: A complexity approach to change.* London, England; New York, NY: Routledge.

Sterin, J., & Choo, R. (2000, January – February). The power of positive deviancy. *Harvard Business Review.* Retrieved from https://hbr.org/2000/01/the-power-of-positive-deviancy

Wenger, E. (1998). *Communities of practice: Learning, meaning, and identity.* Cambridge, England: Cambridge University Press.

Part 2

Psycho–social dynamics in turbulent fields

6   The disruption of relationships and boundaries

To be human is to live in relationship, and our lives are patterns of relationships that we co-create with others. Relatedness, a desire for connection and a need to belong lie at the heart of our existence. We are bound by social ties from the moment of our birth to the end of our lives.

Who we are
Who we love
How we are
How we work

…are inseparable from relationships with others. We are always relating to someone or something other than ourselves.

Connectedness within and beyond ourselves is creative, growth promoting and life enhancing. Equally, the absence, severing or ending of relationships is disturbing, disorienting and painful for us. The psychoanalyst and humanistic philosopher Erich Fromm vividly described how vital connection is to our existence when he wrote:

> One important element is the fact that men cannot live without some sort of co-operation with others. In any conceivable kind of culture man needs to co-operate with others if he wants to survive, whether for the purpose of defending himself against enemies or dangers of nature, or in order that he may be able to work and produce. Even Robinson Crusoe was accompanied by his man Friday; without him he would probably not only have become insane but would actually have died. Each person experiences this need for the help of others very drastically as a child. On account of the factual inability of the human child to take care of itself with regard to the all-important functions, communications with others is a matter of life and death for the child. The possibility of being left alone is necessarily the most serious threat to the child's whole existence.
>
> (Fromm, 1941, p. 19)

Theory and research on child development has, over the past 150 years, uncovered and documented how our psychological health is shaped by our early relationships. The ground-breaking insights and research of the British psychoanalyst and psychologist John Bowlby revealed how attachment to others is fundamental to our psychological well-being and motivational system. Simply put: 'The propensity to make strong emotional bonds to particular individuals [is] a basic component of human nature' (Bowlby, 1988, p. 3). We have an innate psycho-biological system that motivates us as children to seek proximity to significant others in times of emotional need. Attachment behaviour is most obvious whenever the person is frightened, fatigued or sick, and is assuaged by comforting and caregiving (Bowlby, 1988).

We all need a *secure base* from which to explore the world. This represents a relational space where we feel secure and a sense of belonging. When these relationships are threatened, we experience anxiety and act to protect ourselves. Bowlby observed that young children when separated from their parents experience a deep sense of loss, disorientation and confusion, which causes them psychological stress (Bowlby, 1988). Their responses mirror those of the process of grief: anger, despair and detachment.

Our experience of our early attachment relationships influences how we relate to others throughout our lives. If our caregivers are attuned to our emotions and needs, then we are likely to develop a *secure attachment*. We experience the world as ordered, predictable and not chaotic. This helps us to develop a basic trust in the world; expecting disruptions to the status quo to be resolved and a state of equilibrium to be restored. We develop a confidence that we can step beyond the boundaries of the familiar and explore our environments without feeling overwhelmed by anxiety. If, however, we experience prolonged periods of separation, loss of a caregiver or consistent relational trauma, then we develop what Bowlby called an *insecure attachment style*. We are more likely to experience anxieties and fears around rejection, separation and loss. Stepping beyond the familiar can provoke anxieties and fears about our ability to cope.

Bowlby's research highlights how we all have a desire for predictable, reliable and secure relationships. We form emotional attachments with our colleagues and particularly to authority figures, who at an unconscious level meet our dependency needs (Miller, 1993). Physical locations and environments equally become places of emotional attachment which give us a sense of security (Brocato, Baker, & Voorhees, 2015). We turn to others for support in times of stress and change (Bowlby, 1988), and connection with others is one of the clearest predictors of long-term health and emotional well-being. When we feel secure in our environment, we are also more likely to take risks, experiment and exercise creativity. Bowlby's research also helps us to understand how changes and loss in adulthood trigger conscious and unconscious memories of our past experiences of separation and loss. When we experience a loss, all past losses are revived and our primitive fears of abandonment and helplessness return.

The disruption and rupturing of relationships

Disruptive, unexpected and discontinuous change ruptures social relationships. This has profound psychological and social consequences. We use the language of physical injury and pain, such as 'shattered' and 'fracturing', to convey the pain we experience when relationships are 'broken' or 'end'. Whenever a pattern of relationships is disrupted, particularly when we are not prepared, the thread of continuity of experience is attenuated or lost (Marris, 1974). This triggers anxiety, confusion and feelings of loss. For the 30–35% of individuals with an insecure attachment style, the rupturing of relationships is likely to generate intense insecurities. Even the possibility of an imagined ending can provoke anxiety for many people.

The pace of organisational life and the increasingly virtual nature of our interactions make it more difficult for us to meet our need for attachment and intimacy. Connection, relationships and interdependence are undervalued (Fletcher, 1998), whilst independence and competitiveness are promoted. We rarely have time to sit, connect and have meaningful contact with one another. Ongoing reorganisations create temporary, transient and transactional relationships which ultimately do not meet our needs for connection. The less we connect, the more we struggle to understand each other. We become unreliable to each other as we struggle to attune to each other's feelings and anticipate how others will react to events. Consequently, trust breaks down and the threads of the social fabric are weakened, loosened or, in some organisations, ripped apart. To protect ourselves, we withdraw from relationships, which further weakens the social fabric. Isolated, however, we are more likely to perceive others as self-oriented and react by protecting ourselves and our interests. Unsurprisingly, these dynamics act against agility and flexibility, which require people to trust each other.

During change we all have a need for mutual recognition and emotional attunement from others. However, in periods of change and uncertainty, we can expect relational turmoil to emerge. Misunderstandings, impasses and conflict are inevitable as people struggle to recognise others' subjectivities and emotional needs. People need to invest time and attention to understand each other and to repair ruptures in their relationships if trust and mutual understanding is to develop. We need to feel our self is validated and that we are recognised by significant others, such as bosses and peers. If, however, we feel that others fail to acknowledge or attune to our emotional experiences, then we feel violated, shamed or humiliated.

As part of our research during the 2008 financial crisis, Kevin and I (Power & Day, 2009) spoke with an employee in one of the large UK banks that was on the brink of collapse, who offered the following account:

I feel anxious, scared and isolated. With my colleagues I feel disconnected and unclear about how I am to respond. If I am honest I am confused about the messages I am receiving from my leadership. I am being told that I need to worry about the situation and that we need to cut costs, which includes redundancies for some people. My assumption is that this does not mean me; however, I am starting to worry that if things get really bad over the next six months then we may all be suffering. My leadership is not clear about what we can do that is proactive and positive in the situation.

My first response is to look around my organisation for signs that others are responding in ways that engender confidence. My anxiety is further increased, however, when I hear people complaining of the lack of response from our leadership. When we talk about the situation I can sense my colleagues' anxiety and yet I have the distinct impression that they believe that doing what we have always done will be sufficient. It's hard to understand whether we agree on what to do. It feels 'as if' we are all off doing our own thing. What I want more than anything is for the organisation's leadership to state clearly where we are going to focus our efforts and to be clear around how we as an organisation are planning to respond. I pick up that at a senior level people have different views and beliefs about what we should do. Overall, this leaves me feeling helpless, afraid and angry with my leadership for not understanding what I need in this situation.

This account provides an insight into the employee's emotional world during a period of uncertainty. It reveals their and their colleagues' desire for connection, as well as a desire for their leadership to provide them with direction and confidence about the future. Their perception that leaders are unable to meet this desire gives rise to frustration, helplessness and anger.

Whilst researching this book, I interviewed a senior manager at one of the large banks ten years after the financial crisis. He described how 11 banks in the group had been forced into three divisions. Across the bank as a whole there had been close to 300 major restructures over the course of a year. People from different corporate cultures who did not want to work together found themselves in the same teams. The changes released a huge amount of hostility and aggression in people. He described the process as 'pretty horrific'. In his own team, he described how a recent process of redundancies had given individuals 48 hours to leave. This had followed months of speculation about restructures and redundancies. He sadly observed the inhumanity of the organisation's HR processes and how the HR department had taken on the role of the dispassionate executor of the process. He felt that everyone was treated exactly the same, regardless of how they were affected. Any sense of compassion or concern for those affected was missing. In the midst of this turmoil, he reflected that he found it helpful to think that: 'the organisation does not care about me'. However, this way of thinking became a form of self-protection for him. Whilst we can understand people's desire to protect themselves from emotional distress, if it becomes a systemic pattern across a group or organisation, it creates a transactional environment and undermines a sense of community.

Our need to belong

Our need for attachment is also reflected in our need to belong. This is a very powerful impulse (Dalal, 1998) and a sense of community is a human necessity. Belonging to a group provides us with a sense of affiliation, kindredness and identity. When we feel secure in our belonging, we have a much greater sense of safety and of our own agency.

Our desire to belong manifests itself in the process of grouping that happens in all social communities. We differentiate ourselves into in-groups and out-groups. Almost immediately, this triggers what we might call an in-group narcissism, the 'we–they' phenomenon (Levinson, 1994). This is the basis of what we might label our tribal nature. We become unconsciously invested in and emotionally attached to groups. Freud (1921) argued this arises out of the group's identification with an ideal, often represented through the group's leader. This process of identification results in the group members having a strong libidinal tie to both the leader and the other members of the group. This creates a powerful unconscious illusion that the group is an entity. At a primitive level, the survival of the group becomes of the utmost importance to its members (Bion, 1961).

Groups form in a psychological sense when a collection of people perceive their fate depends on the group as a whole (Lewin, 1951). When a collection of people experiences task interdependence – whereby the attainment of a task leads to the achievement of shared goals – then a powerful group dynamic arises. The group becomes a sentient system that is shaped by its members' needs, beliefs and fantasies (Miller & Rice, 1967). This provides the members of a group with a level of emotional gratification. Organisational change, however, often threatens to dilute or diminish the quality of sentience and meaningful connections between people (Krantz, 1998).

For over a decade, I worked for a consultancy that was an independent business unit at a leading business school. This group had a strong sense of its identity and most members were highly invested in the community. The group or, perhaps more accurately, the idea of the group and what it represented – its ideal – was emotionally significant to most members of the community. Or at least this was my perception. When I look back at my membership of the community, I can now see how invested I was in it. I felt pride in who we were and how we were seen by others in our profession. At times, however, the strength of our identification blinded us to our difficulties, challenges and limitations. For instance, I regularly heard from colleagues from other parts of the business school who felt excluded or experienced us as invested in our separateness and felt we were unconcerned about them.

When the executive team of the business school decided to merge the consulting unit with the executive education department, the subsequent sense of loss and anger proved to be overwhelming and devastating to many of us. I, and many of

> *my colleagues, were left feeling that we had lost a place where we belonged and experienced a shared identity and purpose. This sense of loss remained unresolved following the restructuring, which created significant ambivalence towards forming a new group with the executive education faculty. Those outside of the consultancy struggled to understand the strength of our feelings and the depth of loss that we experienced.*

> *One of my clients, a global pharmaceutical business faced with increased competition and concerns about its pipeline of future products and medicines, is attempting to transform itself. A new chief executive introduced widespread changes and initiatives aimed at improving profitability and driving greater commerciality through the business. Many of the middle managers and employees reacted, however, with concerns that the changes threatened the firm's historical values and ideals. These reflected a desire to do 'good in the world' and to make a difference to people's health. The longer-serving employees feared that the greater emphasis on financial performance and deliverables undermined these values. The executive's shift in emphasis and direction was experienced by the group as a threat to its ideals and identity.*

Identifications, boundaries and territory

Groups exist in relation to other groups (Tajfel, 1978) and are part of larger social constellations. To belong to one entity is to not belong to another (Dalal, 1998). Groups construct psychological boundaries with other groups that are symbolically represented through language, artefacts and physical boundaries. These signify who and what belongs to the group; and who and what does not.

Each of us carries with us the groups of which we have been and are a member (Miller & Rice, 1967). These act as markers of our identity and shape our way of relating to others. In different social contexts, different group identifications are called forth. This is partly down to how and with whom with identify with at a moment in time, yet is also in response to how others have formed or are forming into groups. The group identity that is called forth becomes the ground for our perceptions, feelings and behaviour (Lewin, 1951). All social phenomena can be seen therefore both as intergroup and intragroup phenomena (Dalal, 1998).

Where groups perceive they have shared interests and aims, they tend to cooperate; and when they perceive their interests compete, they tend to compete with each other (Sheriff, 1966). The stories and narratives that surround change shape these perceptions.

> *During our research in 2008, Kevin and I observed how in different organisations employees were either 'pulling together' in the face of adversity and uncertainty or 'pulling apart'. In some organisations, the crisis had mobilised a sense of 'esprit de corps' or a sense of 'we are all in it together'. In others, participants reported that the crisis had created a sense of division, blame and competition between employees. We learnt that when employees felt unsafe and in competition with each other, they were more likely to blame each other and look after their interests. Employees and departments tended to perceive their survival rested upon their ability to be seen to out-perform their colleagues. In those organisations in which people were 'pulling together', a sense of a common fate and shared interests pervaded.*

To understand change dynamics, we need to recognise the existing group relations and intergroup tensions. In organisations with long histories, group identities become firmly entrenched. Often, they are reinforced by external reference groups such as professional institutions and trade unions. For instance, in the automotive plants that were introducing self-managed teams, identity groups existed for production workers, skilled trades, process engineers, supervisors and managers. Each of these groups had their respective trade unions. The social fabric of the plant was therefore a complex interweaving of these group relations.

Organisational change, particularly when it is extensive and deep, such as a large-scale reorganisation, requires the redrawing and alteration of group boundaries. When such boundaries change, then groups feel threatened and act to protect their boundaries. If a boundary disappears altogether, for example when two departments are merged or closed down, then the group experiences this psychologically as a death. This generates enormous conscious and unconscious anxiety, anger and fear. Under these conditions, groups are prone to regressing (Bion, 1961), losing their capacity for thought and becoming driven by their primitive emotions and fears. When we experience fear, we tend to retreat back to where we feel safest, which is often the groups to which we feel we belong. Fear limits our ability to step beyond the familiar and to connect with others outside of the boundaries of our group. In the technology company that I referred to in the previous chapter which had experienced several dramatic cycles of downsizing, employees talked of departments 'being collapsed together', 'broken up' or 'disbanded'. The effects of these changes left many groups feeling threatened and protective of their boundaries.

The introduction of new technologies, such as digital processes or artificial intelligence, equally inevitably affects personal and group relations, which has both psychological and social consequences. In many organisations, however, an assumption, often unconscious, is made that the technology determines the form of the organisation. Simply introducing new technology, without consideration of the psycho-social system, is likely to bring about strong resistance to change. In most cases, this results in a failure to harness the full potential of the new technology.

In the early stages of the introduction of self-managed teams at one of the auto-motive plants, individuals' reactions to the changes were strongly influenced by the groups to which they identified. Skilled maintenance technicians saw themselves as a unique group who needed to protect their interests. They perceived the introduction of teamworking to be a threat to their unique role in the plant as some of their responsibilities were to be shared with production workers. The production workers, in contrast, perceived the introduction of teams to be a desirable change since they would be given broader responsibilities and trained in higher-status maintenance tasks. Shopfloor supervisors were concerned about protecting their own interests as a group and wanted reassurances that they would not lose power and influence in the plant. Each group perceived management to be a separate and distinct group that had their own separate interests.

The threat that the maintenance workers experienced to their identity and boundaries was most clearly illustrated to me when I visited one of their rooms next to the production line. The production workers' meeting room was in the adjacent office. The maintenance team had blocked up the windows between the two offices so that the production workers could not look into their space. This act was one means that they had for creating both a psychological and physical boundary with the other group.

As well as being invested in their respective identities, each individual also identified with being a member of the plant as a more encompassing group within the wider organisation. Most of the employees that I engaged with during the period of the project held fears about the long-term future and survival of their plant.[1]

From the perspective of group identification, we can see how people both pulled together when they experienced 'interdependence of fate' and engaged in conflict when groups perceived they were in competition with each other for resources or felt their boundaries or identity were threatened.

I consulted to a public sector agency that was created by merging together teams that previously had been embedded in different government departments. The agency had been formed to create a shared service that could work across government and help realise synergies across government. Following its formation, little or no attention however was given to processing the loss and endings that people experienced as a result of being separated from their departments. Several years after the creation of the agency, morale and engagement were low. The level of identification with the agency was low, as most employees still felt a loyalty to the departments that they had come from. Less than 30% of employees reported feeling personally invested in it. Senior managers and staff groups who were responsible for integrating activities across the organisation experienced passive hostility or resistance. The more that the leadership pushed for a single unifying identity, the more the departments retreated into their traditional identities. This created an underlying competition between departments, which hindered cross-agency collaboration.

Embeddedness in social ecologies

Organisations are part of complex social ecologies. They have a mutual relationship with the local communities in which they operate, being both a place of employment and a contributor to the local economy. At a national, international and global level, corporations and large institutions both influence and are influenced by society.

Organisations in the industrial era typically had a connection to their local communities. Corporations such as Unilever, Cadbury or Ford in the UK, or Bayer, VW and Merck in Germany, equally played central roles in the towns and cities in which their major sites are or were located. To a large degree, this mutual dependency is breaking down. The fragmentation of society and the erosion of social bonds is undermining the sense of community in society (Bauman, 2000). This is wreaking people's sense of belonging and creating a background of anxiety across society. Both employees and organisations perhaps feel less of a sense of obligation and responsibility to local communities. Equally, the forces of global competition exert pressure on corporations to move production to lower-cost countries. Leaders and governments risk treating those affected as if they are 'resources' on a balance sheet rather than human beings with hopes, fears and lives outside of the organisation. When organisations close down operations, this can have a devastating impact on the local community. Many communities in Western Europe and the United States feel left behind as they struggle to adapt to the effects of globalisation.

One of the automotive plants I researched had been part of the local community for 60 years. It closed in 2007, several years after my research, with the loss of 400 jobs. Most of the employees came from the surrounding communities. The plant had been central to the local economy. The explanation for the closure was that the plant was not competitive in the global market. On all accounts the company treated the employees fairly, offering generous redundancy terms. The closure, nonetheless, affected the local community.

To understand the dynamics of disruptive change, we need to see organisations as embedded in social ecologies rather than as independent and closed entities. Employees' anxieties, fears and resistances to organisational change do not just stem from their personal concerns about their jobs but also from the impact that they see of potential changes on the communities to which they belong. There is both a moral and economic case for both governments and organisations to consider the wider societal impacts of disruptive change. If employees feel that changes threaten their wider sense of belonging and identity, they will oppose new technology or structural changes. Take, for instance, the potential impact of artificial intelligence (AI) on the workplace. If, indeed, AI will replace large numbers of administrative and analytic jobs, how can businesses, local and central governments act to minimise the damaging impact this could have on local communities? What responsibilities do global corporations have for the impact of major changes on the local community?

Implications for practice

From a human relations perspective, our rlationships with others provide us with a sense of security, belonging and stability. Those leading or facilitating change need to consider how organisational change will affect social connections and group relations. Change can be undertaken in a manner that acts to strengthen or damage the existing social fabric.

My whole argument can be summarised as follows:

- People form attachments to others, colleagues and bosses, that have emotional significance in an organisation. These meet our needs for belonging, security, recognition and validation. During periods of uncertainty, change or stress, relationships become a source of trust, security and social support. When threatened, they trigger resistance to change and a desire to maintain the status quo.
- To understand how people are participating in organisational change, we need to consider the 'total situation' (Lewin, 1951) – the emotional atmosphere and constellation of tensions the person or group experiences in their social context and surroundings. Individuals interpret events through the lens of their prominent group identities at a given moment and relative to other relevant groups. They react to and respond to events on the basis of comparisons with their perceptions of the behaviour and treatment of other groups. Therefore, their judgements of and reactions to organisational change tend to be based on the relative impact in comparison to other groups rather than the absolute impact.
- The human need to belong gives rise to complex group and intergroup dynamics during periods of organisational change. Changes that support the existing patterns of group relations are therefore more likely to minimise survival anxieties and intergroup rivalries. If groups perceive that

their existence or ideals are threatened then their efforts and energy are invested in their survival. This can either initiate constructive efforts to change in order to survive or defensive responses, such as denial, avoidance or competition with others. Individuals and groups are likely to compete with or blame each other when they feel their boundaries or interests are threatened. Whereas stories that connect people together help people to see common ground and encourage collaboration. For people to work together to develop and change organisations, they need to experience 'commonalities of fate' and perceive they have a common purpose and shared aims.

•   The ending or rupturing of relationships and group boundaries produces both relational turmoil and feelings of loss. The impact of the loss will vary according to its emotional significance for those affected. People need time to grief and time to establish new relationships and group identities. If people are not able to work through their loss, then this limits their willingness and capacity to invest in future relationships.

•   The acknowledgement and recognition of individuals and groups' subjective realities and emotional experience helps them to feel validated, accepted and secure. When breakdowns in mutual recognition or understanding occur, those who feel their experience is invalidated are likely to experience anger, anxiety and alienation. The quality of connection between people is therefore critical to helping people process change. Expression of empathy and mutual recognition by those leading, implementing or facilitating change help those affected to process their pain and distress. This requires an acceptance that people need to speak to 'their truth' and an acceptance that people experience different 'realities'.

Conclusion

Attachment and belonging are central to organisational life. We all have a need to relate, connect and belong. As organisations transition in form from more stable hierarchies to more flexible, fluid and unstable forms, social ties are ruptured and boundaries are eroded and are becoming increasingly temporary. This reconfiguration of the existing social order in many organisations incurs a deep sense of loss as the intangible markers of relationships and community disappear. If responses to change are to be understood and actions taken that facilitate change, then an understanding is required of how change is affecting the existing social system – its social units or groupings. Those leading changes need to recognise both the psychological and social consequences of the breaking of social bonds and help people to process the emotional impact. People need space, time and support to process losses; and are unable to form new connections and relationships before they have processed the ending of past attachments. If losses remain unresolved then they limit employees' capacity to form new groupings at speed and move between different groupings.

Note

1 These fears were realised in 2007, several years after my research, when Ford made the decision to close the Leamington plant.

Works cited

Bauman, Z. (2000). *Liquid modernity*. Cambridge, England: Polity Press.
Bion, W. (1961). *Experiences in groups and other papers*. London, England: Tavistock Publications Ltd.
Bowlby, J. (1988). *A secure base: Clinical applications of attachment theory*. London, England: Psychology Press.
Brocato, E. D., Baker, J., & Voorhees, C. M. (2015). Creating consumer attachment to retail services firms through sense of place. *Journal of the Academy of Marketing Science, 43*(2), 200–220.
Dalal, F. (1998). *Taking the group seriously: Towards a post-Foulkesian group analytic theory*. London, England: Jessica Kingsley.
Fletcher, J. K. (1998). Relational practice: A feminist reconstruction of work. *Journal of Management Inquiry, 7*(2), 163–186.
Freud, S. (1921). *Group psychology and the analysis of the ego*. Vienna, Austria: Internationaler Psychoanalytischer Verlag.
Fromm, E. (1941). *Escape from freedom*. Oxford, England: Farrar & Rinehart.
Krantz, J. (1998). Anxiety and the new order. In E. B. Klein, F. Gabelnick, & P. Herr (Ed.), *The psychodynamics of leadership* (pp. 77–108). Madison, CT: Psychosocial Press.
Levinson, H. (1994). Why the behemoths fell: psychological roots of corporate failure. *American Psychologist, 49*(5), 428–436.
Lewin, K. (1951). *Resolving social conflicts and field theory in social science*. Washington, DC: American Psychological Association.
Marris, P. (1974). *Loss and change*. London, England: Routledge and Kegan.
Miller, E. (1993). *From dependency to autonomy: Studies in organization and change*. London, England: Free Association Books.
Miller, E. J., & Rice, A. K. (1967). *Systems of organization*. London, England: Tavistock Publications.
Power, K., & Day, A. (2009). *In the thick of it part two: The story continues*. Retrieved from http://tools.ashridge.org.uk/Website/Content.nsf/FileLibrary/A11AAC1F0F8F8E E7802575C200486589/$file/Inthethickofit%20Part2.docx.pdf
Sheriff, M. (1966). *Group conflict and cooperation*. London, England: Routledge and Kegan Paul.
Tajfel, H. (1978). *Differentiation between social groups: Studies in the social psychology of intergroup relations*. Salt Lake City, UT: Academic Press.

7 Sensemaking in turbulent fields

Organisations are more than economic or technical entities. They are cultures – patterns of shared meaning – that people create and construct together as they organise. In this sense, they are socially constructed (Gergen, 2015), reflecting the shared beliefs, assumptions and imaginations of their members. They are equally contested spaces in which different actors and groups hold competing views about the nature of the organisation and its effectiveness. These systems of meaning are both disrupted by change and affect how people interpret, make sense of and give meaning to changes, whether they are incremental, sudden or dramatic.

Our sensemaking is patterned and our experience is dependent on how we 'organise' the situation. We see a crowd, not a collection of unique and different individuals. We see the wood and not the single trees. We find meaning, causes and motivations in all sorts of social phenomena, even those that have been artificially constructed by experimenters to have no meaning. For instance, Figure 7.1 is a classic gestalt image – the Rubin Goblet.[1] We can see two different figures depending on how we look at the image – a vase or as two faces. When we see one figure we cannot see the other. In a very simple way, this demonstrates how we actively construct our experiences.

Over time, we take the patterns that we see for granted as our reality (Berger & Luckmann, 1967). We participate therefore in the creation of organisational realities (Weick, 1995) and as we act, so we create our environment. Reality is not thus a given but brought forth in the dynamic interaction of the observer and observed (Rasch & Wolfe, 2000). What we see is relative to our point of view.

Our need for continuity and meaning

To be human is to be confronted with a world that we must interpret in order to act. We all *give* meaning to and search for order in our experience. The human mind perceives order, continuity and pattern across time and space. This impulse to preserve the thread of continuity is a crucial human instinct (Marris, 1974) which creates an inherent tension in our lives. We long for safety, stability and order whilst restlessly exploring beyond the limits of what we currently understand to discover what we do not know. Our underlying motive is to understand our world (Marris, 1974).

Figure 7.1 The Rubin Goblet: A gestalt image

From birth, we are socialised to learn interpretative structures that help us see order, patterns and connections between events. We come to rely on these frameworks to make sense of the world. The child psychologist Jean Piaget (Piaget & Inhelder, 1969) observed how children (and adults) learn through two basic processes. They *assimilate* new information into their existing cognitive structures; and *accommodate* those cognitive structures to fit new experiences which cannot be assimilated into their existing frameworks. This process is inherently conservative, in that its primary function is to make the unfamiliar familiar, to convert novelty to the known (Flavell, 1963).

Our ability to learn from experience relies on the stability of our interpretations of the pattern of events. We cannot therefore easily assimilate change without continuity. Normal events and incremental change can be assimilated into existing structures. Fundamental and unexpected changes which lie outside previous experience need to be accommodated by interpretative frameworks, which requires them firstly to be revised. This disorientates us and requires us to unlearn in order to learn. Events that cannot be explained suggest chaos and meaninglessness to us and leave us feeling disoriented and alarmed. Often our first response to unexpected developments is to ignore them and rationalise away the contradictions and inexplicable side of our experience.

Disruptive, unpredictable and unforeseen changes create a sense of incoherence that result from ambiguities of interpretation. We experience temporal disjunctions in which the smooth flow of the past into the future challenges our taken-for-granted assumptions and beliefs. This throws us into a world of confusion and chaos, as we struggle to make sense of events around us. We are unable to assimilate new information and events into our existing maps of the world. Faced with uncertain, ambiguous and novel situations, we are confronted with multiple competing interpretations and accounts which can leave us unsure of what or who to believe. Under these conditions, our structures of meaning collapse. We feel lost, overwhelmed and frightened. Rather than entering into an emerging and unknown future, we cling to past certainties (Stacey & Mowles, 2015). This phenomenon can be thought of as a form of 'culture shock' or as Alvin Toffler put it, 'future shock' (Toffler, 1984).

Repeated experience of intelligible events undermines our confidence in identifying actions that we can take because we are unable to classify our experience in any meaningful way. This leaves us with fundamental questions about our understanding of events and ability to anticipate the future. Such epistemological anxiety (Cooper & Lousada, 2005) has become central to our experience in organisations.

> *During the start of a consultation with a public sector agency, a group of middle managers explained to myself and a colleague how over several years their teams had been subjected to 'unintelligible change upon unintelligible change' and moved from building to building with little chance to pause to reflect or take stock. This left those affected feeling confused, exhausted and disenchanted. At the end of our two-hour meeting, in which they had openly shared views they had never expressed before to each other, they each commented on how helpful it had been to share their experiences about the changes and hear others' perspectives and accounts. The meeting had helped them make sense of their current experiences and the dynamics that they were experiencing.*

Sensemaking

Under conditions of dynamic complexity, instability and high uncertainty, we have to engage in the process of sensemaking. When a situation changes beyond our recognition, we are confronted with a situation of uncertainty in which no plausible explanation or theory has emerged to guide our actions. Faced with unexpected events or outcomes, we ask ourselves:

What's going on here?
How do I/we describe what is happening?

Followed by an equally important question:

What do I/we do next?

The collapse of Lehman Brothers is an example. Think back to the moment when you first heard the news and recall the anxiety and confusion at the time. How were we to understand this event and what did it mean for the global economy, society and our futures? Different explanations have emerged as to why it happened: the excessive greed and bonuses of bankers, too much deregulation and risk-taking in the financial markets, overly complex financial products that no one fully understood, a highly coupled and complex financial system, etc. We have the need to make sense of events and different accounts emerge that provide us with an explanation of what happened and why.

Sensemaking is an active and interpretative process rather than simply a case of passively receiving information. It is an interplay of both interpretation and action. We have to discern how patterns are changing and to identify new patterns of order. We need to look for connections between events and to understand how relationships are changing. This is often a discombobulating experience because what we are used to seeing or experiencing does not arise and our actions may not lead to the outcomes that we expected. In rapidly evolving situations, we often do not know what action is appropriate. Some form of action may even be required to determine what is the situation.

Sensemaking involves both exploration and discovery through experience and standing back with others to review and reflect on those experiences (see Figure 7.2). This process is conversational, involving the sharing of stories, experiences and interpretations of events.

Sensemaking is, however, challenged by anxiety. Not knowing, having to learn something anew or having to go through a period of feeling incompetent all trigger anxiety. When faced with an unexpected event or a discontinuity of experience, we face a choice: to confront the realities of the challenge or to turn away from reality and avoid the difficulty altogether. The first choice requires us to question our existing assumptions and beliefs about the world. This compels us to tolerate frustration, confusion and anxiety, so that we can reflect and think about what is happening. Whether we are able to learn from

Figure 7.2 The dynamic of sensemaking

experience therefore is dependent on our capacity to tolerate not knowing and being unable to makes sense of the world (Bion, 1967).

If we are unable to bear our frustrations, we resort to neurotic defences by avoiding reality (O'Hara, 2001). We overlook complexities in favour of simplistic solutions or create order where it does not exist. This might involve blaming others, rigidly holding onto our boundaries in an attempt try to stay the same or converging on a course of action because it provides a sense of certainty and takes away the sense of not knowing.

A successful partner in an investment company sought out my help following the abrupt termination of his employment by the senior partner. He had worked for the business close to 20 years and considered himself to be a strong contributor. At a meeting in which he anticipated exploring the business plan for the next year, he was told that the other partners had decided he needed to leave. This event, unsurprisingly, was completely unexpected and triggered a sense of shock. He tried to ask for an explanation but was told simply his returns were not what they expected. In the following days he became increasingly angry about his treatment to the extent that for the first time he experienced symptoms of a panic attack. He was left questioning his sense of his performance at the firm and his relationship with the senior partners, who he had worked with for many years. He experienced symptoms of anxiety and was unable to sleep for a period.

He approached me to help him re-establish his confidence and make sense of what had happened. My judgement was that he was unable to accommodate what had happened in his existing frames of reference. Over a period of months, we were able to look back and piece together different events and conversations to create a possible explanation, which he was able to test out with some of the partners. This helped him to reframe his perceptions of the senior partner and how he was being judged. Through these conversations he started to appreciate some of the hidden dynamics of competition and fear that existed between the partners. He also started to appreciate that he judged his performance against longer-term criteria whilst the senior partner judged him on the basis of the total financial return he personally made to the business each year. As we talked through his experiences, he was able to work through his anger, shame and sense of betrayal. He was also able to recognise that he had overlooked a number of subtle, yet important, signals and political dynamics amongst the partners.

Culture and meaning making

Our interpretative frames are deeply social and cultural. As we engage with others, we construct and co-create cultural patterns (Mead, 1934; Stacey, 2012)[2] that reflect assumptions and beliefs of *how* to behave and models *of* the world (Geertz, 1973). Cultural patterns arise out of ordinary, routine interactions between people. They are expressed through symbols[3] and symbolic action (Geertz, 1973). These include language, objects, rituals, buildings and behaviour.

We can think of culture as a paradigm that shapes how a group or organisation makes sense of the world (Johnson, 1988; McLean, 2013; VanMaanen & Barley, 1984). This is expressed through the behaviour, patterns of interactions and symbols of all its members. These reflect underlying social rules, beliefs and assumptions about the world, including:

- How we see the world and how we act in it;
- What we value, care about and see as important (and what we do not);
- How we interpret others' behaviour and decisions; and
- How we relate to and interact with others and our environment.

A culture develops in support of the organisation's adaptation to its environment and to enable the internal integration of groups within the organisation (Schein, 2010). In other words, it represents collective learning around how to survive and co-exist in a given environment. Cultures evolve to meet the collective need of the group to keep it together (Radcliffe Brown, 1952) and to make coordinated activity possible (Alvesson, 2013). Shared norms, rituals, customs and symbols reflect a shared belief system as to how individual members should behave. These become a solution for regulating anxieties that are associated with being a member of the group (Whitaker & Lieberman, 1964), such as fears around intimacy, struggles around power or competition between individuals. Cultural paradigms therefore enable individuals to relate to each other, to co-exist and to collaborate on complex tasks.

At the business school, faculty worked primarily in one of three roles: executive education, researchers or organisational consultants. The decision to merge the executive education faculty and organisational consultants into a single department created a problem of what to call members of the new group. The executive team made the decision that everyone should call themselves 'faculty'. The intention being not to confuse clients and to create a sense that everyone was part of the same team. Many of the consultants, however, felt that this took away their identity and they continued to refer to themselves as 'consultants' both formally and informally. This presented a problem as the executive team wanted everyone to be part of one group (not two). The problem of language conveyed the deeper problem of unique and separate identities. Changing the name symbolised an eradication of difference, which the consultants – and possibly the executive education faculty – were not willing to accept.

Several years after the introduction of self-managed teams at one of the automotive plants, I witnessed how the cultural interpretations of a management decision had a dramatic effect on how employees engaged with the change process. Over a period of three years, the plant had successfully established wide support for and commitment to team working on the shop floor. Teams of maintenance and production workers had started to jointly hold responsibility for running their stage of the production process. In the early days of the changes, tensions existed between the two groups around who should and could do which types of tasks in the plant. After years of sensitive negotiations between management and the unions, these had more or less subsided. Both groups were collaborating across the plant and effectively working in autonomous teams.

The plant then experienced some economic difficulties requiring production schedules to be reduced. The management team decided that overtime would be restricted only to the maintenance employees in each team. Their reasoning was that this was the most effective expenditure of the limited overtime budget that was available. This gesture was responded to with outrage by the production workers who felt that the decision was unfair because they would forego their overtime whilst the maintenance workers would not. They perceived the decision as demonstrating that the management team was not serious about giving the teams decision-making responsibility. As a group, the production workers across the plant refused to continue to participate in the new working practices. This single decision re-established the historical identities along with the feelings of rivalry, competition and distrust. Whilst the decision on the surface appeared logical from an economic perspective, symbolically it privileged historical identities rather than supporting those of the new teams. The production workers' frame of reference became one of unfairness and injustice, and historical rivalries and distrust were triggered.

In my work with the European telecommunications business, I undertook a project aimed at helping its emerging leaders understand its cultural patterns. The process involved around 60 participants undertaking an ethnographic inquiry in which they were asked to observe meetings and interactions, collect cultural artefacts, and interview individuals who were new to the organisation and long-serving employees about their experience of the culture. The group then came together for a day to explore what they had discovered and work together to represent and describe cultural patterns and assumptions. Through this process, we uncovered widely accepted social rules that they all enacted on a day-to-day basis, such as:

- *Asking for permission from individuals above them in the hierarchy before taking a decision or doing something that was different or unusal. This gave individuals reassurance that they were not going to transgress a rule or upset* someone in senior management. They noticed, however, that this meant that change was slow and radical ideas were quickly filtered out.

- *Avoiding taking actions if the risks of a mistake were high. In the past, the business's success was based on technical excellence and operational reliability. This meant that people were encouraged to apply known solutions and technical knowledge, and exercise caution before taking action that was outside of convention.*
- *Forming close relationships with individuals in their department whilst maintaining a suspicion of individuals in other departments. Individuals were expected to be loyal to their business unit and focused on delivering its objectives, even when they were aware that this led to outcomes that were not in the wider interests of the business.*
- *As a consequence of the above, managers observed how they were expected to be in control and to know all the details of the projects that their teams were working on at any particular time. Their managers would check on them and they would check on their teams.*

As we made sense of their experiences and observations, the participants started to become aware of how they all participated in the creation of these social patterns through their gestures and behaviour, and that these patterns were not something that existed independent of them. To a large extent, these social rules were becoming problematic as their customers needed them to be more dynamic, responsive and creative in how they worked with them. At the same time, they provided a sense of order and predictability to daily life, and not conforming to the rules was perceived to be risky.

If we stand back from these themes, we can get some sense of the challenge confronting what historically has been a bureaucratic organisation with a strong and established culture in becoming more flexible, adaptable and customer oriented. A fundamental change in the cultural paradigm is required if the system is to change in form. This inevitably creates significant tensions between those who are holding onto traditions and established cultural patterns and those who are trying to disrupt them to create change. Both have their value and represent important needs — to maintain order and continuity and to change and adapt to new challenges and demands on the business.

Cultural paradigms, sensemaking and change

Our cultural paradigms are so core to our way of seeing the world that we are hardly aware of their existence. They influence what we see and what we choose to filter out. This can, however, cause us to miss or overlook soft signals and early warnings that a situation is changing. For instance, a researcher at Kodak first developed the digital camera. However, the innovation was rejected as it was seen to be too much of a threat to the existing business. The irony being that the digital camera was developed elsewhere and led to the eventual decline of Kodak.

In my final years at the business school, it was taken over by another business school. In the months following the takeover, I observed that employees became increasingly alarmed and anxious because of how they interpreted their encounters with representatives from the other business school. These encounters could be thought of as a clash of cultural paradigms, with each interpreting the other's actions through a different lens. Historically, faculty had significant levels of autonomy and were relatively free to exercise creativity in their work, particularly in tailoring or adapting what they did for different clients. The other business school, however, valued standardisation, sales and commercial performance. They would question the value of the uniqueness of the service provided to each customer, seeing it as inefficient or uncommercial. They were not inaccurate in their observations and challenges, but our unique proposition to our customers was based on being highly customer oriented and tailored in our services and approach.

Some months into the merger, senior managers in the other school decided to change our branding and marketing brochures. This became a highly symbolic act because it conveyed what they valued and how they made decisions. A small marketing team in Hong Kong redesigned the brochure with little input from those doing the work and any language that they judged to be too complex or abstract was removed to be replaced with more accessible and practical language. At face value this was a sensible commercial decision; however, for many of the faculty the language failed to convey or represent what they believed they were offering to their clients. Most significantly, any involvement or consultation in the changes was minimal. This symbolically and implicitly communicated to us that something fundamental was changing about our influence and what was valued and not valued.

This form of cultural conflict and confusion is all too common in takeovers and mergers. Whenever people do not share the same symbolic code then anxieties of misinterpretation lend themselves to a defensive form of relating – 'I don't understand you and you don't understand me'. At times during the integration process, I literally felt that we spoke different languages.

In their classic book, *Change: Principles of Problem Formation and Problem Resolution*, Paul Watzlawick and his colleagues differentiated between routine adaptation within a paradigm, which they labelled first-order change, with a paradigm shift, or second-order change, that transforms people's fundamental way of seeing, relating and behaving. Routine adaptation, or incremental change, is an attempt to maintain the status quo or social order by restoring continuity, such as the restoration of a social norm when it has been challenged. This is 'tradition preserving'. In this sense, change is 'more of the same' (Watzlawick, Weakland, & Fisch, 1974) or change within a given set of rules and assumptions. The basic rules of behaviour and their meaning remain essentially the same. The existing theories-in-use are maintained (Argyris & Schon, 1978).

Examples of first-order change include:

- When I first joined Ford, most production lines still had a quality control function. Falls in quality were often met by an increased focus on quality control – a common-sense response if you wanted to improve quality. As you would expect, this would often result in an immediate improvement in quality. However, this tended to be temporary and short-lived. Increasing monitoring of quality tended to reduce employees' sense of ownership and responsibility for quality (i.e. quality is someone else's responsibility), which meant that over the longer-term quality would start to fall or remain static.
- Another pattern that I would observe in Ford plants related to managerial behaviour when there was a breakdown on the line. A self-reinforcing loop was established whereby the managers would not trust the production teams to solve the problem. They would therefore intervene and take control. This would set up an expectation from the teams that the managers would take control when there was a problem. The teams would therefore step back and wait when something went wrong in anticipation of the manager telling them what to do. This pattern meant the teams never learnt how to solve production problems nor did they develop confidence in their own expertise or capacity to take responsibility.

Each of these examples is inherently paradoxical in that they are attempts to create change which reinforce the existing social patterns (or social order). Often problems, like the ones described above, emerge because of how we construct or see our world. Ben Ramalingam (2013) in his book *Aid on the Edge of Chaos* described a development intervention in Zimbabwe that transformed 20,000 acres of parched and degraded grasslands into healthy pastures. The transformation, led by Allan Savory's African Centre for Holistic Management, found that the problem arose because animals returned to graze on plants before they had a chance to regrow. This occurred as a result of the introduction of fencing on the lands during colonial times. Prior to this, herds would move around the grasslands with sufficient freedom so that plants had a chance to regrow. The solution was profoundly simple: to herd the cattle in such a way that they only grazed in areas where the plants had regenerated. The problem had arisen because the attempts to manage the land had resulted in unforeseen consequences.

In contrast, second-order change involves a change in being, values and relating which shatters traditions. This requires a qualitative change in the basic underlying assumptions, mental models or metaphor for understanding the world. This is equivalent to what Argyris and Schon (1978) called 'double-loop' learning. Watzlawick and his colleagues observed that when a paradigm shift (Kuhn, 1970) occurs, the rules of the system and hence the system itself change. This disrupts the existing frameworks of meaning rather than maintaining the familiar. Second-order change necessarily alters some fundamental assumptions informing behaviour. For instance, if one is in a nightmare you can run, hide or scream; however, you are still in a nightmare (Watzlawick et al., 1974). A second-order change involves waking up, which terminates the nightmare. Second-order change cannot be accommodated within our existing paradigm and represent a crisis discontinuity. This necessitates a gestalt switch in perception. Change at this level involves a *reframing* of the situation. For instance, an example is the transformation of Ford's levels of quality when production teams were given full responsibility for quality and were given the authority to stop the production line if they received work from other teams that had defects or errors.

Thomas Kuhn argued that scientific revolutions and paradigm shifts do not come about through empirical tests of reality but rather through comparison with other paradigms and through social interaction (Kuhn, 1970). He observed how, before a scientific revolution, competing paradigms co-exist with the predominant paradigm. Anomalies with the dominant paradigm are overlooked until a shift is triggered by a crisis. Kuhn observed that this arises out of 'the growing sense that an existing paradigm has ceased to function adequately in the explanation of an aspect of nature to which the paradigm itself has previously led the way' (p. 92).

Any new paradigm is difficult to grasp, especially for those long familiar with a previous one. Even when the evidence of our experience challenges our paradigms, we tend to revise the meaning of events to minimise dissonance (Festinger, 1957). Paradigms therefore show a resistance to change. We do not readily give them up and resist experiences that require us to do so. At first, people's reaction is often one of shock because what they had accepted as 'true' or unquestionable is challenged. They go on to experience discomfort, confusion and cognitive dissonance (Festinger, 1957) because the accepted frameworks for understanding the world are questioned and challenged. This explains why new technologies that have the potential for disruption tend to be seen as unattractive by established industries.

First attempts to change organisations often reinforce the existing cultural paradigm by responding to change in a habitual manner that reflects unconscious beliefs and assumptions. In other words, attempts to bring about second-order change inadvertently have first-order effects. For instance, I worked for several years with a firm of auditors. They needed to dramatically improve the efficiency and productivity of how they worked to remain competitive. To bring about a change, they established a large programme team that undertook an audit of how they did audit. The irony of this approach was lost on them, as they were so unable to see how their approach was embedded in the very assumptions they needed to challenge. Any suggestion that they could take an alternative approach that was less linear, analytical and controlled proved to be too uncomfortable for them. The programme team produced a rigorous and detailed analysis of the existing approaches and sensible recommendations. However, the ownership for these recommendations resided with the programme team (i.e. the auditors). The project produced some incremental improvements yet in the end they were ultimately disappointed because they were unable to achieve the step change they needed. Transformational change therefore needs to be countercultural if it is to disrupt the established cultural paradigm. New thinking, ideas and approaches tend to emerge from the margins or outside of the core or dominant groups in an organisation because outsiders are not subjected to the same pressures to conform or have access to different perspectives and ways of thinking.

Cultural change therefore involves the emergence of and reconfiguration of dominant ideas, values, metaphors and patterns of behaviour, such that new constructions and interpretations emerge for a community or organisation (McLean, 2013). This requires a raising of collective consciousness of how people act together to maintain culture. This is often brought about through new ways of thinking or external events that challenge the dominant and established patterns in such a way that people conclude that not responding creates a bigger crisis than acting differently.

At the heart of a paradigm shift is loss (Marris, 1974). People have to let go of and give up established beliefs, values and identities. Unsurprisingly, this is highly emotive and destabilising. Tensions inevitably arise between individuals who are invested in the established paradigm and those who take up the role of challenging and questioning traditions and conventional practices. Those who are proponents of alternative paradigms need to be willing to take the risk of not conforming. Scientific breakthroughs by individuals such as Copernicus, Galileo, Darwin and Freud provoked an overwhelming sense of loss, disorientation and mourning as the dominant ways of understanding the world were challenged. If a loss is too painful, we find attempts to maintain the past and to retreat from mourning (Stein, 2004). When this happens, we tend to find splits between groups who are attempting to hold on to the established frameworks and those that are promoting different ways of thinking.

For a period of six months, I consulted to a team at the European telecommunications business that had been asked to help the marketing department to create a new digital marketing platform. The team was given the brief to find ways of disrupting the status quo and to develop innovative, agile and creative solutions that would challenge the established culture. Midway through the project, I facilitated a meeting to help them to review progress. A sense of frustration, confusion and controlled anger pervaded the group. They felt that the project's sponsors were firmly rooted in the established 'ways of doing things' and were not interested in taking any risks or challenging the status quo. The team was highly judgemental and critical of the sponsors. They had, however, not explored their frustrations with the project sponsors because of fears of the consequences of sharing their observations and feelings. This blocked the opportunity to surface and explore the differences in assumptions.

I understood the tension that was emerging between the team and their sponsors as reflecting a wider tension that existed across the organisation between those individuals who remained invested in the traditional cultural paradigm and those individuals who were invested in changing it.

During periods of transformation, projects and local changes become important vehicles for working through and working out cultural paradigms because they provide opportunities for the contained expressions of conflict around beliefs, assumptions and values. The encounters involved in implementing changes translates often abstract concepts or ideas into concrete, tangible and emotive experiences.

Language and framing of change

Language is a specific type of symbol through which we represent our experience to others. Language and discourse order our world and ourselves in relation to it. It places people and objects in categories to which the collective has ascribed meaning. This helps us to find order by making comparisons with other familiar classes of experience.

Metaphors are a form of language that communicates tacit, implicit meanings that are often outside of our immediate awareness. They help us make sense of the world by drawing out similarities and creating meaning by making connections. Metaphors 'structure what we perceive, how we get around in the world, and how we relate to other people' (Lakoff & Johnson, 2003, p. 125). One thing is understood by making associations to another. This helps us to convey insights, ideas and intuitions that are not always possible through rational–logical arguments. For instance, 'cloud computing' is a metaphor that helps society grasp the possibilities of the delivery of computing services over the internet.

Every attempt to change an organisation is informed by one metaphor or another, such as clockwork, construction, revolution, restructure and so on. The metaphors that we use reveals a host of assumptions that we hold about organisations and how to change them. This can help us make sense of our experience whilst also blinding us from what can be obvious through another metaphor (Morgan, 2006). For instance, the metaphor of the organisation as a 'machine' focuses our attention on designing and engineering change, yet hides the human dimensions of organisations. Metaphors can therefore both constrain how we see a situation or open up new possibilities. By using different metaphors, we can give birth to new meanings or ways of seeing a situation (Barrett & Cooperrider, 1990). Metaphors therefore have the potential to disrupt how we see the world.

Organisational change emerges out of new narratives, language and discourses which help people see new possibilities and alternatives for action (Bushe & Marshak, 2015). The ability to manipulate or change language is therefore a powerful act that conveys meaning during periods of change. Whether events and developments are perceived as an opportunity or threat rests upon the language, metaphors and images that are used to describe what is happening and to legitimise the actions taken. Our research into the practice of organisation transformation highlighted that when changes are framed as a future opportunity or a response to an adaptive challenge (i.e. external challenges), employees are much more likely to become energised and engaged (Metalogue Consulting, 2018). If people are going to invest themselves in change then they need to see that it has a purpose that matters to them and appeals to what they care about in their lives and work. In contrast, the use of deficit and critical language (i.e. people are lacking) is more likely to heighten feelings of opposition, resistance or anxiety.

'The Programmable World'

> *The transformation of Nokia was partly inspired by the generative image of 'The Programmable World'. This reflected Nokia's vision of how in the future high levels of network connectivity, through the cloud and mobile sensors technology, would interact to enable intelligent analysis and learning to feed a whole range of devices that will change our lives. This metaphor of the future became central to their transformation as a business.*

The narrative and story that accompanies organisational change efforts needs to help people understand why changes are perceived to be necessary, what is being proposed, how individuals will be affected and how they will be involved in proposed changes. In ambiguous or fast-moving situations, competing narratives co-exist around how to make sense of events and debates arise around what needs to be done and how. Unsurprisingly, disagreements and conflicts arise between individuals and groups with different perspectives. This can be constructive if it helps to surface differences and tacit assumptions. It can equally be problematic when conflict becomes polarised and stuck.

> *A global engineering firm that was experiencing falling margins and profits had launched a series of transformation efforts across parts of its businesses. The executive team had called the programme to improve its support functions' 'fit for growth'. The language surrounding the programme conveyed images of the functions being unfit, over-resourced and lacking in capability. Unsurprisingly, this deficit language left those who were expected to change feeling undervalued, threatened and criticised, which caused them to passively resist and oppose the intended changes. The heads of the functions, many of whom were new to the business, became increasingly frustrated and critical of their teams, which acted to compound the situation.*

Several years ago, I was part of a team that worked with the leadership team of one of the European automotive manufacturers. During an economic downturn, the business had incurred significant and unsustainable losses. The executive team wanted to bring together the top 200 leaders of the business to assess the state of the business, what was happening in the market and to agree on a strategy for improving performance. The event was designed to facilitate the process of sensemaking and decision making. On the first day, they were joined by an external commentator on the automotive industry who gave a perspective on developments in the market, the company's historical positioning and their perspective on the difficulties the company was encountering. The finance vice-president then presented on the financial performance of the business over the long term. Both perspectives helped those at the meeting to see the current challenges in a wider historical context. The group then worked in small functional groups and then cross-functional groups to share their perspectives on the challenges and opportunities facing the business. The small groups then reported their insights and observations back to the large group. Then cross-functional groups were asked to reflect on what they had learnt about the business. Through this process, a shared understanding started to emerge of the challenges facing the business, what were the immediate problems that required fixing and where were some of the longer-term opportunities. The focus of the event then started to move towards action planning. Each functional leadership team was asked to set itself some long-term and short-term goals and then plan actions for realising them. The group then broke into product lines and support functions to repeat the exercise. The action plans were shared and teams invited to request support and help from other teams. The event ended with the executive team making requests of the wider leadership team, in terms of their expectations and the support they needed.

This process helped to create a common understanding of the adaptive challenge facing the organisation and to mobilise collective responsibility for addressing organisation-wide problems.

Implications for practice

Our capacity to see the world symbolically means that we are able to flex and change how we interpret events and situations. By changing language, discourse, rituals and customs and behaviour, we communicate new meanings to each other. This capacity to reframe and shift meaning means that cultural change goes on everywhere and at all times (Malinowski, 1945) as we adapt to technological and environmental changes. Transformation, change and adaptation arises therefore as a process of meaning making and reinterpretation. Action in itself does not bring about change; in fact, if it communicates the existing paradigm it re-enacts existing cultural patterns. Action that expresses a different way of understanding the world is, however, necessary to communicate different meanings and interpretations of a situation.

The following practices help people to process rapid and disruptive change:

Making change meaningful. We cannot assume we know what an event or change will mean for those affected. We need to take the 'native's point of view' (Geertz, 1973), to see the world as they see it, in order to grasp what a change might mean to them. This requires us to inquire into their perspective, to immerse ourselves in their world and to dwell in their experiences. Only when we understand the meaning of the existing cultural patterns can we see what events means to them. Our language or framing of a change will affect how they interpret and respond to our gestures and intentions. Equally, imposing change on others starts from our point of reference, rather than theirs, which results in confusion, misunderstanding and resistance. Working with those affected to help them to make sense and co-create changes increases the likelihood that organisational changes are experienced as meaningful.

Seeing the whole picture. Organisational change can only be achieved if people are able to reflect on and gain new insights into the 'totality' of their situation. We often only see our own narrow window. Complexity requires people to share their perspectives and to try to make sense of how the organisation is being shaped and affected by wider socio-economic patterns. When we see our behaviour in its wider context, we are able to understand how we are participating in maintaining systemic patterns that do not serve our long-term interests or our organisation.

Facilitating sensemaking. The quality of sensemaking depends on the richness of the flow of information. As Gregory Bateson famously argued: 'information is a difference that makes a difference' (Bateson, 2000, p. 25). Change can only happen when we notice what we have previously failed to notice. The richness and quality of information that is available to a group is amplified when differences are noticed and expressed between individuals and groups and between points in time, social contexts and places. Understanding a complex situation, therefore, requires multiple and different perspectives. When faced with new, unknown and unanticipated events we, more often than not, are challenged with finding the words and language to describe what has happened and is happening. Content that is rich in imagery, metaphors and unfolding narratives conveys more information than heavily edited content that is dominated by statistics, lists or generic points (Weick, 1995). Stories and first-hand accounts of experiences aid comprehension and convey meaning and values. They also provide both a description of events, an interpretation, and guidance for action (Weick, 1995). New information also arises when we go and look beyond our usual horizons. Effective sensemaking requires time and space for people to share information, observations and interpretations. Large-group methodologies, such as Future Search (Weisbord & Janoff, 2010) or Open Space (Owen, 2008) help diverse groups to make sense of complex, systemic changes.

Encouraging reflexivity. Without awareness, we become trapped by the images and assumptions we hold of ourselves, others and our organisations (Morgan, 2006). The process of change thus needs to raise people's awareness of their assumptions and how these assumptions influence what they do. Awareness has to happen at an experiential and emotional level, not at just at an abstract rational-logical level, for people to fully engage with change.

Noticing and changing language, narratives and imagery. To bring about change, one must change the words people use and the meaning of the words that are used (Weick, 1995). Vivid words and language draw attention to new possibilities. Those organisations that are able to access a greater variety of images are able to engage in sensemaking that is more adaptive than those with more limited vocabularies (Weick, 1995). Bushe and Marshak (2015) observe how the emergence of a generative image provides new and compelling alternatives for thinking and acting. Such images and metaphors disrupt people's prevailing constructions of reality (Bushe & Storch, 2015) and helps them to see the present differently and, in doing so, see new possibilities for action.

Regulation of anxiety. The desire to make sense is triggered by the experience of anxiety at the point when we struggle to understand events yet, as we have seen, if anxiety becomes overwhelming for those affected then psychological defences start to act against sensemaking. Those leading and facilitating changes need to create environments and spaces that contain people's anxieties and minimise their fears of being judged, feeling incompetent and being vulnerable. Having the capacity to bear anxiety, however, is central to our growth and learning as individuals. By moving through, not away, from anxiety we develop and enlarge our view of the world (May, 1977).

Conclusion

Adaptive change and transformation involve a shift in our cultural paradigm and interpretative frames. This necessarily disturbs and dislocates the thread of continuity in our experiences and patterns of meaning. To make sense of changes, we need to draw on our established frames of reference yet we also need to let go of these to change. This is easier said than done. Disruptions to our interpretative frames trigger overwhelming anxieties in organisations because they challenge our desire for order, certainty and continuity. More often than not, this results in attempts to simply complexity and restore some semblance of certainty. The process of sensemaking, however, requires us to move towards the unknown and our anxieties by exploring, inquiring and reflecting with others to interpret events and discover emerging patterns. A central challenge facing organisations, in turbulent fields, is how to help people to make sense of their experience and to find a thread of continuity between the past, present and future.

Notes

1 Named after the Danish psychologist Edgar Rubin, who publicised it in 1915.
2 Stacey (2012, p. 24), building on this principle, observes that:

> meaning does not lie in the gesture alone but in the social act as a whole; meaning arises in the responsive social interaction… meaning is located not just in the past (gesture) or the future (response) but also in the interaction between the two… no matter how clearly worded the communication is, it will be interpreted in many different ways.

3 A symbol is anything that signifies meaning in a given social context. A red flag is a symbol of danger on a beach, a white one surrender on a battlefield.

Works cited

Alvesson, M. (2013). *Understanding organizational culture* (2nd ed.). London, England: Sage.
Argyris, C., & Schon, D. (1978). *Organizational learning: A theory of action perspective.* Reading, England: Addison-Wesley.
Barrett, F. J., & Cooperrider, D. L. (1990). Generative metaphor intervention: A new approach for working with systems divided by conflict and caught in defensive perception. *Journal of Applied Behavioral Science, 26*(2), 219–239.
Bateson, G. (2000). *Steps to an ecology of mind.* Chicago, IL: University of Chicago Press.
Berger, P. L., & Luckmann, T. (1967). *The social construction of reality.* New York, NY: Doubleday Anchor.
Bion, W. (1967). *Second thoughts.* London: Karnac.
Bushe, G. R., & Marshak, R. J. (2015). *Dialogic organization development: The theory and practice of transformational change.* Oakland, CA: Berrett-Koehler.
Bushe, G., & Storch, J. (2015). Generative image: Sourcing novelty. In G. R. Bushe, & R. J. Marshak (Eds.), *Dialogic organization development: The theory and practice of transformational change.* Oakland, CA: Berrett-Koehler.
Capra, F., & Luisi, P. L. (2014). *The systems view of life: A unifying vision.* Cambridge, England: Cambridge University Press.
Cooper, A., & Lousada, J. (2005). *Borderline welfare: Feeling and fear of feeling in modern welfare.* London, England: Karnac Books.
Festinger, L. (1954). *A theory of cognitive dissonance.* Stanford, CA: Stanford University Press.
Flavell, J. H. (1963). *Developmental psychology of Jean Piaget.* Princeton, NJ: D. Van Nostrand.
Geertz, C. (1973). *The interpretation of cultures.* New York, NY: Basic Books.
Gergen, K. (2015). *An invitation to social construction* (3rd ed.). Los Angeles, CA: Sage Publications.
Johnson, G. (1988). Re-thinking incrementalism. *Strategic Management Journal, 9,* 75–91.
Kuhn, T. (1970). *The structure of scientific revolutions.* Chicago, IL: University of Chicago Press.
Lakoff, G., & Johnson, M. (2003). *Metaphors we live by.* Chicago, IL: University of Chicago Press.
Malinowski, B. (1945). *The dynamics of culture change.* New Haven, CT: Yale University Press.
Marris, P. (1974). *Loss and change.* London: Routledge and Kegan.

May, R. (1977). *The meaning of anxiety* (revised ed.). New York, NY: Norton.

McLean, A. (2013). *Leadership & cultural webs in organisations: Weavers' tales*. Emerald.

Mead, G. H. (1934). *Mind, self and society from the standpoint of a behaviorist*. Chicago, IL: University of Chicago.

Metalogue Consulting. (2018). *Organisation transformation: "Fateful framings"*. Retrieved from https://metalogue.co.uk/Metalogue-Report-on-Transformation-Dec-2018.pdf

Morgan, G. (2006). *Images of organization*. London, England: Sage Publications.

O'Hara, M. (2001). *Alternative psychological scenarios for the coming global age*. Retrieved from http://citeseerx.ist.psu.edu/viewdoc/download?doi=10.1.1.475.6830&rep=rep1&type=pdf

Owen, H. (2008). *Open space technology: A user's guide*. San Francisco, CA: Berrett-Koehler.

Piaget, J., & Inhelder, B. (1969). *The psychology of the child*. New York, NY: Basic Books.

Radcliffe Brown, A. R. (1952). *Structure and function in primitive society, essays and addresses*. London, England: Cohen & West.

Ramalingam, B. (2013). *Aid on the edge of chaos*. Oxford, England: Oxford University Press.

Rasch, W., & Wolfe, C. (2000). Introduction: Systems theory and the politics of post-modernity. In W. Rasch, & C. Wolfe (Eds.), *Observing complexity: Systems theory and postmodernity* (pp. 1–32). Minneapolis, MN: University of Minnesota Press.

Schein, E. (2010). *Organizional culture and leadership*. The Jossey-Bass Business & Management Series. San Francisco, CA: Jossey-Bass.

Stacey, R. (2012). *Tools and techniques of leadership and management: Meeting the challenge of complexity*. London, England; New York, NY: Routledge.

Stacey, R. D., & Mowles, C. (2015). *Strategic management and organisational dynamics*. Harlow, England: Pearson Education.

Stein, H. F. (2004). *Beneath the crust of culture: Psychoanalytic anthropology and the cultural unconscious in American life*. Amsterdam, the Netherlands: Brill Academic Publishers.

Toffler, A. (1984). *Future shock*. New York, NY: Bantam USA.

VanMaanen, J., & Barley, S. R. (1984). Occupational communities: Culture and control in organizations. In B. M. Staw, & L. L. Cummings (Eds.), *Research in organisational behaviour* (Vol. 6, pp. 287–365). Greenwich, CT: JAI Press.

Watzlawick, P., Weakland, J., & Fisch, R. (1974). *Change: Principles of problem formation and problem resolution*. New York, NY: W.W. Norton Company.

Weick, K. E. (1995). *Sensemaking in organizations*. Thousand Oaks, CA: Sage Publications.

Weisbord, M., & Janoff, S. (2010). *Future search: Getting the whole system in the room for vision, commitment and action*. San Francisco, CA: Berrett-Koehler.

Whitaker, D. S., & Lieberman, M. A. (1964). Psychotherapy through the group process. Oxford, England: Atherton Press.

8   Altered images

Identity construction and fragmentation

Identity is at the heart of human existence. We all have a desire to be recognised and seen by others as we want to be seen; and we act in ways that help to cultivate a recognisable and stable sense of self. This forms the basis of our self-esteem. One way we express our identity is through our work; and organisations are places where we enact our identities. We equally construct our identities in relation to the identities of our organisations (Alvesson, 2013).

Identity can be the driving force for organisational change if it is perceived to enhance employees' identity or enable them to live up to their ideals. However, organisational change often challenges and threatens our identity. When this happens, we deploy a range of psychological defences in an attempt to protect our self-esteem (Brown & Starkey, 2000). For instance, we might deny what is happening or hold rigidly onto our identity in an attempt to preserve our sense of self.

One of the principal struggles for both myself and many of my colleagues following the takeover of the business school where I worked was a question of identity. Being 'taken over' represented a failure of which we were, to some degree, ashamed. We had described ourselves as a 'leading international business school' yet here we were being taken over by another business school. This was not something that was publicly talked about or acknowledged. Yet it emerged through informal conversations or could be sensed from the reactions of employees, particularly the management and professional staff, to the announcement.

As the takeover unfolded, fundamental differences in values and beliefs about the world became apparent and what it meant to work for the business school started to change. As we interacted with senior managers from the other organisation, we became aware that how we saw ourselves was not how they saw us. This process was very disorientating and unsettling for many employees. The challenge to our identity produced feelings not just about ourselves but also towards the other business school such as anger, hurt and fear. We made judgements of 'them', and my experience was that 'they' made judgements of 'us'.

This account is itself a reflection of how I want to construct my identity to you – the reader – and how I classified others in relation to myself in the context of the takeover.

Identity, whether it is of the individual, group or organisation, implies characteristics that are distinctive and enduring. It reflects our desire to belong and our need for order, classification and boundaries. Identity helps us to locate ourselves and others in the social order by producing contrasts, distinctions and classifications. Orthodox and traditional categories, such as professions, social class and nationality, create fixed coordinates, or social anchors, in social life. These provide us with a sense of stability and, thereby, security. We become emotionally committed to these social locations and passionately invested in them.

In society and organisations, identities are becoming fluid, negotiated and temporal choices (Bauman, 2004). Our identity is more uncertain than in the past. Social change, in all its forms, challenges taken-for-granted assumptions about how we define ourselves and others. As the established social order is disrupted, our identities are altered, disturbed and challenged. This introduces uncertainty and disorder into our identities, which most people experience as a threat to who they are. Social positions may be altered, challenged or destroyed altogether. During transitions, we feel betwixt and between identities, neither being who we were nor who we will be. If during this process, our existing identities are not recognised, we feel disoriented, thrown off balance and invalidated. This leaves us feeling lost and even bereft. Who we thought we were and how others perceived us is different.

During periods of disruption, we therefore search for reference points that help us maintain a feeling of sense and coherence. These become points of security that will provide us with an anchor for a recognisable identity. If these anchors are lost, we can experience an absence of a coherent identity which leaves us feeling insecure and helpless.

The social construction of identity

Historically, psychology has, in the main, viewed identity as something that we possess, is internal to us, and is relatively enduring throughout our lives. Identity was seen as a 'thing' that is static, stable and bounded. This perhaps reflected the stability of the times. The postmodern view of identity challenges and questions this assumption. Identity is conceptualised as an ongoing process in which we actively adopt our identities. Identity is as much an invention as a possession. We choose, consciously and unconsciously, how we want to construct ourselves, to see ourselves and to be seen. We locate ourselves in specific identity positions which can be fluid and contradictory (Frosh, 2010). Language creates categories and conveys characteristics that construct our identities in specific social contexts. Symbols, customs and rituals equally express and confirm identities.

Identity is intersubjective in nature. Our identities are constructed in and through everyday relationships with others. We can think of identity as an image that we produce for the Other (Dashtipour, 2012). These images reflect our ideal self or group – how we want to be seen – and how we believe we are seen by others. Our identity equally comes from outside of ourselves, and others become the mirror in which we see ourselves, reflecting back to us images of how they see us. Identity is thus both a self-ascription and ascribed by others. I can see myself as a white, middle-class, British, middle-aged psychologist. In doing so, I locate myself in particular categories of an existing social order. Others may construct me in other ways that compete with this identity. I could, for instance, be seen as a member of the dominant, privileged elite or perhaps as a somewhat conservative, uninteresting and conforming member of society. Who or what we identify with at any one point depends on which social categories and images are most salient to us and the other actors in the situation.

Organisational change invariably mobilises group identities because it invokes language, symbols and images that talk to identities. This can trigger anxieties and regressive behaviour when groups perceive that their boundaries or identity are threatened. It can equally energise people to participate in change if images and language appeal to desired identities or ideals. The fluidity of language and images also enables identities to flex and adapt to changing circumstances. Identities can change when we change the labels that we give ourselves or others or when we change the meaning that we associate with these labels (Gioia, Schultz, & Corley, 2000).

In the automotive plants that were introducing self-managed teams, the maintenance workers had an image of themselves as highly skilled and of higher status than the 'production' workers. This reflected their high skill levels and their importance to the running of the plant. The introduction of new ways of categorising and representing both professional groups through the introduction of work groups brought about a disturbance in the identities of the respective groups because their identities were mutually dependent on each other. At first, many of the maintenance group workers resisted and opposed the introduction of teamworking because of what they felt was an undermining of their identity and status. The management invested considerable time in positioning the changes as central to the future of the plant, arguing that productivity improvements were required if the plant was going to have a secure future. This appealed to a signifier of identity at the plant level by presenting a shared sense of purpose. By mobilising employees' identification with the plant and their fears about the future, the maintenance workers became more accepting of and committed to the proposed changes.

The politics of identity

We are engaged in a constant struggle to express ourselves and to be recognised for who we feel we are in the face of others' classifications, perceptions and projections. In this sense, identity is highly politicised. As the world changes, so the symbolic order presents us with new choices and opportunities to construct who we are, yet, equally, it eradicates, alters or takes away signifiers of our identities. In contemporary society and organisations, many people are experiencing a crisis of identity, as they are confronted with the challenge of how to represent themselves against a backdrop of constantly shifting identities.

Social media and the internet are helping to break down the established and rigid identities of modernism of class and nation (Castells, 2015). Equally, they facilitate the creation of niche identities and amplify a global discourse around signifiers of identities such as gender, race and sexuality. Traditional identities increasingly feel precarious. Globalisation as a process is stirring up anxieties and fears as it threatens to eradicate cultural differences. In direct contrast, complex and fluid identities are also emerging. Each of us now has greater degrees of freedom as to how we take up and express our identity. This opens up a creative potential for all of us; no longer constrained by tradition, we can, to a much larger degree, choose who we want to be both at work and more generally. This process, however, has a darker side to it. Many groups in societies are starting to feel marginalised and negated. In reaction to globalisation, multiculturalism and cultural fluidity, we are witnessing a corresponding rise in fundamentalism and nationalism. This can be understood as a protest against a sense of invalidation of people's identity and an attempt to re-establish historical identities.

Images often act as a disruptive and destabilising force on identity (Gioia et al., 2000). Changes within an organisation will either mirror an image to those affected that is reflective of their self-image or challenge it. During periods of upheaval, the images of ourselves that are reflected back to us start to change. Changes that alter and challenge a person or group's identity will necessarily be harder to accept and accommodate. Such changes incur a loss to those affected that is often hard to process. An organisation, which for many years has seen itself as leading-edge and successful, may suddenly find itself being seen as outdated and unfashionable. This may trigger defensiveness if employees are not willing to accept or recognise the image. It may equally trigger a desire for change to restore a desired or ideal image. The imposition of new identities or the reshuffling of people, as if they were cards in the pack, plays havoc with their identities. Ongoing ambivalence around our identity is notoriously hard to endure.

Where individuals or groups experience negative images being reflected back to them, this tends to be psychologically disturbing, as their self-image is challenged or undermined. For instance, I recently heard a CEO declare that 'our staff groups are over-resourced and not best in class'. This statement appeared to me to be an attempt to legitimise cutting costs and reorganising different functions. More often than not, rather than producing energy for change, presenting negative images triggers resistance to the message because groups engage in face saving. Either the group has to reject the arguments or reject its self-image.

> *I can recall the day when driving into business school that the sign in front of the main building had been changed. I was not aware that this was going to happen and I recall feeling taken aback in the moment. My initial reaction was one of anger – how could 'they' change 'our' name? The sign itself was an important signifier of how the identity of the institution was changing. In hindsight, my moral outrage was a confrontation with reality. Our identity had and was changing, whether I liked it or not.*

Social comparison and differentiation

The philosopher Pierre Bourdieu (Bourdieu, 1984) observed that the basis of social identity lies in difference, and difference is asserted against what is closest. Groups make comparisons with other similar groups on characteristics that are of importance to them, such as ability or status (Festinger, 1954). In the automotive plants, the maintenance workers acted to differentiate themselves from the production workers. The introduction of self-managed teams, however, challenged this process as it introduced a shared work group identity which would need to become more significant than occupational identities.

Our desire to differentiate creates social categories. Individuals within a social category are perceived to be similar and those outside of it are perceived to be different. This is a process of depersonalisation, as it de-emphasises the uniqueness of individuals. A social category, or signifier, comes to represent an identity for both those individuals within and outside a category. When organisations change, the meaning of these signifiers of identity is changed and this has meaning for those affected. When the sign outside of business school changed, our identities changed with it. Anyone who has worked for a company that has been merged with another or been taken over will recognise the importance of a name and the sense of loss that is experienced when the name is changed. When Guinness and Grand Metropolitan merged in 1997, they created a new name – 'Diageo' – to signify the creation of a new entity. This helped employees come together in the creation of a new organisation, rather than feel that they were being consumed by another.

This process of differentiation usually happens with the groups that are closest to our own. Because of this, our identity is most threatened and challenged by those who are closest to us. Our fiercest relationships are often with individuals, groups or communities that differ very little from us and with whom we are more similar than perhaps different. Freud (1921, p. 102) called this process 'the narcissism of minor differences', observing that:

> Of two neighbouring towns each is the other's most jealous rival; every little canton looks down upon the others with contempt. Closely related races keep one another at arm's length; the South German cannot endure

the North German, the Englishman casts every kind of aspersion upon the Scot, the Spaniard despises the Portuguese.

Once a group is named as 'US', then the world is divided into two regions – an 'us' and a 'not us' or 'THEM'. The 'not us' tends to represent what we do not want to be, the qualities of ourselves that we wish to disown. The moment of becoming an 'US' brings anxiety, as in this moment, a 'NOT US' is created that represents what we do not want to be and this is a threat to our identity (Dalal, 1998). The more we reject the other group, the more we feel a tie to the group to which we feel we belong, yet this comes at the cost of anxiety.

Groups and individuals in this way use other groups to maintain their self-esteem or protect their identities when they feel threatened. By projecting their negative feelings about themselves onto others, they are able to maintain their identity and see others as possessing the negative characteristics or images that they would rather not see in themselves. Stereotypes thus serve the purpose of making us feel superior to others and protect our identity. More confident and secure individuals and groups are less prone to projecting fears and hostilities onto other groups. Strongly cohesive yet insecure individuals and groups, however, need an 'other' against whom to define themselves. When people feel their identity is threatened during periods of upheaval and change, then this can trigger prejudice and hostility towards others. In organisations that are under pressure or struggling to change, it is not uncommon to find a higher prevalence of bullying and harassment or incidences of discrimination and prejudice towards minority groups.

Classic social psychology experiments demonstrate that competition emerges between groups when they perceive that if the other gains, they will lose (Campbell, 1965); Sheriff, 1966). Under these conditions, they behave in such a way as to protect or safeguard their interests. When change creates clear 'winners' and 'losers', then competition, rivalry and hostility arise. In contrast, when groups perceive they have shared interests in achieving an outcome or a common fate, they are more likely to cooperate and conflict tends to reduce (Sheriff, 1966). Where groups perceive that they have common ground in creating a preferred future (Weisbord & Janoff, 2010), we can therefore expect that they will cooperate and work together. This is by no means guaranteed as collaboration may threaten a group's identity to such an extent that groups become more invested in protecting their identity.

The blurring and fragmentation of identities as social boundaries change and disappear leaves us with fundamental questions around:

Who am I?
Who are we?
Where do I belong?

Instability, economic insecurity and uncertainty about one's place in the world creates confusion and fear. Not knowing who we are in relation to others is traumatic and unbearable for us, inviting feelings of shame and humiliation. This engenders a powerful desire to restore our psychological security and self-esteem. If we experience too much existential anxiety, we retreat into rigid positions in an attempt to hold on to some semblance of an identity. This causes groups to search out stable, known and secure identities, particularly where they experience a loss of differentiation with important reference groups. Often this results in the devaluing and degrading of other groups to shore up the in-group's esteem. We can expect therefore for change that threatens identities to be associated with conflict, aggression and hostilities between groups. The challenge for organisations is how to achieve unity across differences and how to preserve differences whilst creating a sense of unity.

Status difference, power and identity

Status transactions are part of human relating. Every interaction, inflection and movement imply status (Johnstone, 2017). These micro-interactions give rise to and maintain stratification patterns in social systems. Identity is therefore inextricably connected to status and power dynamics in any social system. Members of higher-status groups tend to have higher levels of self-esteem than members of low-status groups (Turner, 1982). Groups in power therefore act to maintain their status.

Status differences are often communicated by symbols and signs in organisations. Organisation charts can be thought of as cultural artefacts that signify power and status. When I first started working at Ford, I soon learnt that I could fairly accurately work out the grade of a manager from the size, location and position of their office and the type of plants that were in the office. These symbols communicated to others the importance of the individual and the relative level of deference that was expected.

An internal consultant at a global technology company described to me how two design teams in the medical appliances division were involved in a heated and intractable argument about the naming of their products. Both products were based on similar technology yet were designed to address very different medical problems. The marketing department had seen that by marketing the two products under a common brand and reframing the purpose of the devices, a wider and broader market could be served. The two products were to be given the same name with the only differentiator an extra '0' on the end of one of the devices. Neither team would accept to be the one without the extra '0'. This symbol conveyed to the teams which device was considered to be superior and of higher status. The '0' therefore became a symbol of great importance.

In 1965, Norbert Elias and John Scotson, in what has become a classic socio-logical enquiry, studied two adjoining working-class neighbourhoods in an English town in the Midlands (Elias & Scotson, 1994). They found that 'the established' neighbourhood who had lived in the town for many years excluded and stigmatised the other neighbourhood that had only been established a few years previously. The 'established' working-class families were more organised and this enabled them to exclude the newcomers who had lower social cohe-sion. Elias and Scotson described how the 'established' group maintained power differentials with the 'newcomers' by using ideology and gossip about their superiority over the newcomers. This became 'a means of preserving the current social order by making it seem natural, unquestionable, by convincing all that participants that it is so' (Dalal, 1998, p. 116). People therefore do not just gather or form groups because of similarity; they group around the vortices of power using their similarity to hide the vortices from view and deny their existence (Dalal, 1998). Groups thus use identity to create and maintain power and status differentials (Elias & Scotson, 1994).

Most change disrupts the established power structures that define social identities. We can therefore expect groups to use their power to maintain the status quo, to protect their power and status. This can put them at odds with managers who are trying to introduce changes or other groups who may stand to gain power and status as a result of changes in the organisation.

Organisational identity

Organisations are also social objects that produce identities. These relate to the characteristics, values and ideals that different stakeholders associate with the institution and act to create. An organisational identity represents how its members see themselves as a social group and how they see themselves to be different to other organisations (Haslam, 2004). We can think of this as the stories that the organisation tells itself about itself (Smircich, 1983) and the assertions organisational members make about who-they-are-as-an-organisation. These are often linked to the history of the organisation and how people remember its past.

By acting into an image of the organisation, employees create and main-tain an identity and uphold shared ideals. Equally, investors, customers, the media and the public relate to an organisation with an image of it in mind. The form and nature of these images influence how employees relate to the organisation and their emotional investment, sense of belonging and commitment. Through advertising and public relations, organisations go to great lengths to communicate and promote particular images of themselves. High-profile organisations, such as Nike, Apple, Ford, Facebook or the NHS, are all seen in particular ways by the wider public. Other organisations, such as Greenpeace or trade unions, may equally promote alternative images and discourses about a particular organisation or sector to mobilise them to act in particular ways.

Employees identify with and relate to their organisations to a greater or lesser degree. In socially cohesive organisations, employees are more likely to identify with the organisation and its ideals. This has consequences for social capital. High levels of identification correlate with higher levels of job satisfaction, performance, citizenship behaviour, and lower absenteeism and turnover (Riketta, 2005) – all of which are likely contribute to the long-term success of an organisation. In many organisations, such as Ford, Apple or BP, identification can be strong with the organisation and its ideals. Employees take pride in the image of the organisation and become invested in the success of the institution. For instance, the identity of Ford Motor Company is partly cultivated through stories of Henry Ford and his founding of the business; these were often recounted at critical events. At the company's headquarters in Dearborn in the United States, a museum tells the history of Henry Ford and the company itself. These stories and the sense of history create a strong sense of pride and loyalty to the organisation.

Excessive identification with an organisation and its ideals, however, can be narcissistic in nature (Schwartz, 1990) and therefore problematic. This can lead employees as a group to distort how they see the organisation, resulting in a loss of reality testing. The organisation is seen as 'perfect'. This restricts employees' ability to critically evaluate what the organisation does, its effectiveness and impact in the world. Instead, attempts are made to preserve the illusion that the organisation has attained its ideal (Schwartz, 1990); problems or failure are thereby overlooked. Highly cohesive groups with strong identities are likely to filter out information or deny threats to their self-esteem (Janis, 1972). This limits their capacity to learn and to adapt. Over-identification with the identity of the organisation is likely therefore to impede its ability to adapt and renew itself. This can often be the case with highly successful organisations where an inflated belief in the capacity of the firm to survive becomes the seed for its longer-term decline.

Attempts to change organisations are often associated with 'projected images' and symbolic representations of the organisation in the future (Gioia et al., 2000). These may be bona fide attempts to uphold important values or ideals or to change the identity of the organisation. They may also reflect attempts by leaders to manage impressions for internal or external audiences by projecting inaccurate or even false images. When this happens, change becomes a public relations exercise. When employees perceive the narrative of change as inauthentic and incongruent with their experience, then this generates cynicism and mistrust.

A desire to maintain or enhance an organisation's identity, ideals and image can drive high levels of energy and motivation to change. For instance, in my work with BP since the Gulf of Mexico disaster, I observed across the organisation genuine effort and commitment to restoring its reputation and make reparation for the damage that the disaster had caused. Equally, fundamental changes alter the identity of an organisation. If this is of a form that employees do not recognise, then it risks undermining their emotional investment in the organisation.

Constant and disruptive change has undermined and weakened employees' identification with their organisations. When the purpose and ideals of an organisation change, employees feel disoriented, disenchanted and alienated. The head of organisation development at one of the large banks described to me how the business's fall from grace during the financial crisis, criticism in the media and subsequent downsizing had left employees feeling ashamed, cynical and guilty. They had been advised not to wear any symbols of their membership to the organisation in public. Partly out of necessity, executives also had to be ruthless in making people redundant over a very short time period. This had left employees feeling that they did not matter to the organisation.

> *An ex-colleague who left the business school soon after the takeover confided in me: 'I don't belong to what the institution has become'. Two years after the take-over, close to 50% of the faculty had left. For many, this was because they were either no longer seen to fit or did not feel that they identified with the ideals of the organisation. Those who were able to adapt tended to be newer arrivals or were more able to flex their identity to accommodate the changes.*

> *I worked with a group of leaders across the UK's National Health Service to help them make sense of changes across the system. As part of the work, we explored in depth different cultures and sub-cultures and how these shaped how employees were responding to different changes. One of the themes that emerged were the strong ideals and values around caring that were part of the culture. This proved to be a double-edged sword. In part, they generated high levels of commitment to patients and moments of compassion. The leaders also noticed, however, that they experienced shame, guilt and anger when the system failed patients and these ideals were not met. Many of them had been patients themselves or had family members who had suffered poor care or treatment because of organisational failings. Employees also had to contend with criticisms from patients or families when things went wrong or mistakes were made. The anger, guilt and shame appeared to lie behind aggressive and bullying behaviour on the part of managers or colleagues in the system.*

Transformation of identities

Turbulence, uncertainty and disruption calls for identity to be dynamic and flexible yet maintain an inherent consistency. Such an 'adaptive instability' (Gioia et al., 2000) gives identity both continuity and adaptability. Nokia is a case in point. The organisation has successfully transformed itself throughout its history whilst maintaining a coherent sense of its identity.

Discontinuities in the social order open up 'identity gaps' (Reger, Gustafson, Demarie, & Mullane, 1994), creating a space between our experience of our current identity and our desired identity – our ideal self. This dissonance can motivate people to engage in change as it calls for some form of transformation of identity for individuals, groups and the organisation. Both change and continuity are required, as people need to adapt yet equally preserve a sense of self. This requires a process of self-reflexivity involving self-examination, debate around the fundamental premise of the organisation and a questioning of existing identities. This is an unsettling of the self and the collective. However, if this process becomes too threatening of the collective self-esteem, resulting in humiliation or shame – then we find a regressive retreat from the threat and an opposition to change. I have recently witnessed this process at a global pharmaceuticals business that is trying to transform itself. The board and the executive are calling for the organisation to be more commercial in response to frustrations from shareholders about the long-term profitability of the business. This demand is being heard by long-standing employees as putting at risk their image of themselves as being scientifically rigorous and philanthropic.

Leaders, by shifting and altering the images they project about the organisation, are able to project a compelling and desirable future image of the organisation. Generative images enable people to see the organisation differently and open up possibilities for actions (Bushe & Marshak, 2015). Such images point to a future that people care about and contain signifiers with which they identify. They convey ideals for the social group that unite people behind a shared desire for change. Whether employees are receptive to such projected images depends heavily on whether they identify with the images. They are also likely to be most receptive when they feel the existing identity and image of the organisation is destabilised (Gioia et al., 2000). This is both a proactive and reactive process. Identity is destabilised yet also created through attempts to redefine and reconstruct it.

We do, however, require time to find and adjust our identity. We need to try it on, see if it fits and whether we like it, let go of past identity and get used to how others might see us differently. The adjustment and adaptation of identity requires us to reinterpret the meaning of different signifiers of identity. This process takes place through social interaction and discourse. At one of the automotive plants, the production and maintenance workers' identities did change; however, this emerged over a period of years rather than overnight.

Implications for practice

Those leading change need to recognise how change is both an enactment of identity and alters existing identities. The process of adaptation to disruptive changes requires individuals and groups to engage in identity work. This necessitates a willingness on the part of those affected to question who they are, how they see themselves and how they are seen by others. This is a highly sensitive process because it brings into question our sense of self and touches our self-esteem, either enhancing it or harming it. Those leading or facilitating change can help people to find continuity of identity and to adapt their identities by:

Understanding and acting on relevant social identities. If organisations are made up of multiple and complex identities then before we start to attempt to change them, it makes sense to understand what they are and how they matter to people. It is critical to understand the important markers of a group's identity and the boundaries between groups. This is best achieved by connecting with groups directly and trying to understand how they see themselves in relation to other groups. It is important to recognise that different groups have different interests, agendas and frames of reference. It makes little sense to assume that what matters to shareholders will be important to other stakeholders. The process of change can be facilitated if those making changes anticipate how different groups will be affected by the changes and involve them in working out how to make changes. For some changes, this may involve tough discussions and negotiations; however, usually this leads to more constructive outcomes than avoiding or putting off difficult conversations.

Validating and honouring identities. Providing space for identity groups to express themselves in the change process both helps them to feel recognised and validated and helps them to make sense of changes. Ignoring their existence equally leaves groups feeling negated, causing them to feel their very existence is threatened. The acknowledgement of identities, differences and boundaries helps to build esteem and minimises fears. This increases the likelihood that groups will be open to other groups and less defensive in their relating. Change that builds self-esteem and pride is far more likely to be supported than changes that diminish or invalidate individual or group identities.

Enabling identity work. All organisational change involves identity work as those affected are challenged with letting go of their established identity and finding and negotiating a new one. The questions of: who are we? and who do we want to be? need to be worked through as part of the process of change. As people engage in making decisions about the future, creating new organisational forms and adapting to changes, they are simultaneously crafting new identities. Psychologically safe environments that support the expression of uncertainties, emotions and vulnerabilities are central to the reformulation of identities. People are able to flex and shift their identities when they can find a sense of continuity with the past. As identities are socially constructed, this process happens through interaction, negotiation and confrontation with others. Space and time need to be provided for people to grieve and mourn their loss.

Finding common ground. Through the exploration of similarities and differences, groups can find issues of mutual concern and common ground

(Weisbord & Janoff, 2010) which represent shared interests, aspirations and goals. We can only find these areas if we are willing to be clear about our differences and what we do not agree on. We may still have differences of perspective and opinion; however, finding common ground helps us to collaborate and work together in the face of change and disruption. Leaders can also encourage collaboration by appealing to collective signifiers of identity, such as company ideals or shared values, that connect people together across an organisation.

Projecting a desirable image of the organisation. In times of change, employees can be mobilised in the process of change if they feel they are maintaining and creating an identity that matters to them. Leaders need to engage employees in a conversation about who we now are and who we want to be. People are motivated to participate in changes when they perceive them as being in support of their identity, ideals and values, such as providing a great service to customers, caring for patients or designing innovative products. Equally, when changes undermine or threaten such ideals then this is likely to create opposition, cynicism and resistance. The generation of new ideals or the re-establishment or confirmation of past ideals can energise groups to act differently by changing their self-image.

Conclusion

A central paradox of identity is its recognisable stability and its inherent fluidity. Our identity can and does adapt to change. It is malleable and it endures because it changes. So, whilst people and social groups find change to their identities difficult and challenging, they do and can adapt and change. This happens as the discourse around signifiers of identity change, bringing forward different images and associations. This process is, however, inherently contested and political as different groups are assigned identities by others or are used to protect their interests, status and self-esteem.

Changes that threaten the deeper aspects of individuals or groups' identities and sense of self will be more strongly resisted. This is particularly the case when individuals or groups feel that their self-esteem is diminished because they feel judged, criticised or rejected on the basis of who they are perceived to be by others. When people feel their identities are fundamentally threatened, they become rigid and inflexible as they attempt to hold on to and preserve their identity. In contrast, an individual or group is far more able, it seems, to make changes to and accommodate change when they feel it supports or develops their existing identity. Equally, when individuals feel they are able to project an image that represents how they want to be seen and have that recognised by others, they are likely to be more commited to and less threatened by changes. Imposing images on people as to how they should be seen tends to create anxiety and resistance.

Works cited

Alvesson, M. (2013). *Understanding organizational culture* (2nd ed.). London, England: Sage.

Bauman, Z. (2004). *Identity: Conversations with Benedetto Vecchi*. Cambridge, England; Malden, MA: Polity.

Bourdieu, P. (1984). *Distinction: A social critique of the judgement of taste*. Cambridge, MA: Harvard University Press.

Brown, A. D., & Starkey, K. (2000). Organizational identity and learning: A psychodynamic perspective. *Academy of Management Review, 25*(1), 102–120.

Bushe, G. R., & Marshak, R. J. (2015). *Dialogic organization development: The theory and practice of transformational change*. Oakland, CA: Berrett-Koehler.

Campbell, D. T. (1965). Ethnocentric and other altruistic motives. In D. Levine (Ed.), *Nebraska symposium on motivation* (pp. 382–311). Lincoln, NE: University of Nebraska Press.

Castells, M. (2015). *Networks of outrage and hope: Social movements in the internet age* (2nd ed.). Cambridge, England: Polity Press.

Dalal, F. (1998). *Taking the group seriously: Towards a post-Foulkesian group analytic theory*. London, England: Jessica Kingsley.

Dashtipour, P. (2012). *Social identity in question: Construction, subjectivity and critique*. Abingdon, England: Routledge.

Elias, N., & Scotson, J. L. (1994). *The established and the outsiders*. London, England: Sage Publications.

Festinger, L. (1954). *A theory of cognitive dissonance*. Stanford, CA: Stanford University Press.

Freud, S. (1921). *Group psychology and the analysis of the ego*. Vienna, Austria: Internationaler Psychoanalytischer Verlag.

Frosh, S. (2010). *Psychoanalysis outside the clinic: Interventions in psychosocial studies*. London, England: Palgrave.

Gioia, D., Schultz, M., & Corley, K. (2000). Organizational identity, image, and adaptive instability. *Academy of Management Review, 25*(1), 63–81.

Haslam, A. (2004). *Psychology of organizations* (2nd ed.). London, England: Sage.

Janis, I. I. (1972). *Victims of group think*. Boston, MA: Houghton Mifflin.

Johnstone, K. (2017). *Improvisation and the theatre*. London, England: Bloomsbury Methuen Drama.

Reger, R., Gustafson, L. T., Demarie, S., & Mullane, J. V. (1994). Reframing the organisation: Why implementing total quality is easier said than done. *Academy of Management Review, 19*(3), 565–584.

Riketta, M. (2005). Organizational identification: A meta-analysis. *Journal of Vocational Behavior, 66*, 358–384.

Schwartz, H. S. (1990). *Narcissistic process and corporate decay: The theory of the organizational ideal*. New York, NY: New York University Press.

Sheriff, M. (1966). *Group conflict and cooperation*. London, England: Routledge and Kegan Paul.

Smircich, L. (1983). Concepts of culture and organizational analysis. *Administrative Science Quarterly, 28*(3), 339–358.

Turner, J. C. (1982). Towards a cognitive redefinition of the social group. In H. Tajfel (Ed.), *Social identity and intergroup relations* (pp. 15–40). Cambridge, England: Cambridge University Press.

Weisbord, M., & Janoff, S. (2010). *Future search: Getting the whole system in the room for vision, commitment and action.* San Francisco, CA: Berrett-Koehler.

9 Loss, mourning and the inability to mourn

Any passionate investment or attachment leaves us vulnerable to loss. To live we must both risk and suffer the pain of loss. Before something new begins, something first has to end (Bridges, 2003). Loss creates an emptiness – a lacunae in our experience. We feel deprived of what we have lost (A. Freud, 1967). What we possessed, or knew, has gone. This we experience as a disruption to our very existence. Yet, growth, development and change involve loss and endings. All of life's major transitions, such as birth, going to school, becoming an adult or parent require us to let go of something that is important to us, so that we can gain. Change is therefore an inevitability of life and loss is an inevitable consequence of change. Our fear of loss is what makes change threatening to us.

Constant, ongoing and disruptive change means that we are continually having to process loss. Most of us are now grappling with multiple, simultaneous and overlapping transitions. The speed and pace of life, however, means that we rarely have time to mourn our losses before we are into the next cycle of change. Losses therefore remain unresolved, existing as ghosts that haunt us, and creating an emotional heaviness which sucks vitality and energy from the present.

Disruption, transformation and loss

Disruptive and transformational change incurs losses at multiple levels and in different forms. These have a tangible form, whether it is a change in role, the closure of a site, a fall in financial rewards or benefits, or an office move. Every loss also has a more imperceptible, symbolic form that is psychological, emotional and social. Moreover, deep change to paradigms requires us to give up our assumptions, beliefs and ways of making sense of our experience.

People are often surprised and decentred by change because it exposes assumptions, beliefs and fantasies about the world that are not realistic. In many large and stable organisations, for instance, people may hold unconscious beliefs that the organisation will endure forever or that they or their department is indispensable and therefore not at risk. Such unconscious illusions can be painful to let go of.

Structures, roles and boundaries are powerful psychological anchors that provide us with a sense of security, identity and self-worth. The more significant these anchors, the greater the psychological impact the loss has on us. Sudden and unanticipated changes prove to be extremely disorientating for people. Without time to anticipate loss and prepare ourselves emotionally, we can be overwhelmed by its impact.

Our experience of loss is not only a response to what is lost in the present. Every time we encounter a loss, memories of past losses are awakened. A senior manager, for instance, at a UK county council recounted to me that whilst the current restructuring had been handled well, her team was nevertheless overwhelmed with anxiety because the process had triggered painful memories of the last reorganisation that had been poorly managed and destructive. Our experience of loss in adulthood has echoes of losses that we experience in infancy. Primitive and unconscious fears of abandonment and helplessness are evoked. For many people, with histories of insecure attachments or traumatic losses, change can trigger overwhelming anxiety.

The impact of technological change: the case of the coal miners

Eric Trist and Ken Bamforth (Trist & Bamforth, 1951), of the Tavistock Institute, observed the disruptive impact of the introduction of new technology to a social system in the 1950s. They studied the effects of the introduction of a new form of technology – called longwall mining – that used new cutting machinery. This transformed work processes, offering the opportunity to mine a large coal face rather than a smaller one using hand tools. However, the new technology resulted in a range of problems, including lower than expected productivity, worker dissatisfaction and increased turnover. In trying to understand what was happening, Trist and Bamforth studied how the technology was introduced in the different coal mines. Their research uncovered that those mines that adopted the new technology in a form that allocated individuals to specific roles, and distributed responsibility for the mining of a coal face across three shifts, were experiencing a norm of low productivity. This new form of organising broke up the established work groups and social structures. An environment was created of 'reactive individualism', non-cooperation and mutual scapegoating and high absenteeism. In mines where the existing small work group was retained to operate the new technology, both productivity and morale were higher than in the other mines.

Trist and Bamforth understood that the introduction of longwall mining technology and the corresponding changes to the work system destroyed the existing social order and the sense of community. Pointedly, they observed:

> Anyone who has listened to the talk of the older miners who have experienced in their own working-lives the changeover to the longwall

cannot fail to be impressed by the confused mourning for the past that still goes on in them, together with a dismay over the present coloured by despair and indignation

(Trist & Bamforth, 1951, p. 10)

This timeless study points to the importance of considering the disruption that technology can have on the social system of an organisation. Digital technologies, robots and artificial intelligence are the modern-day equivalent of long-wall mining. Their introduction can either respect the existing social system and attempt to anticipate and process the losses that are experienced; or be done in a manner that gives scant regard to their impact on the existing social system.

Change in organisations incurs loss at both the individual and collective level. In the case of the coal miners, the loss was a collective loss, the meaning of which can only be understood at the level of the social system. Collective loss extends beyond the aggregation of individual losses. Often what is lost is a collective ideal, identity or sense of purpose (S. Freud, 1917). Freud (ibid.) referred to this as the psychology of disillusionment. Such losses are symbolic in nature (Homans, 2000), giving meaning to a group or community. The loss is sociohistorical in its nature. Symbolic losses are hard to register and mourn because they exist outside of our conscious awareness.

When the consulting unit merged with the executive education department, I felt we lost an identity that was linked to an unconscious and shared ideal. We saw ourselves to be an innovative, radical and leading-edge consulting practice. To maintain this identity, we had to differentiate ourselves from other consultancies and business schools. This included the executive education faculty at the business school. The integration of the two departments to create three new departments was met with despair and dismay by members of both groups. The sense of loss that the consulting community experienced was overwhelming and a trauma from which it struggled to recover. I experienced a period of intense confusion around my identity and frustration that something that I valued and cared deeply about had been taken away from me for reasons that did not make sense to me. The denial of the loss by those in positions of leadership meant that no space or time was given to listening to those affected and processing the emotional dynamics of the reorganisation. For several years, a sense of disillusionment and disenchantment prevailed. Many of those who had the strongest identification with the ideals of the consultancy either withdrew from organisational life, became associates or left the organisation altogether.

Grief: a natural response to change

When we experience loss, even though we might desire change, we experience a grief response that follows a similar path to that of bereavement (Marris, 1974; Parkes & Prigerson, 2010). Change is experienced as a symbolic death – a 'little death' (Weisbord, 2012). The observations of Marc Fried (1962) [reported in Parkes and Prigerson (2010), p. 151] of this parallel are revealing. He studied the relocation of slum dwellers in North America, concluding that:

> While there are wide variations in the success of post-relocation adjustment and considerable variation in the depth and quality of the loss experience, it seems quite precise to refer to the reactions of the majority as grief: these are manifest in the feelings of painful loss, the continued longing, the general depressive tone, frequent symptoms of psychological, social or somatic distress, the active work required in adapting to the altered situation, the sense of helplessness, the occasional expressions of both direct and displaced anger, and tendencies to idealize the lost place... 46% gave evidence of a fairly severe grief reaction or worse.

Indeed, grief appears to be a universal response to loss and one we need to experience in order to re-establish a sense of meaning in our lives (Marris, 1974). For instance, the following is a quote from an employee recounting the final days of the closure of a retail chain:

> The last day was awful. We used to have music playing in the shop, and we put on Everything Must Go by the Manic Street Preachers just to add to the melancholy. I remember locking the door for the last time in tears. I don't want to sound overdramatic, but it was like a bereavement after such a long time.[1]

John Bowlby (1980) in his studies on grief and loss observed that we move through a series of overlapping phases. The first stage involves shock and denial of reality in which we struggle to accept the loss. This is followed by a period of protest in which we try to protect ourselves against the pain of the loss. Next follows a period of confusion and disorientation, during which we are adjusting to the reality of our situation; and finally, we move into a phase of letting go and reorganisation, which involves letting go of our memories and hopes and reinvesting our energy in new relationships and plans. This model is very similar to Elizabeth Kübler-Ross's (1969) stages of bereavement, which has been adapted and popularised as a framework in organisations. Kübler-Ross observed that we move through shock/denial, anger, bargaining, depression, and finally onto acceptance and integration of the loss.

The confusion, pain and distress of loss arises from the presence of two contradictory and conflicting impulses (see Figure 9.1) – to consolidate all that is valuable and important in the past and to preserve it from loss, whilst moving

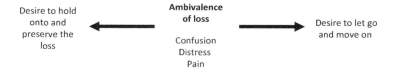

Figure 9.1 The ambivalence of loss

on and re-establishing a meaningful pattern of relationships (Marris, 1974). S. Freud (1919) observed that grief demands that we let go of the loss, which 'arouses understandable opposition' (p. 244) as most of us do not willingly give up our passions or our emotional attachments.[2] Rather than face reality, we cling to who or what we have lost (S. Freud, 1919), to the extent that we might even distort or deny the reality of our experiences.

> *One of my coaching clients, a successful lawyer, upon receiving news that he had been made a partner in a leading international law firm, found that in the months following the news he experienced intense feelings of sadness and depression that surprised and alarmed him. He could not understand how achieving an ambition and goal that he had invested himself in for the past 20 or so years could have such an impact on him. We were able to make sense of his reactions as a form of grief for what he had lost in achieving his goal. His relationship had changed with his peers, his goal that was driving him had gone and his identity had changed as had expectations upon him. I also wondered whether achieving his ambitions had confronted him with a reality that shattered an illusion that becoming a partner would make him happy and give him a sense of self-worth. In this context, his grief was a natural reaction and part of a process of adaptation.*

Mourning: the working through of grief

All change is loss, and all loss must be mourned if the resulting depressive feelings are not to retard adaptation and change (Levinson, 1994). Mourning is the process we go through to adjust our inner world and adapt emotionally, behaviourally and socially to the new reality. It involves repeated memories of the past that are contradicted by experience. Successful mourning involves the recognition, acknowledgement and acceptance of the loss (S. Freud, 1917). As Judith Butler (2004) observed:

> …one mourns when one accepts that by the loss one undergoes one will be changed, possibly for ever. Perhaps mourning has to do with agreeing

to undergo a transformation (perhaps one should say submitting to a transformation) the full result of which one cannot know in advance.

(Butler, 2004, p. 21)

Most conventional thinking (such as Bowlby's or Kübler-Ross's models) on
grief and mourning suggest that people move through a series of recognisable
and predictable phases (Hagman, 2001). However, contemporary research now
suggests that the working through of grief is a highly dynamic and personal
process in which we cycle between working through, accepting and making
sense of the loss whilst attempting to restore a sense of meaning and engaging
with the everyday demands of life (Stroebe & Schut, 1999). This cyclical process
can be confusing for all concerned. One day a person or group can appear to
be deeply affected by a sense of loss, whilst another day they may come across
as relatively unaffected by events.

Working through, registering and accepting the loss

In grief, we experience the ambivalent desires to cling to the past whilst also
wanting to forget about it altogether (Marris, 1974). Each of these impulses is a
defence mechanism, involving a denial of the loss. We may also displace our distress onto others, seeing their distress but not our own. I recall for instance that a
member of my team repeatedly expressed her concerns about the distress of the
administrators following the closure of the consulting group. She felt that no one
was witnessing their distress or caring about them. Her concerns were no doubt
justified; however, subsequent interactions and conversations revealed to me that
she too was experiencing a deep sense of loss and pain around the changes.
Below the surface, in grief we experience a deep ambivalence. To mourn a loss,
however, requires us to experience the pain, discomfort and distress of the loss.

Intense emotional responses are a signal that we have started to register a loss
and to allow ourselves to experience what it means to us. We can find ourselves
surprised by the intensity of our emotions in grief; almost out of nowhere
we can be engulfed by emotion. I recall breaking down, overwhelmed by my
emotions, during a check-in with a team of close colleagues with whom I was
working some six months after the closure of the consulting department. The
depth of anger, frustration, disappointment and sadness that I had been holding
onto whilst trying to lead my department abruptly surfaced, taking both myself
and my colleagues by surprise. My emotional turmoil perhaps mirrored those
of the people I led. In this moment of catharsis, I was able to recognise both
the pain I had been experiencing and my unconscious attempts to help people
to hold on to the past. Following this moment, I felt lighter, as if a burden had
been lifted from my shoulders, and clearer on what was possible and realistic.

The avoidance of loss can ultimately prove to be self-destructive because we
need to recognise and express our ambivalence. This, however, means we have to
confront our pain and distress. We cannot move unless we express our disappointment, regret, anger and sorrow. If this does not happen, then the loss becomes

idealised, untouchable and unable to be replaced. It is not uncommon to hear employees talking about 'the good old days' – close examination of which typically reveals a more complex, less simple picture. Moving forward may require us to forgive ourselves or others whom we blamed for inflicting our loss. The former often requires us to overcome unconscious feelings of guilt for the damage we might have done through our thoughts, words or actions (Klein, 1998).

Witnessing and representing the loss

What we have lost is not immediately obvious or clear. When we are grieving, we experience that something is missing; there is a void or a sense of emptiness. However, a loss needs to be discovered, registered and represented (Leader, 2009). We need to give meaning to what we have lost. Looking back, I needed time – 18 months maybe – to really understand what the closure of the consultancy meant to me. I lost a group of colleagues with whom I felt a deep connection and with whom I had many happy (and not so happy) memories; I had lost a sense of belonging to a group that I valued; I lost a future that I had imagined; I lost an aspect of my identity in my professional field and I lost a sense of security and safety in knowing that what I did was valued by my institution. I could list many other aspects of the loss. I am not sure I could have articulated these, however, in the months immediately after the reorganisation.

The making sense of loss is a social process, not just a psychological one. We need others to witness our sense of loss, to confirm it and make it real (Leader, 2009). Loss needs to be represented both socially and symbolically. Communities create symbols, rituals and ceremonies to help them to represent loss and render it memorable, meaningful and thereby bearable (Homans, 2000). These appear as universal practices in human societies as a mechanism for processing loss. They help a loss to be represented and mark a point of transition.

Art is another form of expression that communities use to represent loss. During the Industrial Revolution, the new industrial landscape of smokestacks, railways, tracts and workshops became prevalent in literature and art. These works became a means by which society was able to symbolise and process the dramatic changes they were experiencing. New inventions and technologies that threatened individuals' sensibilities, such as trains and railroads, were often represented as demons, monsters or other forms of disturbing imagery. In a similar way, clients are often more able to access deeper and more unconscious emotions and thoughts through drawing and expressive form. The picture in Figure 9.2, for instance, was drawn by a group of managers in a large charity that had been formed through the merger of two smaller, rival charities. The drawing is a representation of their experience of the organisation. In talking about the image, they described how it revealed two sides to the organisation: a surface level, of warmth and friendliness; and a darker vicious and dangerous side that could appear suddenly. They associated these feelings with the underlying anger and division that remained unresolved from the merger that had taken place a few years previously.

Figure 9.2 A drawing made by managers in a charity to represent their experience of their organisation

Rituals and ceremonies provide a structure that acts as a container for the loss (Homans, 2000). This helps the mourner to bear their loss and to face their chaotic and confusing emotions. Rituals act as a path into the unknown, a passage for the mourner to make a transition to a new state (Leader, 2009). They create a liminal or transitional space in which the participants are between the past and the future. Here, a person can let go of their pre-existing status, position or identity and an ambiguous and creative space is opened up. In transition, we are betwixt and between the familiar and the unknown.

Social groupings and communities do seem to naturally and spontaneously create and enact rituals and ceremonies to facilitate endings. I was working at Ford Motor Company in 2002 when the company announced its plans to close its assembly plant in Dagenham. The plant had opened in 1931 and was the first to build Ford cars outside of the United States. The announcement therefore was hugely symbolic for Ford, the local community in Dagenham and for the UK's car industry. To mark the ending, all the employees who worked at the plant were invited to be present to see the last car come off the production line. Each of them was given the opportunity to sign the car. Retired workers were also invited. The ceremony itself was kept private and the press and outsiders were not present. This created a space where the past could be acknowledged and celebrated and the loss mourned. A union con- venor describing the atmosphere inside the plant said it ranged from 'dis- appointment to disbelief, to anger and panic'.[3]. The car itself – a cherry red Fiesta – is still kept at the Dagenham site, with other vintage cars produced at Dagenham, as a symbol of the significant role that the plant played in the organisation and the local community.

Similar rituals have also been reported at other significant and symbolic closures. For instance, following the collapse of MG Rover in 2005, on the Sunday following the announcement a group of workers travelled in a convoy of over 300 vehicles to the gates of its Birmingham factory. Flowers were laid and a banner with the epitaph 'Rest in Peace MG' was hung across the gates.

Restoration of meaning, identity and purpose

In mourning, we encounter a crisis of meaning which requires us to reformu- late our sense of self, our identity and our plans for the future. When we accept that we will be changed by a loss, then this process can be transformational. In this sense, the processing of loss can become a creative process in which we are discovering a new purpose and finding a new way of being in the world.

To mourn a loss, we must uncover what was most important to us from the past to find some sense of continuity between the past, the present and the future. Often, we have to reframe our perceptions of the past; perhaps we were not as effective, happy or content with it as we led ourselves to believe at the time. We also need to revise our perception of our current situation, our assumptions and beliefs and sense of purpose. This process requires us to symbolise what has been lost and abstract a purpose from what has been lost (Marris, 1974).

Darian Leader (2009) observed that the fundamental crisis of mourning is not so much the loss itself, but the loss of self. We tend to think of a loss as happening outside of ourselves. However, Leader points out that mourning requires us to give up an image we hold of ourselves and the image that others have of us. Grief involves a crisis of identity. After leaving the business school, I lost my identity as head of the organisation development department and an employee of a leading business school – an institution with which I had identi- fied strongly. In the following months, I experienced a sense of being somewhat lost and unsure of my professional identity. I was unclear of and confused about where or what I belonged to, and felt isolated.

Individuals and groups that experience change need to restore a sense of their identity. This can manifest itself as attempts to reassert and maintain an existing identity. The process of change, however, needs to accommodate the renegotiation of identities as the relationships between individuals and groups change. At the automotive plants the process of change to self-managed teams required the management, supervisors, maintenance engineers and produc- tion workers to renegotiate their identities, boundaries and expectations of each other. All groups incurred loss as well as gains. This process took place through formal management–union negotiations as well as in informal day-to-day interactions and conversations in local work groups. Both conflict and negotiations are necessary to find meaningful resolutions to questions of identity and purpose.

The ambivalence of mourning, however, can be expressed as conflict between groups. One group denies its loss by holding on to the past whilst the other denies the past by focusing on the future. Both groups split off unwanted emotions, thereby relieving themselves of the distress and pain of mourning. This process can feel confusing to all involved as denial keeps the recognition of loss outside of people's conscious awareness. I have observed this dynamic in many organisations whereby one group – 'the reformers' – focus on planning for the future and changing the organisation, whilst another – 'the resistors' – are labelled as being 'unmotivated' and 'resistant to change'. This process involves the process of 'splitting' (Klein, 1998) whereby each group sees itself as 'good' and the other as 'bad'. Each retreats to 'tribal' boundaries whereby they displace one side of their ambivalence about loss onto the other group. The reformulation of meaning requires the ambivalence and contradictory feelings that lie behind such conflicts to be acknowledged, expressed and resolved.

If we are able to mourn a loss, then a sense of mature hope (Lemma, 2003) is able to develop. This is a hope that is rooted in reality, rather than a fantasy of restoring the past. As we withdraw our energy from the past, we are able to look towards the future. We become open to seeing things differently and are more able to see new possibilities and opportunities. The experience of mourning a loss can therefore generate the potential for creativity and transformation.

Several years ago, I consulted to a UK publisher that had grown rapidly across the globe over the preceding decade. The organisation was over two hundred years old and was highly traditional and respected internationally for its standards and reputation. Power and decision making had always been highly concentrated in the centre of the institution. The expansion of the business across the world and the success of some of the national businesses created a desire for more autonomy and influence in the regions. A clear split had started to emerge between leaders at the centre who were anxious about what they were losing, particularly around the uniqueness of the culture, its traditions and identity. The regions, moreover, were focused on how the business needed to move forward and appeared relatively unconcerned about loss in any form. The regional offices perceived themselves as being 'progressive' and perceived the centre to be 'conservative' and unwilling to change. Whilst each group saw the other as the problem, the underlying ambivalence around loss could not be acknowledged and a new relationship could not be negotiated between the centre and the regions.

Inability to mourn and melancholia

If the pain of mourning is too much for people to bear then the normal process of grief is blocked. The 'fear of loss' leads us to avoid 'experiencing loss' (Steiner, 1993). We substitute the loss with an illusion and a defensive adaptation prevails. Such a refusal to mourn involves a disavowal of the loss itself. The loss becomes lost, hidden within an absence. It is neither seen nor expressed, nor consciously experienced. If individuals or groups do not accept a loss, they continue to experience a longing for it. S. Freud (1917) observed how the unacknowledged unmourned loss leads to melancholia and depressive feelings. This means that those affected cannot consciously perceive what it is that they have lost (S. Freud, 1917). I am reminded of interviewing a maintenance worker about his experience of the introduction of work groups at one of the automotive plants. He exclaimed that 'it was the worst thing that had happened at the plant'. When I then asked him how long he had been in a work group, he replied ten years. This conversation, and the individual's anger and sadness, has remained with me for many years. He could not fully explain to me what was so terrible about the experience beyond feeling that it had been unfairly introduced and was 'wrong'.

This inability to mourn is to be in mourning, yet to be unable to mourn (Steiner, 1993). The underlying grief remains unresolved. Such unmourned losses continue, however, to haunt a group or organisation (Rizq, 2012). In organisations, this gives rise to what Gabriel (1999) calls a state of 'organizational miasma' whereby dramatic losses are not recognised or honoured and grief is repressed. This is a state of organisational melancholia – a sense of a collective unconscious loss (Rizq, 2012) in which mourning is blocked. The past, where it is represented by leaders, practices or people, is denigrated (Gabriel, 1999) in favour of narratives that privilege a new future or ideals (i.e. 'We will be an agile and innovative organisation'). On the surface, normality may prevail, whilst people are experiencing helplessness, disenchantment, disillusionment and despair at a deeper level.

This inability to mourn tends to manifest itself in a form of collective mania (Mitscherlich & Mitscherlich, 1975). People focus on the 'outer' world, avoiding reflecting on their experience, so they do not have to engage with their emotional world. Their frantic activity and busyness allows them to keep their pain, anger, fear and sadness out of conscious awareness. Mania also serves to ward off feelings of guilt that are linked to their anger towards the lost object or those who are seen to have inflicted the loss (Klein, 1998). On the face of it, mania can be highly productive yet it has an unreal quality to it and results in unhealthy consequences, such as burnout, or an absence of reflection or creativity.

If changes are dramatic, leading to the end of a group or community, then collective trauma often ensues (Erikson, 1994). The level of distress that is generated exceeds the group's ability to cope with the experience, overwhelming them with anxiety. The trauma itself is caused not so much from the event itself as the absence of acknowledging and recognising the event. Any experience that contradicts the dominant narrative becomes dislocated, incommunicable and irresolvable, alienating those affected. It is this act of overlooking the event that turns the pain of loss into trauma (Balint, 1969). This is what I think was most distressing about the takeover of the business school where I worked; we were unable to discuss or explore what was happening and its meaning without censoring ourselves. Trauma often arises following large and dramatic restructuring and downsizing efforts when the attachments that bind a group of people together are shattered. The collective shock and realisation that the community no longer exists (Erikson, 1994) becomes a trauma. For those affected, part of the self feels as if it has disappeared, as the entity that gave them an identity no longer exists.

Modernity, with its emphasis on the known and the rational, has led to the decline of rituals and ceremony with their emphasis on the symbolic and emotional aspects of life (Homans, 2000). In the modern corporation, the expression of emotions is all too often suppressed or avoided. The public working through of loss and change is assumed to be a private matter and individuals are left on their own to deal with their feelings of loss. The popular and ironic idiom 'SUMO', or 'Shut up and move on', seems to capture the sentiments of contemporary management culture. As a consequence, we increasingly find that the disavowal of feelings of loss is associated with feelings of helplessness, disillusionment and despair.

The government agency, referred to earlier, that was formed by integrating multiple departments, suffered from a deep sense of low morale, cynicism and disengagement two years into its creation. The creation of the agency meant that each department had to let go of their (local) status, autonomy and unique ways of working. The underlying emotions and reactions, including repressed anger, resistance to central leadership and general disaffection, could be understood as unresolved grief. These dynamics had remained stuck for some time without any apparent resolution. The leadership team were angry, frustrated and somewhat helpless in the face of the widespread intransigence. The sense of loss, however, remained undiscussed and avoided as a topic of discussion or exploration. In our consultations with the leadership team, we made some progress in helping people to talk about the history of the organisation and the underlying emotional dynamics. Whilst we had some success in this regard, we found it hard to influence the board and the executive that the difficulties they were experiencing existed at a deep emotional level and were not simply reflective of 'poor' leadership or the organisation's structure – the latter being more an expression of the unresolved grief and ambivalence around belonging to the agency.

Implications for practice

Those who are leading, facilitating or affected by disruptive changes need to recognise that widespread and systemic collective losses will be central to people's lived experience. Before they are able to move on, they first need to mourn what they have lost. Under pressure to adapt, however, the temptation is to focus on the future. Rather than facilitating change, this paradoxically risks leaving people stuck in the past. The facilitation of change thus needs to start with where people are emotionally, giving them space to recognise, process and express their lived experience. Simply put, this involves helping people to talk about their experience of change. This can be done by:

Acknowledging the existence of and significance of an ending. To grieve and work through a loss, we first need to acknowledge that something has ended. Leaders or change agents can help individuals or groups to recognise that something has ended and to start the process of understanding what it means to them.

Providing space and time to work through loss. The process of mourning requires time for people to come to terms with what has come to an end. When under pressure, managers or those seeking to make change often try to push changes forward before people are ready. This tends to be counter-productive as it takes away space and opportunities for working through grief.

Creating rituals and ceremonies. The creation of social processes that facilitate the witnessing of loss helps to facilitates its registration. The purpose of mourning rituals is to support the expression of grief in all its forms and to create a liminal space in which the people can creatively explore possibilities and new identities. Whilst it is tempting when bringing people together to focus on what needs to be done, this closes down the opportunities for people to explore and register what has been lost.

Saying goodbye. Most organisational change involves a departure or ending (Bridges, 2003) of some shape or form, whether it is people leaving, an office move, a merger or divestment of a business unit. The act of saying 'goodbye' marks the ending, which helps to make it 'real' for those affected. We are all ambivalent about saying goodbye because it brings to the surface painful feelings. It is all too easy therefore to let it slip yet doing so obscures the ending, making mourning more difficult for both the 'leaver' and the 'left'.

Involving people in the process of change. Impersonal and rational arguments about the interests of the business or its shareholders do not help people to reconcile themselves to the loss of the familiar (Marris, 1974). They need to find their own meaning in changes before they can live with them. This requires those who are leading changes to be willing to listen, accommodate their ideas and renegotiate their proposals.

Facilitating the expression and exploration of conflict. The restoration of a sense of meaning and purpose requires individuals and groups to renegotiate their boundaries, relationships and identities. Time and attention therefore need to be given to bringing individuals and groups together, formally and informally, to explore their needs, to surface differences and to work out together new relationships. The avoidance of conflict simply maintains underlying ambivalences, tensions and fears.

Finding continuity and purpose. We are more able to navigate and make sense of change when we are able to take what we valued from the past and discover how we can meaningfully create it in the future. This requires those involved to honour, celebrate and understand the past so they can abstract a sense of purpose and to make choices about what they need to let go of and what they can take forward into the future.

Preparing for the future. Once a loss has been recognised and registered, people need to look to the future and prepare for what comes next. When people are ready to move forward, their attention starts to shift from the past to the future. At this point they are more ready and able to explore what they will need to do differently and what they will need to learn. Individuals may experience doubts about their capacity to adapt or have questions about what the future will mean for them.

Conclusion

The transformation of both societies and organisations is without doubt resulting in widespread and deep feelings of loss and grief. We could perhaps see the fast pace of modern life as being a manic defence against recognising what we are losing. Whether this is the case or not, it is evident that both the speed of change and rationality prevent us from registering and mourning our losses in organisations. Rather than accelerating change, this slows it down. We hold on to the past and protect it from loss, and this limits our capacity to be creative in how we organise and adapt to changes. Where loss remains unmourned, we find disaffection, helplessness and disillusionment. Such climates can only be associated with unhappiness and longer-term decline.

The adaptive capacity of an organisation rests upon its capacity to process loss. This requires a culture in which people are willing to be vulnerable and can both express their emotions and recognise others' grief. When the anxieties of loss are understood, the tenacity of conservatism and the ambivalence of transition become clearer (Marris, 1974). We need to acknowledge loss and endings, provide space for the expression of grief and meet each other's pain with compassion, understanding above all else humanity. After all, loss is something that we all know and understand.

Notes

1 'Death of the high street: How it feels to lose your job when a big chain closes', www.theguardian.com/business/2019/mar/06/death-of-the-high-street-how-it-feels-to-lose-your-job-when-a-big-chain-closes
2 From S. Freud's (1916) paper 'On transience'.
3 'Final car rolls off Dagenham production line', www.dailymail.co.uk/news/article-101274/Final-car-rolls-Dagenham-production-line.html

Works cited

Balint, M. (1969). Trauma and object relationship. *International Journal of Psychoanalysis*, *50*, 429–435.

Bowlby, J. (1980). *Attachment and loss. Volume 3: Loss: sadness and depression*. New York: Basic Books.

Bridges, W. (2003). *Managing transitions*. London, England: Nicholas Brealey Publishing.

Butler, J. (2004). *Precarious life: The powers of mourning and violence*. London, England; New York, NY: Verso.

Erikson, K. (1994). *A new species of trauma: The human experience of modern disasters*. New York, NY: W. W. Horton.

Freud, A. (1967). About losing and being lost. *The Psychoanalytic Study of the Child*, *22*(1), 321–333.

Freud, S. (1916). On transience. In J. Strachey, A. Freud, A. Strachey, & A. Tyson (Eds.), *The standard edition of the complete psychological works of Sigmund Freud, Volume XIV (1914–1916): On the history of the psycho-analytic movement, papers on metapsychology and other works* (trans. J. Strachey) (pp. 304–307). London, England: Hogarth Press.

Freud, S. (1917). Mourning and melancholia. In J. Strachey, A. Freud, A. Strachey, & A. Tyson (Eds.), *The standard edition of the complete psychological works of Sigmund Freud, Volume XIV (1914–1916): On the history of the psycho-analytic movement, papers on metapsychology and other works* (trans. J. Strachey) (pp. 243–259). London, England: Hogarth Press.

Freud, S. (1919). The 'uncanny'. In J. Strachey, A. Freud, A. Strachey, & A. Tyson (Eds.), *The standard edition of the complete psychological Works of Sigmund Freud, Volume XVII (1917–1919): An infantile neurosis and other works* (trans. J. Strachey) (pp. 217–256). London, England: Hogarth Press.

Gabriel, Y. (1999). *Organizations in depth: The psychoanalysis of organizations* (1st ed.). London, England: Sage Publications.

Hagman, G. (2001). Beyond decathexis: Toward a new psychoanalytic understanding and treatment of mourning. In R. A. Neimeyer (Ed.), *Meaning reconstruction & the experience of loss* (pp. 13–31). Washington, DC: American Psychological Association.

Homans, P. (2000). *Symbolic loss: The ambiguity of mourning and memory at the century's end*. Charlottesville, VA: University Press of Virginia.

Klein, M. (1998). *Love, guilt and reparation*. London, England: Vintage.

Kübler-Ross, E. (1969). *On death and dying*. New York, NY: Macmillan.

Leader, D. (2009). *The new black: Mourning, melancholia and depression*. London, England: Penguin.

Lemma, A. (2003). *Introduction to the practice of psychoanalytic psychotherapy: A practical treatment handbook*. Chichester, England: John Wiley & Sons.

Levinson, H. (1994). Why the behemoths fell: Psychological roots of corporate failure. *American Psychologist, 49*(5), 428–436.

Marris, P. (1974). *Loss and change*. London, England: Routledge & Keegan Paul.

Mitscherlich, A., & Mitscherlich, M. (1975). *The inability to mourn: Principles of collective behaviour*. New York, NY: Grove Press.

Parkes, C. M., & Prigerson, H. G. (2010). *Bereavement: studies of grief in adult life bereavement* (4th ed.). London, England: Penguin Books.

Rizq, R. (2012). The ghost in the machine: IAPT and organizational melancholia. *British Journal of Psychotherapy, 28*(3), 319–335.

Stroebe, M., & Schut, H. (1999). The dual process model of coping with bereavement: Rationale and description. *Death Studies, 23*(3), 197–213.

Trist, E., & Bamforth, K. W. (1951). Some social and psychological consequences of the long wall method of coal getting. *Human Relations, 4*, 3–38.

Weisbord, M. (2012). *Productive workplaces: Dignity, meaning and community* (3rd ed.). San Francisco, CA: John Wiley & Sons.

10 Alienation, anomie and anxiety

Several years ago, I was involved in a consulting project with a UK university. Under financial pressure, the leadership had decided to outsource all of the basic services that were required for running the university such as catering, cleaning and porters. A colleague and I were asked to provide support to employees whose jobs were being outsourced to help them process the impact of the changes and work through the transition. As I listened to the stories of those affected, I began to learn how they felt a deep sense of betrayal and were struggling with making sense of the change. They feared that their terms and conditions, pay and longer-term benefits would be gradually eroded under the new outsourced arrangements. They had not been involved in making the decision and students, unions, academics and employees were united in opposition to the decision. This compounded their sense of anger and confusion. What became apparent to us in our work with them was the symbiotic relationship they had with the students. For many of the students, this was the first time they had moved away from home, and the cleaners and porters took on a pastoral role of supporting them. Friendships formed and the spirit of the institution was maintained through their relationships. An underlying fear of the staff was that whoever managed their service in the future would not value this intangible, yet important, cultural role. I felt that the changes had been done in a manner that was both inhumane and damaging to the institution. No doubt, economic pressures lay behind the decision to outsource what were perceived to be non-core services. However, those affected by the changes were left feeling unwanted and rejected from the organisation. Our advice to the client was that the Vice Chancellor and the Pro-Vice-Chancellor needed to meet directly with the staff to hear and acknowledge their anger, explain to them the reasons for their decisions and listen to their concerns. Regrettably, we were unable to convince them that this was a necessary and helpful exercise.

At the heart of this change was a sense of injustice, betrayal and a deep distress at feeling unvalued. Those affected felt their self-esteem was being diminished. At a fundamental time for the institution, the changes also surfaced questions around identity, meaning and purpose for the university as an institution. Was it a place for developing young adults and creating a community for critical inquiry or a degree-awarding business who train adults at a competitive price?

Myself and colleagues were asked to help a new public sector agency to address problems with low engagement and morale across its staff. At the time of our involvement, the staff survey had revealed that engagement levels were amongst the lowest across the UK civil service. Further investigation revealed that behind the low levels of morale and engagement existed frustrations with how the organisation functioned, exclusion and disrespect of some groups and aggressive behaviour from some managers. Senior managers and employees pointed to the history of how the organisation had been formed as being critical to the low levels of morale and engagement. This had been done by integrating a collection of departments from across the civil service. Historically, each department's identity was tied up with that of the civil service department that it serviced. They also had autonomy to make their own decisions, status within their department and their own working practices. These were all lost with the merging of these unique groups together. However, little space had been given to processing the impact of these changes on those who were affected. Nor were any mechanisms put in place to agree how to develop the new agency to create a common culture, identity and shared work practices. This left many unable to mourn their losses, frustrated with the organisation they now found themselves in and hostile to their new bosses and the other departments.

These two cases are illustrative of a growing crisis of psychological distress, low morale and disengagement that is arising in organisations as they struggle to adapt. This is evidenced by a range of indicators of psychological health and well-being in organisations, including:

- Both employee engagement and job satisfaction have been falling. According to Gallup's 2017 *State of the Global Workplace report*, only 13% of employees worldwide are engaged at work. This is based on research across 142 countries. In other words, only about one in eight employees are psychologically committed to their jobs. An earlier study by Gallup in 2013, titled the *State of the American Workplace*, revealed that *only* 30% of workers were engaged. This figure for US workers has remained static now for several decades, despite the rise in popularity of employee engagement initiatives. A similar study by Tower Watson in 2012[1] across 29 countries found that more employees are 'detached' or 'disengaged' (43%) than are engaged (35%).
- One in four employees feel unhappy or depressed by their jobs (Balaram & Wallace-Stephens, 2018) and close to 50% of employees feel their jobs do not provide their life with meaning or purpose (ibid.). Employee commitment is also deteriorating across organisations (Baruch, 1998; Kalleberg, 2001).

- Over recent decades, stress and anxiety levels have been increasing at work in the developed economies. Research shows that the stress levels of managers and professionals are increasing, which is causing psychological distress and health problems (Antoniou & Cooper, 2005; Cooper, Quick, & Schabracq, 2009). Since the 2008–09 economic crisis, there has been a steep increase in work stressors such as job insecurity, work intensity and interpersonal conflict at work (Chandola, 2010). In 2015–16, work-related stress accounted for 37% of all work-related ill-health cases and for 45% of all working days lost due to ill-health (Executive, 2016).[2] The number of sick days lost to stress, depression and anxiety are estimated to have increased by 24% between 2009 and 2013.[3] The number of female employees suffering from job-strain, an indicator of work stress, tripled from around 8% to almost 25% between 1992 and 2006. Furthermore, middle managers have been shown to be more likely to suffer symptoms of depression and anxiety than their counterparts at the top or bottom of the workplace hierarchy[4] (Bates, Keyes, & Muntaner, 2015).
- A report from the Rotman School of Management, in 2016 (McCarthy & Trougakos, 2016), indicated that 41% of employees reported high levels of anxiety. Every year, 4 in 15 Europeans will be affected by depression or an anxiety disorder (WHO, 2001). By 2020, the World Health Organisation anticipates that depression will be second only to heart disease as a source of illness in the world (WHO, 2001).
- Loneliness is becoming endemic in our workplaces. A recent *Harvard Business Review* article (Murthy, 2017) reported that 40% of adults in the United States feel lonely at work.

These trends are symptoms of an underlying psychological and social distress in both society and organisations. People are struggling emotionally and psychologically because of the levels of uncertainty, insecurity and complexity that confront them. The Harvard psychologist Robert Kegan (1994) in his book *In Over Our Heads* argues that most people have not attained a level of psychological development to be able to cope with this level of complexity and uncertainty. Many of us are struggling at both an emotional and cognitive level to make sense of and respond to the demands caused by the degree of change and disruption in our lives.

The current era could be, and has been, termed the 'age of anxiety'.[5] We are observing endemic levels of anxiety in organisations and wider society. We know from personal experience how periods of upheaval and uncertainty cause anxiety. When we feel unable to cope with the demands of our environment, we experience anxiety (May, 1977). Uncertainty and unpredictable events stir up primitive anxieties that centre around fears of collapse, annihilation, disintegration, destruction and loss of identity. As anxiety grows, it spreads rapidly through social contagion. For instance, during the 2008 economic crisis anxiety spread like wildfire across organisations as they experienced a sudden and dramatic rise in uncertainty about the future (Day & Power, 2009).

Research also has demonstrated the psychological costs of organisational change and restructuring initiatives on employees; for instance:

- Reorganisations have been shown to have a detrimental effect on employees' health and psychological well-being, particularly when those affected feel they have limited control over events (Bamberger, et al., 2012; Oreg, Vakola, & Armenakis, 2011; Vahtera, Kivimaki, & Pentti, 1997).
- Repeated or multiple experiences of organisational change have long-term detrimental effects on employees' mental health (Flovik, Knardahl, & Christensen, 2018).
- Job insecurity is one of the most significant stressors at work. Research demonstrates that employees who feel insecure in their jobs report lower job satisfaction, high psychological distress, lower well-being and feel less committed to their organisations (Probst, 2002; Sverke, Hellgren, & Näswall, 2002).
- Following downsizing and staff layoffs, those who remain have been shown to suffer from what has been called 'survivor syndrome' (Applebaum, Delage, Labib, & Gault, 1997; Wolfe, 2004). This is a form of trauma whereby people struggle to cope psychologically in the aftermath of redundancy programmes, experiencing guilt, anger, anxiety, and fear and apprehension about the future.

Without doubt, uncertainties and changes in society are contributing to the emotional climate in organisations. Bauman (2006) observed how interhuman bonds, community and the foundations of social solidarity are increasingly frail and temporary. He observes how social fluidity erodes self-assurance, shared meanings and elevates anxiety. The changes that are happening in organisations are part of this process and the effects of these changes permeate the boundaries of organisations. Outside of work, support is less available to individuals to help them to cope with the pressures within work. At the same time, the fragmentation of society unsettles individuals and creates anxieties that permeate the workplace. Isolation leaves individuals without a sense that their world will protect them; whilst social support is linked to psychological health (Baumeister & Leary, 1995; Emery, 1959; House, 1981). When we feel disconnected from others then our capacity to respond to crisis, difficulty or change is diminished. We know, for instance, that individuals with strong social ties have mortality rates of half or one-third of those with weak ties (Whitehead & Diderichsen, 2001).

Over the years, I have seen clients in my therapy practice who are experiencing difficulties with anxiety linked to their employer's plans to reorganise. Their experiences in the present trigger painful memories and associations with early formative experiences in their lives.

One very successful manager, a winner in all intents and purposes, feared that he was going to be asked to leave when he first heard a rumour of a restructure. He had a similar fear during every restructure that had happened throughout his career. He would report feeling powerless whilst he had to wait for an announcement to be made about what would happen to his role. He would struggle to sleep at night and feel distracted by his fears for much of the time. His anxieties were associated with a childhood memory of seeing his father, who was a successful executive, coming home having been asked to leave his job. He had seen his father change from a confident man to one who felt he had lost his purpose in life and everything he had worked so hard to achieve.

Another client spent a year worrying about how he would be impacted by a planned restructure and relocation of his department. He also felt powerless and at the mercy of the powerful. For him, the restructuring brought back painful memories of family separations and frequent house moves when he would be thrown into a new school and neighbourhood where he would not know anyone and have to struggle with the loss of his friends.

I am sure that each of these clients kept their anxieties hidden at work, as I am sure did many of their colleagues. It is a reminder that we often do not see others' suffering or anxieties.

Alienation and anomie

One explanation of the above trends is that discontinuous change is separating people from their basic human needs and undermining social integration, cohesion and solidarity in organisations. This alienates employees, creating a state of 'anomie' (Durkheim, 1897 [1951]) – or normlessness.

Alienation is signified by a sense of detachment, despondency and general disinterest. It manifests itself as low job satisfaction, disengagement and burnout. Karl Marx (1844) first introduced the concept of alienation in his early writings on the effects of industrialisation, the division of labour and the emergence of capitalism. He argued that alienation separates us from our true nature. The person gives up the desire for self-expression and control over his or her own fate at work (O'Donohue & Nelson, 2014), experiencing a sense of despair and pointlessness.

Marx observed that by treating workers as machinery, they were robbed of their human essence and estranged from the kind of life they were capable of living. The conditions of work separated them from their basic human qualities. This he attributed to employees producing products that did not reflect their creative energies, the failure of work to meet their basic needs, an absence of a 'common purpose' which debased social relationships, and, finally, 'alienation from humanity', which he attributed to the long hours that the workers had to endure in early industrial organisations. Blauner (1964), taking more of a psychological stance, argued that alienation in the workplace has four elements:

1. A sense of powerlessness due to being controlled by others and because of an absence of autonomy and discretion in how work is performed.
2. Meaninglessness arising from a lack of a sense of how our work contributes to a bigger whole. Work either makes our lives richer and more fulfilling or it strips it of purpose, dignity and social value.
3. The loss of a sense of a community and belonging, which causes isolation, loneliness and anxiety.
4. Self-estrangement, detachment and an absence of a sense of identity and personal fulfilment. The individual experiences a disconnection between the inner 'self' and the 'self' created by work and the organisational environment. In essence, alienation arises because the conditions of work require an individual to present a 'false' self, a defensive façade, and find they are unable to express their 'true' self (Winnicott, 1960).

In the 1960s, 1970s and 1980s, concern about the de-humanising characteristics of bureaucratic and mass production processes, particularly levels of employee satisfaction and commitment, led to research into the design of workplaces (e.g. Trist & Bamforth, 1951; Hackman & Oldham, 1980; Walker & Guest, 1952) and the Quality of Work Life movement (Davis & Cherns, 1975; Lawler, 1982). For instance, Fred Emery (1993) identified that employees are motivated when the content of their job is reasonably demanding, provides some variety, creates opportunities to learn and to make decisions, provides social support and recognition, enables the person to make a meaningful social contribution, and finally, leads to some sort of a desirable future.

One of the major functions of work therefore is to connect people to concerns that transcend their own limited personal existence (Jahoda, 1981). As Freud said, 'Liebe und Arbeit' – 'Love and work' – 'are the cornerstones of our humanness'. Life and work, however, increasingly disrupt the bonds and social ties that historically 'gave meaning and security to life' (Fromm, 1941, p. 253). As the existentialist philosopher and psychiatrist Viktor Frankl (1978) argued: '...the self-transcendence of existence denotes the fundamental fact that being human means relating to something, or someone, other than oneself, be it a meaning to fulfil, or human beings to encounter. And existence falters and collapses unless this self-transcendant quality is lived out' (Frankl, 1978, p. 47). If our work has little meaning or purpose, then we experience alienation from our essential nature. And it is this threat of the meaninglessness of existence that gives rise to anxiety (Kierkegaard, 2015).

Alienation accelerates as people withdraw to protect themselves against incurring further pain of separation and isolation from others. This creates a vicious cycle whereby withdrawal creates isolation, which in turn tends to initiate further withdrawal, and so on.

When I took over the management of the newly formed organisation devel-opment department at the business school following the reorganisation, I spoke to each individual about what they wanted and needed from the department. One request from many of was to feel like a department again. When we held department meetings, however, more than half the department failed to turn up. When I followed up with those who did not come, I learnt from a few individuals that their underlying concern was that others would not turn up. Turning up when others chose not to intensified individuals' feelings of isolation. So better to stay away. My sensemaking of this dynamic was that even though staying away compounded the sense of alienation within the group, it protected the group from further disappointment.

The breakdown of social solidarity, integration and cohesion

The French sociologist Emile Durkheim observed how social integration and cohesion break down during periods of rapid and dramatic social change. He named this process 'anomie', which roughly translates to mean a state of 'normlessness' and an *absence* of social solidarity in society. Durkheim made this observation during his research into the industrialisation in French cities at the turn of the last century. He linked anomie to a breakdown of standards, values and a sense of a common purpose. The outcome of this Durkheim argued to be *alienation* of the individual from the social group. He observed how those affected were left confused and isolated from others.

Durkheim theorised that as values and norms change, people are unsure of what is expected of them and what is 'right' or 'wrong'. *Anomie* creates a sense of social uncertainty and unpredictability. Individuals feel unsure of how to interpret social expectations and are unsure of how their behaviour will be interpreted by others. 'Anomie' therefore occurs when the 'normal' ways of integrating a social system are disturbed or interrupted during periods of severe crisis or instability (Wilke, 2015). The social rules that govern how we interact together start to disintegrate and people become unclear as to how to behave. Durkheim observed that anomie left individuals feeling that they are not part of the collective, invoking states of aimlessness, futility, hopelessness and despair.

During periods of disruptive change, employees are likely to experience a sense of disembeddedness and their sense of relatedness to their organisations is diluted and diminished (Krantz, 2013). Whilst the existing social order is disintegrating, a space is created in which new social forms can emerge. For instance, the NHS is experiencing a period of transformation as it adapts to societal change. Norms that used to apply no longer apply; and new ones are emerging. The sense of shared purpose that served as an ideal across the service is being challenged, leaving employees struggling to find a sense of meaning.

We have also witnessed a trend towards creating competitive work environments that are reinforced by targets, bonus systems and forced ranking performance management systems. Such hyper-competition undermines social cohesion and risks being pathological in nature. Individuals need to win (and avoid losing) at any cost to maintain or enhance their self-worth. Such conditions create a ground of competitive anxiety and individuals respond by focusing on demonstrating their worth. The delivery of results takes precedence over all else, including the long-term development and health of the organisation.

The de-humanising effects of constant change

The current crisis in psychological well-being appears therefore to stem not so much from the de-humanising effects of bureaucracy than from several emerging patterns. Firstly, technology is increasing the pace of work and minutely monitoring employees' behaviour. A survey by the Royal Society for Arts (RSA), for instance, found that 50% of employees fear that technology will lead to excessive monitoring, checking and control.[6] This leaves the individual feeling de-humanised and controlled by others. Secondly, constant reorganisations, outsourcing and downsizing are breaking bonds, social ties and group boundaries. This is weakening any sense of belonging, causing isolation and creating confusion around social norms and expectations. Thirdly, the creation of competitive environments in which employees have to constantly prove themselves and demonstrate that they are 'performing' generates an underlying sense of anxiety and fear in organisations. Finally, how organisational change is undertaken is alienating those affected because the process of change does not account for their fundamental human needs.

The impact of these effects tends not to be equally distributed. Those in positions of power often have time to process, discuss and prepare for changes. This gives them a greater sense of being in control of their experience. Individuals who see little chance of winning, such as the cleaners, caterers and porters at the university described at the start of the chapter, inevitably start to feel alienated and marginalised.

Alienation due to the process of change

Alienation and anxiety arise in modern organisations because the process of change is de-humanising, lacks meaning and is experienced as unfair and unjust by those affected. All of the evidence would seem to suggest to that employees' needs, despite the rhetoric, are not recognised or considered during periods of change. At both the university and the public sector agency described earlier in this chapter, the changes had little genuine meaning for the staff and the process of change did not meet their need to be treated humanely and with respect.

In organisations that have undergone successive cycles of widespread change, employees often start to experience change fatigue, particularly when the changes lack purpose or substance to them. This leaves them experiencing a sense of malaise, frustration, distrust and cynicism around change efforts. This manifests itself as a general indifference towards change. Behind the fatigue often lies a history of changes that has led to an accumulation of unmourned and unresolved losses.

Anxious and fearful managers have a greater propensity to resort to the use of power to make rapid changes. Those with more paternalistic tendencies tend to exclude people from the process of change because they are aware that individuals may experience uncomfortable or painful emotions. Others may fall back on forms of domination and coercion to drive through change despite underlying resistance and opposition. Others see the use of power as simply an expedient way of achieving their aims and are relatively unconcerned about the consequences. Some managers perhaps lack the management and social skill to lead complex changes through more consultative and democratic means. The weakening of unions in the UK and the US has generally eroded workers' capacity to resist or stand up to management. Forms of domination and suppression of resistance or dissent alienate individuals through the non-recognition of their point of view and subjective experience. Self-estrangement arises when we participate in the distortion of communication or when our disagreement is silenced with such distortions. This only acts to amplify our sense of powerlessness and alienation.

One of the consequences of radical or constant change is an almost inevitable breaking of the psychological contract (Rousseau, 1995) that exists between employee and employer. This challenges the implicit expectations and assumptions that employees and employer hold of each other. Changes that dramatically alter relationships both expose and undermine the implicit expectations that each has of the other. In many hierarchies, for instance, an implicit paternalistic contract existed between employer and employee, whereby the employer looked after and protected the employee. Sometimes, however, senior managers have little or no alternative but to break the psychological contract, particularly when economic factors require laying-off workers. Betrayal is both necessary and inevitable.

When the psychological contract is transgressed, people generally experience a sense of injustice and anger. When both the process of change and the outcomes of change are perceived to be unfair (Novelli, Kirkman, & Shapiro, 1995; Tyler, 1994) people feel de-valued, angry and resentful. Change is experienced as an act of betrayal. Each violation of the psychological contract undermines trust and makes future changes less likely to be accepted by employees. The opposite equally applies: when changes are perceived as being fair both in terms of how they happen and what happens, employees tend to experience increased self-esteem, feel respected and experience pride in the group (Tyler, Degeoy, & Smith, 1996).

In an area of one of the automotive plants which had implemented self-managed teams, a pervasive sense of unfairness and injustice existed because of how the changes were perceived to have been introduced. Prior to the changes, the maintenance workers had a rest area, known as a 'crib', which was based away from the line. They tended to leave it only when responding to a machine breakdown. With the introduction of the autonomous work groups, management removed these rest areas. Managers now expected maintenance workers to work on the line to help the work group cover absence and complete preventative maintenance routines and other production jobs, such as cleaning machines and housekeeping. In practice, a number of maintenance specialists commented that they spent much of their time operating machines. Additionally, the younger maintenance craftsmen, who had recently graduated from the apprentice school, spent the majority of their time operating machines. The plant's management explained that this was because of a shortage of available maintenance positions in the plant. The maintenance specialists thought they should not be expected to perform such tasks. During the research, individuals expressed the following frustrations:

> '...you can stand there and load on a hundred blocks, which I didn't do an apprenticeship to do. I could have left school straight away, come in here and done that, but I did a four-year apprenticeship so I could get a trade but unfortunately I don't think a trade counts for anything in here anymore.'
>
> 'I didn't in my view train for four or five years to hump heads on and off the line or gauge for an entire day. I think I'm worth more than that really.'
>
> 'You could be doing a grade 3 job and that's soul destroying.'

Behind their accounts was a perception that their status had been lowered. These individuals were angry and resentful about the changes to their role. Those who been working at the plant for the longest held the strongest beliefs about their role, whilst those who joined after the changes did not have anywhere near the same strength of feeling.

As a group, the maintenance specialists felt that they had been 'coerced' or 'forced' by management to go into work groups when they were originally introduced almost ten years earlier. They felt exploited and devalued.

> '...the older people, that come from the days of operators and maintenance, have been forced, not forced, well they have been forced into going into a team. They've still got a big attitude about doing team work...'
>
> 'Basically, they said to us: "we want you to be a team. It's either that or go on the day work". So, it was almost forced upon us like that. The unions agreed with it... didn't involve us with that side of things but they said: "do it or go on the days", and for those that couldn't afford to go onto days it was a case of having to. So, it was forced upon us and from the start it was a bad air.'

We can hear in their accounts how they felt alienated from their identities and devalued as a group. They believed they had been forced to work in the new system and treated as if they were objects rather than human beings with needs, identities and expectations. The strength of their feeling is highlighted by the fact that team working was introduced into this area of the plant more than ten years before the study took place. These accounts illustrate the importance of employees' experiences of <u>how</u> they feel they are treated by those in power during periods of change.

Nokia's Bridge programme[7,8]

In 2011, Nokia embarked on the closure of R&D centres and factories across 13 different countries as it exited the mobile devices market. Eventually, these changes would affect 18,000 employees. In some locations, Nokia was by far the biggest employer and the closures threatened to have a significant impact on the local communities.

The board of Nokia wanted to make these changes in a manner that was congruent with their values and Nokia's tradition of social responsibility and desire to treat employees fairly. They chose to proactively engage employees, local stakeholders and government bodies in a programme of change, which they called 'Bridge' – a symbol of transition. The aims of the programme were to:

1. *Assist individuals and teams to utilise their capabilities to the fullest;*
2. *Continue to build the local economies in which Nokia played a key role; and*
3. *Support and enable Nokia's renewal.*

The programme offered those employees who were affected five paths:

1. *To find an alternative job within Nokia;*
2. *To find a new job outside Nokia;*
3. *To start a new business;*
4. *To learn a new skill or vocation; or*
5. *To create their own path.*

Those affected were offered various forms of support that they could draw upon, including career coaching, career services, jobs fairs, social media support to find roles inside or outside the firm, training programmes or funding for retraining, coaching on starting a business, for new ventures an opportunity to join local incubators and the offer of start-up grants or seed capital. By the end of the programme, Nokia had invested 300 million euros in supporting new businesses and 800 million euros in training, coaching and career advisory services (Siilasmaa, 2018).

> In total, the programme was available to 18,000 employees across 13 countries. It helped to ensure that 60% of employees had found their next opportunity by the time their employment ended. The programme also helped create 1,000 new start-up companies. An evaluation of the programme by Aalto University in Finland in 2015 showed that by 2015, 91% of these businesses were still active. 85% of employees were satisfied with their treatment by Nokia and most felt supported by the organisation in their transition (Ronnquist, Hakonen, & Vartianen, 2015). The evaluation found that the programme gave those affected mental resources, diminished feelings of uncertainty and insecurity and helped them cope with the transition (Ronnquist, Hakonen, & Vartianen, 2015). Nokia reported that the programme helped to maintain their external reputation and close sites without disrupting operations.
>
> Nokia's approach illustrates how organisations are able to restructure and make layoffs in a manner that is perceived to be fair, responsible and humane. Judging by the positive reporting of the Bridge programme across the internet and in the media, the programme has enhanced the firm's reputation. No doubt the fairness of the programme also strengthened the sense of connection that those employees who remained with Nokia had experienced with the company.

Questions of meaning around the contribution of organisations to society and the planet

At a deeper level, the pervasiveness of alienation and anxiety at work is reflective of more fundamental questions of meaning that we all face in the modern era. We are aware that economic growth and consumerism is destroying the eco-system. At the same time, organisations have an almost fetish-like focus on economic and financial returns. This creates a pseudo-purpose that undermines a sense of genuine meaning or social contribution. It is hard for people to find a sense of purpose when we are aware, at some level, that our work is contributing to the destruction of the planet, damaging society or affecting people's health. Even if people are not consciously experiencing anxiety around these issues, they are responding at an embodied and unconscious level, overwhelmed by their sense of impotence and helplessness in the face of such existential threats.

Implications for practice

We need to find ways of humanising change so that the process of change is experienced as meaningful and engages those involved, rather than alienates them. This requires attention to be paid to the purpose, values and intent that lie behind our plans and actions, the quality of relationships, and the psychological and social needs of employees. There is no simple recipe for doing this, beyond connecting with people and finding what people truly care about and want to create together. The following in my experience are helpful principles that help to make change meaningful to those affected:

Imagining, framing and planning for a future that people care about. During periods of uncertainty and change, we all need hope that together with others we can create a meaningful future. It is the absence of such a hope that creates despair and helplessness. Helping a group to create a clear picture, image and outline of their preferred future creates a sense of shared purpose. This can help people endure the hardship and difficulties of change.

Treating employees as self-motivated and willing to take responsibility. If the desired outcome is that employees are motivated, take initiative and collaborate with each other, then the process of change needs to invite those involved to do so. In the 1960s the psychologist Douglas McGregor (1960) in his book *The Human Side of Enterprise* observed that if managers believe that employees are not motivated and will not take responsibility, which he called Theory X, then this becomes a self-fulfilling prophecy. If, on the other hand, managers believe that employees are self-directed, self-motivated and want to feel responsible, Theory Y, then individuals tend to respond accordingly. McGregor argued that Theory Y challenges managers 'to innovate, to discover new ways of organising and directing human effort, even though we recognise that the perfect organisation, like the perfect vacuum, is practically out of reach'.

Encouraging direct and open communication. To feel recognised and seen as a human being, we need others to listen to and witness our subjectivity and hear our voice. This requires a willingness to hear difficult truths about the present. To create such a space, we need to be prepared to say what we think and feel; and to be prepared to hear what others have to say. This statement is very easy to write and very hard to apply in practice. We have all sorts of fears and anxieties about what would happen if we were open and candid in what we say to others. Most workplaces have a norm of politeness or moderation of strong or challenging opinions. We equally do not tend to have a problem listening to individuals who share our view of the world, yet we find it very challenging when we disagree or feel challenged by what they have to say. A tension therefore always exists between what *can* be spoken about in a group and what *needs* to be spoken about.

Involving people in the process of change. One of the central findings on the effectiveness of organisational change processes is the role of involvement, participation and giving those affected choice in both the process and form of the change (Hartley, 1996; Lewin, 1947). Participation improves both the likelihood of acceptance of changes and their ultimate effectiveness (Hartley, 1996). Indeed, if there was one finding that stands out from the research on organisational change, it is the importance of participation in the process of change. A 60-year review of research into change recipients' reactions to organisational change demonstrated this very clearly. It concluded that high levels of participation resulted in higher readiness and acceptance of change, lower stress levels, stronger overall support for the change, a greater understanding of the meaning of change, the realisation of possible gains associated with the changes, improved interpersonal trust and increased attachment to the organisation (Oreg, Vakola, & Armenakis, 2011).

Paying attention to fairness and social justice. Transgressions of the psychological contract can be minimised if leaders pay attention to the implicit and explicit expectations that employees hold about their relationship with the organisation. This requires some attention to how history and past events have shaped employees' expectations. Ensuring the process and outcomes of changes helps develop trust and engage employees. This necessitates the management of expectations and direct conversations where the expectations are changing.

Designing organisations with people's needs in mind. Organic and networked organisational forms also in theory offer the potential to humanise work. Theoretically, they meet many of employees' socio-psychological needs, such as the need for autonomy, variety and to learn. Those creating new designs or structures, rather than assuming they know people's needs, need to proactively consult with and involve those affected in the process. Involving employees in the process of organisation redesign not only leads to more satisfied employees but also more productive workplaces (Weisbord, 2012).

Using new technologies to enrich jobs. Whilst the technologies are different, much of the research that was done on designing jobs in the Industrial Age is applicable in the digital age. If there is one lesson from the research into work design, it is that technology can enrich jobs or de-humanise them. Proponents of artificial intelligence and machine learning argue that these technologies have the capacity to replace mundane and routine administrative tasks. This potentially could create more challenging, enriching and complex roles that are more motivating and engaging for employees. This does, however, require that those using technologies to create new work systems involve those who will be doing the work and understand how new work systems can be developed that meet their needs.

Conclusion

In this chapter, I have tried to illustrate that alienation and disengagement can be understood as arising from the social reconfiguration that is taking place within and across organisations and society. We are all entangled in this process of social upheaval which is played out in our everyday lives. The disintegration and collapse of the existing social order is generating overwhelming anxieties that affect our psychological well-being and engagement with our work. It is tempting to pin the blame on 'bad' management or 'insensitive' executives for the health of our organisations. They are, however, just as overwhelmed as everyone else. Sure, they have their responsibilities; however, they are also caught up in the same dynamics of social ambiguity, uncertainty and unpredictability. I do not see any simple solutions for resolving this crisis beyond acknowledging its existence and recognising ours and others' basic human needs for connection, belonging, self-direction and, fundamentally, meaning in our/their lives.

Notes

1 Reported in Laloux (2014).
2 Wolfe, H. (2004), 'Survivor syndrome: Key considerations and practical steps', www. employment-studies.co.uk/system/files/resources/files/mp28.pdf
3 'Anxiety: The office fear factor', www.ft.com/content/75b99926-77da-11e5-a95a-27d368e1ddf7
4 Reported in *The Washington Post* (2015), 'The perilous plight of middle managers: Exploitation, domination and depression', www.washingtonpost.com/news/to-your-health/wp/2015/08/20/why-middle-managers-are-more-likely-to-be-depressed/?noredirect=on&utm_term=.d2fc46b0ea56
5 Although it should be noted that others have referred to the start of the 20th century and the middle of the 20th century as the 'age of anxiety' (May, 1977).
6 'Good work in an age of radical technologies', https://medium.com/@thersa/good-work-in-an-age-of-radical-technologies-52c7bc6b8cc2
7 *The Bridge Programme – participant perspectives*, https://aaltodoc.aalto.fi/bitstream/handle/123456789/16082/isbn9789526062129.pdf
8 'Nokia's pain becomes Finland's', www.wsj.com/articles/SB1000142405270230456 31045763597439265256766

Works cited

Antoniou, A. S., & Cooper, C. L. (2005). *Research companion to organizational health psychology*. Cheltenham, England: Edward Elgar.

Applebaum, S. H., Delage, C., Labib, N., & Gault, G. (1997). The survivor syndrome: The aftermath of downsizing. *Career Development International*, 2(6), 278–286.

Balaram, B., & Wallace-Stephens, F. (2018, January). *Thriving, striving, or just about surviving? Seven portraits of economic security and modern work in the UK*. Retrieved from www.thersa.org/globalassets/pdfs/reports/rsa_7-portraits-of-modern-work-report.pdf

Bamberger, S. G., Vinding, A. L., Larsen, A., Nielsen, P., Fonager, K., & Nielsen, R. (2012). Impact of organisational change on mental health: A systematic review. *Occupational and Environmental Medicine*, 69(8), 592–598.

Baruch, Y. (1998). The rise and fall of organizational commitment. *Human Systems Management*, 17(2), 135–143.

Bates, L. M., Keyes, K. M., & Muntaner, C. (2015, November). Anxious? Depressed? You might be suffering from capitalism: Contradictory class locations and the prevalence of depression and anxiety in the USA. *Sociology of Health & Illness*, 1352–1372.

Bauman, Z. (2005). *Liquid life*. Cambridge, England: Polity Press.

Baumeister, R. F., & Leary, M. R. (1995). The need to belong. *Psychological Bulletin, 117*, 497–529.

Blauner, R. (1964). *Alienation and freedom: The factory worker and his industry*. Chicago, IL: University of Chicago Press.

Chandola, T. (2010). *Stress at work: A report prepared for the British Academy*. London, England: The British Academy.

Cooper, C. L., Quick, J. C., & Schabracq, M. J. (2009). *The international handbook of work and health psychology*. New York, NY: John Wiley.

Davis, L. E., & Cherns, A. (1975). *The quality of working life*. New York, NY: Free Press.

Day, A., & Power, K. (2009). Developing leaders for a world of uncertainty, complexity and ambiguity. *The Ashridge Journal*, Winter 2009–2010.

Durkheim, E. ((1897) [1951]). *Suicide: A study in sociology*. New York, NY: The Free Press.

Emery, F. E. ((1959) [1978]). Characteristics of socio-technical systems. In F. Emery (Ed.), *The emergence of a new paradigm of work* (pp. 38–86). Canberra, Australia: Centre for Continuing Education, Australian National University.

Emery, F. E. (1993). Characteristics of sociotechnical systems. In E. L. Trist, H. Murray, & B. Trist (Eds.), *The social engagement of social science: A Tavistock anthology. Volume II: The socio-technical perspective* (pp. 157–186). Philadelphia, PA: University of Pennsylvania Press.

Flovik, L., Knardahl, S., & Christensen, J. O. (2018, October). Organizational change and employee mental health: A prospective multilevel study of the association between organizational changes and clinically relevant mental distress. *A Scandinavian Journal of Work and Environmental Health*, *45*(2), 1–12.

Frankl, V. (1978). *Man's search for meaning*. Reading, England: Rider.

Fromm, E. (1941). *Escape from freedom*. Oxford, England: Farrar & Rinehart.

Gallup (2013). *State of the American workplace*. Retrieved from https://news.gallup.com/reports/178514/state-american-workplace.aspx

Gallup (2017). *State of the global workplace*. Retrieved from www.gallup.com/workplace/238079/state-global-workplace-2017.aspx

Hackman, J. R., & Oldham, G. R. (1980). *Work redesign*. New York, NY: Addison-Wesley.

Hartley, J. (1996). Organisational change and development. In P. Warr (Ed.), *Psychology at work* (pp. 399–426). London, England: Penguin Press.

Health & Safety Executive (2016). *Work related stress, anxiety and depression statistics in Great Britain 2016*. Retrieved from www.cwumeridian.org.uk/hse-work-related-stress-anxiety-depresssion-stats-in-gb-2016-report.pdf

House, J. S. (1981). *Work stress and social support*. Reading, MA: Addison-Wesley.

Jahoda, M. (1981). Work, employment, and unemployment: Values, theories, and approaches in social research. *American Psychologist*, *36*(2), 184–191.

Kalleberg, A. L. (2001). Farewell to commitment? Changing employment relations and labor markets in the United States. *Contemporary Sociology*, *30*(1), 9–12.

Kegan, R. (1994). *In over our heads: The mental demands of modern life*. Cambridge, MA: Harvard University Press.

Kierkegaard, S. (2015). *The concept of anxiety* (originally published in 1844). (T. B. Harvey, Ed.). New York, NY: Liveright.

Krantz, J. (2013). Approaching twenty-first century, information-based organisations. In L. Vansina (Ed.), *Humanness in organisations: A psychodynamic contribution* (pp. 51–69). London, England: Karnac.

Laloux, F. (2014). *Reinventing organizations: A guide to creating organizations inspired by the next generation of human consciousness*. Brussels, Belgium: Nelson Parker.

Lawler, E. E. (1982). Strategies for improving the quality of work life. *American Psychologist, 37*, 486–493.

Lewin, K. (1947). Frontiers in group dynamics: Concept, method and reality in social science; social equilibria and social change. *Human Relations, 1*(1), 5–41.

Marx, K. (1974). *Economic and philosophical manuscripts of 1844*. London, England: Lawrence Wishart.

May, R. (1977). *The meaning of anxiety* (revised ed.). New York, NY: Norton.

McCarthy, J., & Trougakos, J. (2016). How workplace anxiety fuels emotional exhaustion. Retrieved from www.forbesindia.com/article/rotman/how-workplace-anxiety-fuels-emotional-exhaustion/43553/1

McGregor, D. (1960). *The human side of enterprise*. New York, NY: McGraw-Hill.

Murthy, V. (2017). Work and the loneliness epidemic: Reducing isolation at work is good for business. *Harvard Business Review: The Bid Idea*. Retrieved from https://hbr.org/cover-story/2017/09/work-and-the-loneliness-epidemic

Novelli, L., Kirkman, B., & Shapiro, D. (1995). Effective implementation of organizational change: An organizational justice perspective. In C. Cooper, & D. Rousseau (Eds.), *Trends in organizational behaviour* (pp. 15–36). Chichester, England: John Wiley & Sons.

O'Donohue, W., & Nelson, L. (2014). Alienation: An old concept with contemporary relevance for human resource management. *International Journal of Organizational Analysis, 22*(3), 301–316.

Oreg, S., Vakola, M., & Armenakis, A. (2011). Change recipients' reactions to organizational change: A 60-year review of quantitative studies. *Journal of Applied Behavioral Science, 47*, 461–524.

Probst, T. M. (2002, August). Layoffs and tradeoffs: Production, quality, and safety demands under the threat of job loss. *Journal of Occupational Health, 7*(3), 211–220.

Ronnquist, R., Hakonen, A., & Vartianen, M. (2015). *The Bridge Program –Participant perspectives*. Retrieved from https://aaltodoc.aalto.fi/bitstream/handle/123456789/16082/isbn9789526062129.pdf

Rousseau, D. (1995). *Psychological contracts in organizations: Understanding written and unwritten agreements*. Newbury Park, CA: Sage Publications.

Siilasmaa, R. (2018). *Transforming NOKIA: The power of paranoid optimism to lead through colossal change*. New York, NY: McGraw-Hill Education.

Sverke, M., Hellgren, J., & Näswall, K. (2002, July). No security: A meta-analysis and review of job insecurity and its consequences. *Journal of Occupational Health, 7*(3), 242–264.

Trist, E., & Bamforth, W. (1951). Some social and psychological consequences of the long wall method of coal-getting. *Human Relations, 4*, 3–38.

Tyler, T. R. (1994). Psychological models of the justice motive: Antecedents of distributive and procedural justice. *Journal of Personality and Social Psychology, 64*, 850–863.

Tyler, T., Degeoy, P., & Smith, H. (1996). Understanding why the justice of group procedures matters: A test of the psychological dynamics of the group value model. *Journal of Personality and Social Psychology, 70*(5), 913–930.

Vahtera, J., Kivimaki, M., & Pentti, J. (1997). Effects of organisational downsizing on health of employees. *The Lancet, 350*, 1124–1228.

Walker, C. R., & Guest, R. H. (1952). *The man on the assembly line*. Cambridge, MA: Harvard University Press.

Weisbord, M. (2012). *Productive workplaces: Dignity, meaning and Community* (3rd ed.). San Franscisco, CA: John Wiley & Sons.

Whitehead, M., & Diderichsen, F. (2001). Social capital and health: Tip-toeing through the minefield of evidence. *The Lancet, 358*(9277), 165–166.

World Health Organization (WHO). (2001). *Mental health: New understanding, new hope.* World Health Organization report. Retrieved from www.who.int/whr/2001/en/

Wilke, G. (2015). *The art of group analysis in organisations: The use of intuitive and experiential knowledge.* London, England: Routledge.

Winnicott, D. (1960). Ego distortion in terms of true and false self. In *The maturational processes and the facilitating environment* (pp. 140–152). New York, NY: International Universities Press.

Wolfe, H. (2004). *Survivor syndrome: Key considerations and practical steps.* Brighton, England: Institute for Employment Studies.

Part 3

Transformation, learning and adaptation

11 Creativity, imagination and transformation

Permanence, equilibrium and stability is not a natural state of life. The biologist and complexity theorist Fritjof Capra perceived creativity – the generation of new forms – to be a critical characteristic of life (Capra & Luisi, 2014). A living system changes in order to adapt to and change its environment, and in doing so preserve itself. Creative adaptation is therefore the natural order of life. Organisations – like living systems – evolve and creatively adapt to their environments in unplanned and unpredictable ways. This becomes all the more important for their survival and success when the environment becomes unstable and turbulent. Repeating what worked in the past simply leads to decline and entropy.

As I have argued, human beings have a desire for order and continuity; however, part of the human condition is our impulse to explore our environments, to learn and to be creative. The psychoanalyst Donald Winnicott (1971) believed that it is the capacity for creative living that makes the individual feel that life is worth living. He believed that each of us has a creative potential, our 'true' self, and that it is important for us to make sense of experiences and assimilate new ideas into our existing ways of understanding the world. Expressing our creative potential gives us a sense of vitality.

Transformation, creativity and emergence

Organisation transformation and change is fundamentally a process of discovery, creativity and collective learning that involves discovering something new and different about ourselves and our worlds. It requires us to imagine new possibilities and identify where we place limits on our perceptions and our ability to act, and to explore the consequences of removing them. This is both a psychological and social process, challenging us to shift our inner world, our beliefs and assumptions about ourselves and others; and at the social level, to reconfigure the social rules and norms that govern how we organise ourselves. These necessitate that we move outside of our zone of comfort and to step into the unknown. It is in this space – between what is known and what is not known – that learning happens.

Transformation starts when patterns of conversation, thinking and interaction start to shift. Small acts or ideas can trigger responses that eventually trigger the emergence of new system-wide patterns of behaviour. New forms of organising start to emerge in the form of new practices, processes and structures. This is a messy, dynamic and unpredictable process. Patterns of interaction can suddenly collapse, shift and emerge. In this sense, organisational change is more a process of improvisation than of implementation. Individual acts of brilliance often get the attention yet the reality is that new organisational forms, products or services emerge through complex interactions across and between organisations.

The emergence of new patterns, ideas and forms of organising requires instability in the existing patterns and order (Capra & Luisi, 2014). This is when the potential for creative change is at its highest. This is the 'edge of chaos' (Kauffman, 1993; Waldrop, 1992) – a state in which established patterns start to disintegrate and a level of disorder is present (Stacey, 2003). It is a space in which creative responses are possible and necessary. Uncertainty, disorder and confusion are therefore at the heart of human creativity. Rather than being a problem that needs to be controlled or fixed, they generate a creative potential (Stacey, 2003) from which a new order or form can emerge. A level of disruption to the existing social order is thus required for transformation to emerge.

Creative potential, hope and anxiety

Our ability to *imagine* alternative futures is at the heart of the creative process. The tension between the present as it is experienced and an imagined future creates a creative potential (Fritz, 1989). Once a meaningful intention emerges, it starts to act like an unfulfilled need for those involved. This gives rise to a tension in the individual or group to move towards their desired goal (Lewin, 1951). The tension remains whilst the intention remains unresolved. Acts of social creativity emerge, therefore, when we can imagine a preferred future that is *felt* to be in tension with our 'current reality' (Fritz, 1989). In Nokia's transformation, for instance, a group of people were able to imagine how they could transform from a producer of mobile handsets to a provider of network services. It is this dissonance and tension between our current experience and our imagined future that generates the creative energy that is necessary for social transformations and change.

A process for generating a creative tension[1]

- Bring a large group (between 40–60 people) together who represent the stakeholders from inside and outside of the organisation who care about and have a stake in the organisation or part of the organisation.
- Explore how the 'current' reality emerged from the past, recognising key events, moments and points of transition.

- Identify together the existing context of the organisation, including wider socio-economic, political and technological trends. Assess the implications of these in terms of the opportunities and threats they present.
- Envisage/articulate the long-term adaptive challenge facing the organisation or part of the organisation.
- Imagine together what the organisation could look like in the future. Identifying the principles and themes that are commonly agreed on and supported.
- Brainstorm and agree the actions and next steps that would involve others and mobile people to act differently.

Imagining a realistic, yet alternative, future is important because people act into the future they imagine. For instance, if design engineers in a car company envisage a future made up of driverless, electric cars, they start to act differently in the present than if they imagine a future that is not much different to today. This creative tension opens up a desire to learn and motivates us unconsciously to strive for our desired future. Many change efforts fail to engage people because they are based on rational-logical plans that do not generate a creative tension for those who need to change.

This sense of possibility is an invitation to step into the unknown. Whenever we visualise possibility, both excitement and anxiety are present, and acts that matter to us are necessarily grounded in anxiety. Anxiety, however, signifies that we are ready to learn (Perls & Hefferline, 1951) and reveals the 'the possibility of freedom' (Kierkegaard, 2015). However, we fear stepping into uncertainty and try to evade anxiety. Kierkegaard argued that anxiety can be constrictive and uncreative, causing the individual to choose not to move forward (May, 1977). We follow rules and obey authority, real or imagined, to deny our freedom and choice. If anxiety becomes excessive, our thinking becomes concrete and rigid (Segal, 1974). Psychological defences therefore impair our creative capacities.

If we are to learn and change, we need to step into this unknown possibility. It is through confronting and moving towards anxiety (Kierkegaard, 2015) that we realise our creative potential. A transformative response leads us to question ourselves, to experiment, to take risk and be creative (O'Hara, 2001). By confronting our anxiety, we deepen our capacity to deal with the challenges of life and work. This requires people to be:

- Vulnerable without feeling persecuted so that they can learn from experience;
- Curious about, rather than fearful of, the unknown;
- Able to link with others across important differences; and
- Realistically connected to the genuine challenges and opportunities they face (Krantz, 1998).

To hold this position, our desire for change needs to exceed the fear and anxiety of changing. The process of reconstructing a way of understanding and seeing the world tends to be painful, disorienting and anxiety provoking. Old patterns need to dissolve and reconfigure for new ones to emerge and form. As the gestalt psychologist Max Wertheimer (1945) observed: 'Creativity is the process of destroying one's gestalt in favour of a better one'. Creative acts therefore also incur loss.

If people are going to step into the unknown, they need to reconnect with a sense of hope. Hope combines with the anxieties associated with the current reality to generate energy to overcome people's fears and anxieties of letting go of the familiar. If we feel hopeless we hold on to certainties, even if this certainty resides only in our own minds (Lemma, 2003). People also need to feel that they are able to take the risk of making the first necessary steps for change. They may need encouragement and support from their leadership or peers to do something that they have not done before and risk feeling vulnerable in the process.

Design thinking: a method for creative design

One method for enabling the creative potential of a group of people is *design thinking* (Brown, 2009; Simon, 1969). This method helps a group to understand the needs of a customer group, understand the problems they want to solve and then imagine how they can create products or services that address these needs. Design thinking is a deliberate effort to expand the range of ideas rather than to constrain them. It is a 'human-centred' approach to design – starting with the user rather than the technology. The approach can be used for developing organisations (i.e. systems, processes and structures) or new products and services.

The process brings together a group who understand the customer and possess diverse expertise. It helps the group to develop innovative and creative solutions by working in short cycles of design, experimentation and review. The basic steps are as follows:

1. Develop an empathic and intuitive understanding of the customer by observing them and speaking to them in naturalistic environments.
2. Describe and frame the problem or difficulty that they are experiencing for which the product or service is a solution.
3. Generate as many creative and imaginative ideas as possible (uncensored for practicality or utility).
4. Develop prototypes of the service or product that can be tested directly and quickly with the customer.
5. Test the prototype with the customers or end users and use feedback to refine the prototype.
6. Further testing and refinement of the prototype with the customers until there is clear convergence on a product or service that can be piloted.

Design thinking as a method requires those involved to feel safe to experiment, to take risks and to be imaginative. This requires the creation of a psychological space in which individuals feel they can express ideas without judgement or criticism from others. Without these conditions, the process tends to produce ideas that do not challenge the existing boundaries of thinking and practice.

Transitional space

We have the capacity to reflect on our behaviour, how we interact with others and the social rules that inform these interactions. In doing so, we learn about how together we preserve the status quo. By heightening our awareness, we create the possibility that together with others we can create new social patterns. This requires us to interrupt what we are doing (technically or practically) to reflect on and explore its nature, dynamics and worth (Kemmis, 2001). It is only by examining our taken-for-granted assumptions, habits and ideologies that we can consider what kind of collective social action might be necessary to transform things for the better (Kemmis, 2001). It is through such reflective dialogue that critical consciousness emerges (Habermas, 1984), which is necessary for collaborative acts of change.

Transformation requires space and time for us to explore the *inherent tensions* that exist between our existing purposes and the emerging external challenges (Bridger, 2001). This is facilitated by the creation of social spaces where the current ways of doing things can be suspended to allow for a playful and creative atmosphere in which new ideas and possibilities can be explored. Winnicott (1953) called such an environment a *transitional space* (Winnicott, 1953). This is a psychological space of potential – a zone of transition – where an individual can play, and imagination and illusion can flourish. Here, the pressures of the immediate demands of reality can be put on hold, to enable people to explore what they are doing together – its nature, dynamics and worth. One method of facilitating transitional space is the process of a 'group review' (Bridger, 2001). This requires suspension of the 'business agenda' to allow space for a group to explore how they are working together and relating to their environment.

Transitional spaces help people to work through the tensions of moving from the past to a future that is only partly known and largely imagined (Vansina & Schruijer, 2013) and to process the losses that change incurs. They create an opportunity for people to exercise their imagination by adopting a position between social 'reality' and 'inner' experience (Winnicott, 1971). The presence of such spaces provides a community with 'restorative capacity' (Fischer, 2012) in which connections, trust and shared understanding can develop.

Dialogue

Facilitating communication and dialogue helps to contain people's anxieties, which overcomes a group's regressive tendencies. Dialogue enables people to retain the capacity to think and act creatively, particularly when a group is able to suspend judgement, listen to each other and be receptive to different perspectives. The quality of dialogue influences both the quantity and richness of information that is shared between people. When people from diverse backgrounds and different parts of the system are brought together, this also amplifies both the quality and quantity of information that is potentially available to a group. As a group exchanges perspectives and ideas freely, the potential for new insights and patterns of interaction to emerge increases. As people think together, they are more able to see how they are connected and part of wider patterns and dynamics in a system.

> *Margaret Wheatley (2007) describes her experience of working with communities in Zimbabwe during a period of society collapse, terror and brutality. She describes the power of bringing people together to connect and reclaim their imagination for themselves. She observed how communities would sit together in a circle and reflect together to hold each other's grief and anxiety. By coming together, individuals were able to reclaim their sense of self and rediscover their strength and resolve.*

Bringing people together has its risks. Being in a group, even a small one, can trigger considerable anxiety as individuals struggle with issues such as control, rejection, judgement, acceptance and recognition. As a group becomes larger, levels of anxieties tend to increase and become harder to contain. As it regresses, it loses its capacity to make reasoned decisions. If anxiety gets too overwhelming, a 'perverse space' (Fischer, 2012) can develop, where people or sub-groups become so frustrated and scared that they blame others and become aggressive. This leads to splits and fragmentation between individuals and groups. Persecutory aggressor–victim dynamics emerge, fuelled by hostile projections, in which 'others' are seen to be 'bad' and 'the problem'. Ultimately, this leads to mutually destructive conflict and outcomes. Alternatively, groups can deal with anxiety by avoiding 'reality' so they do not have to encounter what is causing them to feel anxious. They may pursue hopelessly optimistic ideas or place constraints on their conversations. When avoiding their anxieties, a group's exchanges remain superficial and on familiar, safe territory. Rather than confronting difficult issues or dilemmas, the group colludes to focus their attention on topics and subjects that feel safe. Their conversations become stale and mundane as conflicts, disagreements and emotions are evaded.

The higher the level of trust and psychological safety that exists within a group, the more individuals are willing to share information and insights that they have been withholding, such as fears, resentments, controversial observations or unconventional ideas. People need to feel they can express themselves without judgement or risk of attack from others. This is encouraged when a group feels safe and its environment feels dependable and secure. Winnicott called this a 'holding environment' (Winnicott, 1971). This is a space where emotions and anxieties can be expressed and met, without interference, so that 'natural' growth processes can reassert themselves. We can think of the holding environment as a space where paradoxically there is sufficient reliability, order and dependability for disturbance, uncertainty and movement to occur. The presence of a consultant or facilitator who takes responsibility for the process of the meeting can help contain anxieties and structure interactions to enable dialogue.

Implications for practice

During periods of change and transformation, therefore, we need to take care to establish social spaces in which people feel sufficiently safe to be able to be vulnerable, to hear others and to acknowledge difficulties. A transitional space is most likely to emerge when the group experiences a sense of a shared purpose in meeting together, 'good enough' trust and clear boundaries of time, place and participation. The space itself needs to:

- Be sanctioned to give it legitimacy and acceptance within the wider system;
- Focus on addressing issues of mutual concern to those present;
- Be held in a physical space that enables free-flowing communication, privacy and prevents impingements from the external world;
- Create a climate of safety to allow those present to express themselves, including their fantasies, assumptions and emotional experiences;
- Provide time for free and uninhibited reflection, discovery and sharing of insight and ideas;
- Have minimal yet sufficient structure to enable uninhibited conversation and expression whilst not creating excessive anxieties around control and inclusion;
- Facilitate the expression of conflict to help people work through the tension between holding on to the past and moving on;
- Allow individuals to feel heard, to find their own meaning and not be subjected to ideology or rational arguments as to why they must change; and
- Give individuals a free and informed choice (Argyris, 1970) to decide for themselves the actions and changes they wish to make.

There are a range of methods and approaches that have been developed for creating these conditions in small (Isaacs, 1999)) and large groups (Bunker & Alban, 1996), such as Future Search (Weisbord & Janoff, 2010) and Open Space (Owen, 2008).

A long-standing colleague of mine, Adrian McLean (2013), describes in his book Leadership & Cultural Webs in Organisations how he helped facilitate the merger of Nokia and Siemens Communications to form Nokia Siemens Networks

(NSN). This is the joint venture that is referred to in earlier chapters that was central to Nokia's transformation.

Adrian's role was to be a consultant on the cultural aspects of the merger, working closely with an internal consultant, Alistair Moffat. He describes the intention to engage the 60,000 members of the new company in an active conversation about the creation of a culture that was distinctive to the new organisation. The project involved a series of phases that explored and surfaced the cultural patterns of Nokia Networks and Siemens Communications and started to formulate themes as to the culture that employees wanted to create in the future.

To widen the conversation and involve employees in the process of co-creating the new culture, the company set up a social networking site. This online forum created a virtual space – called The Culture Square – where employees could engage in the exchange of ideas around the culture and support the formation of cultural patterns and norms. Over a period of time, a dynamic and unfolding conversation developed about the merger and the developing culture. Initially, contributions were engaged in the process; however, after a few weeks, a theme of cynicism and mistrust emerged with individuals questioning the intention behind the initiative. A large number of silent 'lurkers' followed the discussions but did not actively participate. Adrian interpreted these dynamics as testing whether the forum was safe to express oneself. After five to six weeks, the pattern of the conversation started to shift and contributions became more constructive. Proposals developed to initiate meetings with management to develop ideas that were emerging in the conversations. A series of further developments arose on the back of this event. One of these was a company-wide three-day conversation facilitated by IBM's JAM – a social networking technology – on four specific topics:

- Getting closer to customers;
- Enabling people to flourish;
- Making NSN different; and
- Becoming ONE great company.

Senior management participated in the conversation throughout the three days. The conversation self-organised and unfolded as sub-groups emerged and topics of conversations developed. The central themes that surfaced were reviewed by the board and this led to a series of project groups supported by volunteers from the JAM conversation. A year later, a survey showed that 82% of employees 'fully supported the values' that were articulated through the process.

The NSN case demonstrates how new technology can support the creation of a transitional space which enables connection, sensemaking and the co-creation of new meanings. It demonstrates that it is possible to facilitate disruptive change in a way that recognises people's fundamental needs for connection, belonging, identity and meaning.

Experimentation, muddling through and reviewing

Complexity theory helps us to understand how change evolves in unpredictable ways that we cannot fully comprehend as it is happening. Because complex systems change in unexpected ways, we need to act and pay close attention to what happens. Kurt Lewin famously said: 'you cannot understand a system until you try to change it'. What he meant by this statement was that intervention or action was necessary to disturb a social system in order to learn about it. This simple idea was the basis of Lewin's method of action research. To bring about change we need to work in cycles of action and review (see Figure 11.1), helping people to study the impact of their behaviour and to modify it. Change is therefore a process of experimentation, learning and improvisation in response to feedback. Muddling through with an intent, perhaps, rather than a result of rational planning and implementation. All attempts therefore to bring about change are experiments that create the possibility that those involved can learn about how to change the organisation. In a similar manner, methodologies for working in dynamic environments, such as agile methods, rapid proto-typing or design thinking, encourage people to work in short iterative cycles of design and testing with customers or users to develop new solutions.

We learn about change by reviewing what we have learnt from experience. Reviewing is therefore central to the process of organisation development. This step is, however, very often missed. People's attention tends to be directed towards tangible actions or changes rather than on learning. Regular, disciplined and rigorous learning reviews, however, are critical to the process of transformation. They help those involved to make sense of change and identify intended and unintended consequences of their interventions. The process

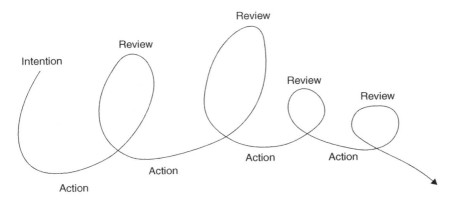

Figure 11.1 Action research cycles

of reviewing needs to attend to both the 'task-work' and how people work together on the task (Bridger, 2001). It is a process of making sense of experience and involves looking back at events, interactions and outcomes to support future actions. Typical questions that are explored include:

- What did we do?
- What impact did it have – what changed and what did not?
- What is our understanding of what enabled change?
- How did we work together?
- What are we learning?
- What do we therefore need to stop doing, start doing or do more of?

The review process needs to encourage a climate of reflection and learning rather than judgement and evaluation. Otherwise, the process can easily become a persecutory space in which those involved find excuses, blame others or attack each other. Reviewing can help sustain the process of change and transformation by providing support to those who are attempting to affect change (Vansina & Vansina-Cobbaert, 2008).

The process of review needs to be a systematic and comprehensive process. Complex and widespread change requires learning reviews at multiple levels and in different parts of the system. Reviews that bring together representatives from across boundaries are necessary to explore and develop an understanding of systemic interdependencies between different parts.

> *With a colleague, I consulted to an NHS Mental Health Trust to support a process of organisation development and cultural development. The executive board had established a group of 50 internal change agents who were working across the Trust to engage staff in the process of change. We helped them design and run a highly participative approach in which employees were encouraged to gather stories of effective performance. They were asked to identify small actions and interventions that would amplify the behaviours and values they perceive to represent effective practice. This process enabled individuals to express themselves whilst also communicating to staff that the senior management trusted them. Over time, we observed that more and more staff became engaged in the process, taking responsibility for initiating improvements at a local level. By focusing on what was working, teams learnt about how to improve services for service users. By telling stories of success across the Trust, a shared narrative started to emerge around how the Trust made a difference to people's lives in the community. This created a virtuous cycle of growing confidence and pride in the work of the organisation.*

In our consulting work with the European telecommunications company at regular intervals, we brought together the project teams to reflect on what they were learning about changing the organisation. We also convened meetings with all the teams from the cohort, members of the executive, past alumni from the programme and other stakeholders to share what they were doing and to reflect together on what they were learning about change. By creating these spaces in which people felt safe to share their experiences, we helped to create a transitional space in which learning and a commitment to change could be fostered. From these processes, hope started to develop that change was possible and ideas were developed for enabling the process of change.

Conclusion

Disruption opens up the possibility for creativity, learning and transformation. To many of us, it often feels forced upon us, yet change and adaptation are central to living. We are constantly adapting to events and life itself is a creative process of adjustment. The gap between our desires for the future and our current experiences creates a tension that generates both anxiety and a creative potential. When we are willing to step into the unknown and face our anxieties, we grow, develop and transform. We stretch and challenge ourselves and in doing so, learn something about ourselves, our assumptions and our environments. Disruptive change therefore offers us the opportunity for creative self-expression and self-development. This is most likely to arise if we are able to create transitional spaces and environments that encourage people to play, experiment and to take personal risks without fear of judgement or punishment. If, however, people become overwhelmed by anxiety, they lose their capacity to be creative and to learn from experience. An organisation's adaptive capacity thus reflects its ability to create the conditions that allow employees to realise their creative potential.

Note

1 Influenced by the Future Search (Weisbord & Janoff, 2010) and Search Conference principles (Emery & Purser, 1996).

Works cited

Argyris, C. (1970). *Intervention theory and method: Behavioural science view.* Reading, MA: Addison-Wesley Longman.

Bridger, H. (2001). Foreword. In G. Amado, A. Ambrose, & R. Amato (Eds.), *The transitional approach to change* (pp. xi–xiv). London, England: Karnac.

Brown, T. (2009). *Change by design: How design thinking transforms organizations and inspires innovation*. New York, NY: Harper Business.

Bunker, B., & Alban, B. (1996). *Large group interventions: Engaging the whole system for rapid change*. San Francisco, CA: Jossey-Bass.

Capra, F., & Luisi, P. L. (2014). *The systems view of life: A unifying vision*. Cambridge, England: Cambridge University Press.

Emery, M., & Purser, R. (1996). *The search conference: A powerful method for planning organizational change and community action* (1st ed.). San Francisco, CA: Jossey-Bass.

Fischer, M. (2012). Organizational turbulence, trouble and trauma: Theorizing the collapse of a mental health setting. *Organisational Studies, 33*(9), 1153–1173.

Fritz, R. (1989). *The path of least resistance: Learning to become the creative force in your own life*. New York, NY: Fawcett.

Habermas, J. (1984). *The theory of communicative action: Volume 1 – Reason and the rationalization of society* (trans. T. McCarthy). Boston, MA: Beacon Press.

Isaacs, W. (1999). *Dialogue and the art of thinking together: A pioneering approach to communicating in business*. New York, NY: Doubleday.

Kauffman, S. (1993). *The origins of order: Self-organization and selection in evolution*. Oxford, England: Oxford University Press.

Keegan, R. (1994). *In over our heads: The mental demands of modern life*. Cambridge, MA: Harvard University Press.

Kemmis, S. (2001). Exploring the relevance of critical theory for action research: Emancipatory action research in the footsteps of Jürgen Habermas. In P. Reason & H. Bradbury (Eds.), *Handbook of action research: Participative inquiry and practice* (pp. 94–105). London, England: Routledge.

Kierkegaard, S. (2015). *The concept of anxiety* (originally published in 1844). (T. B. Harvey, Ed.). New York, NY: Liveright.

Krantz, J. (1998). Anxiety and the new order. In E. B. Klein, F. Gabelnick, & P. Herr (Eds.), *The psychodynamics of leadership* (pp. 77–107). Madison, CT: Psychosocial Press.

Lemma, A. (2003). *Introduction to the practice of psychoanalytic psychotherapy: A practical treatment handbook*. Chichester, England: John Wiley & Sons.

Lewin, K. (1951). Intention, will and need. In D. Rapaport (Ed.), *Organization and pathology of thought* (pp. 95–153). New York, NY: Columbia University Press.

May, R. (1977). *The meaning of anxiety* (revised ed.). New York, NY: Norton.

McLean, A. (2013). *Leadership & cultural webs in organisations: Weavers' tales*. Emerald.

O'Hara, M. (2001). *Alternative psychological scenarios for the coming global age*. Retrieved from http://citeseerx.ist.psu.edu/viewdoc/download?doi=10.1.1.475.6830&rep=r ep1&type=pdf

Owen, H. (2008). *Open Space technology: A user's guide*. San Francisco, CA: Berrett-Koehler.

Perls, F., & R. Hefferline, F. G. (1951). *Gestalt therapy*. New York, NY: Julian Press.

Segal, H. (1974). *Introduction to the work of Melanie Klein*. New York, NY: Basic Books.

Simon, H. A. (1969). *The sciences of the artificial*. Cambridge, MA: MIT Press.

Stacey, R. (2003). *Strategic management and organisational dynamics: The challenge of complexity*. Harlow, England: FT/Prentice-Hall.

Vansina, L. S., & Vansina-Cobbaert, M.-J. (2008). *Psychodynamics for consultants and managers*. Chichester, England: Wiley-Blackwell.

Vansina, L., & Schruijer, S. G. (2013). Facilitating transitional change. In L. Vansina (Ed.), *Humaness in organisations: A psychodynamic contribution* (pp. 125–138). London, England: Karnac.

Waldrop, M. M. (1992). *Complexity: The emerging science at the edge of order and chaos.* London, England: Penguin.

Weisbord, M., & Janoff, S. (2010). *Future search: Getting the whole system in the room for vision, commitment and action.* San Francisco, CA: Berrett-Koehler.

Wertheimer, M. (1945). *Productive thinking.* New York, NY: Harper.

Wheatley, M. J. (2007). *Finding our way: Leadership for uncertain times.* San Francisco, CA: Berrett-Koehler.

Winnicott, D. W. (1953). Transitional objects and transitional phenomena. *International Journal of Psychoanalysis, 34,* 89–97.

Winnicott, D. W. (1971). *Playing and reality.* London; England; New York, NY: Tavistock Publications.

12 Leading through disruption and change

The role of leadership is to represent a group of people, whether this is a team, department or organisation, with the intent of enabling it to achieve its shared aims and maintain itself as an entity. Leaders therefore need to attend both to the internal dynamics of the social group and its relationship to its environment. From this perspective, leadership is a process of representation and a dynamic that is inseparable from the followership of a social group. It is based on a compact that binds those who lead and those who follow into the same moral, intellectual and emotional commitment (Zaleznik, 1991). To fulfil this compact, leaders need to represent the group's ideals, identity and needs to an extent that the group perceives they are acting with their needs and interests at heart.

Acts of leadership are therefore bound up in the dynamics of the group. To lead, in the true sense of the word, a group needs to see a leader as 'one of us' and to exemplify what makes 'us' different to a salient other (Haslam, Reicher, & Platow, 2011), whether this is the competition or another department. Groups give leaders authority and legitimacy when they perceive they will and are able to act in their interests. Those who influence do so because they appeal to and shape the group's identity. Leaders thus need to be attuned to the group to ensure their actions reflect its desires, mood and ideals.

The language and actions of the leaders are deeply symbolic and convey meaning to the group around its identity and purpose. These can either reflect and reinforce the group's identity – providing a sense of continuity – or appeal to what the group can become.

Who are 'we'? and
What do 'we' want to become or achieve?

....are critical questions during periods of change, when people are likely to feel that their identities are under threat. Leaders convey they are acting on behalf of the 'common good' and reflecting the interests of a broad set of stakeholders.

A change in the meaning of 'leadership'

The role of leadership in organisations, not that it was ever easy, is becoming increasingly challenging. There is a general trend to ascribe increasing importance to the role of leaders in the success of organisations (Alvesson, 2013), which perhaps reflects the individualistic developments of society. Leaders are expected to live up to a range of ideals and prescriptions about what they should be doing (Flinn, 2018), such as being transformational visionaries who determine the fate of their organisations. These ideals, however, bear little resemblance to what is realistically possible or what leaders actually do in practice (Alvesson & Jonsson, 2016).

Many of our assumptions and beliefs about what makes an effective leader are embedded in the bureaucratic paradigm. In the past, leadership was about managing a steady state whilst encouraging incremental adaptation to external developments. It was based on an authority that came with a position in the hierarchy and claims to truth based on knowledge and expertise. Leaders were expected to be in control, to organise people, to set the strategic direction of the organisation and inspire people through their vision and charisma. This form of leadership rewarded the creation of order, coherence and clarity of direction. However, the rules of leadership are being rewritten and the meaning of 'leadership' as a concept is changing. We currently inhabit a transitional space where a new set of assumptions and beliefs are emerging. This is creating confusion and ambiguity for both leaders and followers:

Who can and does lead?
What can leaders expect of their followers?
What do followers expect of their leaders?

Both these unrealistic expectations and the level of confusion around the nature of leadership has contributed to the greater levels of distrust in authority and the general cynicism about leadership. This, in turn, makes it harder for leaders to claim and exercise authority.

In a fluid, uncertain and unpredictable world, control and order are not possible. Decision making breaks down when it relies on a small group of individuals making the critical decisions for the whole organisation. How can they be informed and abreast of fast-moving, local events? Exerting too much control over others simply creates greater chaos (Wheatley & Frieze, 2011). Leadership thus needs to be distributed and decentralised across complex systems, rather than being a defined role in a stable structure. Equally, the shift to more organic, self-organising and decentralised forms of organising requires a different form of leadership than in hierarchical structures. Authority is temporary and ambiguous and needs to be negotiated, determined as much by the task, the individual's capabilities and relationships. This raises the question of who is able to shape how change happens in an organisation. From a complexity perspective, acts of leadership can be observed in the local interactions between people as they attempt to organise themselves. We need to speak less of leadership as a role occupied by the few and see it more as a process that is enacted by the many.

In the face of change, leaders need to find a balance in relation to people's ambivalence to change, choosing what is important for people to hold on to whilst embracing the emergence of new cultural patterns. Confronted with complexity, they need to improvise as they respond to uncertainty and act into the unknown (Flinn, 2018). Leadership becomes less about applying what worked in the past, or a set of rules, and more about making judgements. They need to act on the basis of what they understand and to learn through experience. This calls on them to adjust, adapt and creatively respond in the face of unexpected and emerging events (Barrett, 2012). Ralph Stacey calls this 'practical judgement' – mindful action involving ongoing reflection on judgements and their consequence (Stacey, 2012). In dynamic and uncertain contexts, leaders need to develop and exercise a capacity for self-awareness and critical reflection.

I facilitated a meeting of around 70 change agents in a global corporation that was one year into a transformation. The aim of the day was to help those present to make sense of the changes and their experience of supporting change projects. The design involved individuals working in divisional groups to share stories of how the change was progressing and then to notice patterns and themes in their conversations. We then spent time in plenary sharing and making connections. In the first plenary session, a theme quickly emerged of widespread discontent and dissatisfaction with the senior leadership at 'the top' of the business. Several of the groups spoke of a 'lack' of leadership. The sense in the room was that the top team was 'failing' and not 'living up to expectations'. When I drew attention to the references to 'lack of leadership', people were unable to clearly put into words what was missing, just the sense of frustration that people felt with the change process. Further exploration indicated that people were feeling under pressure from the executive for not making faster progress with the change. The executive team were felt to be 'imposing' changes and pushing hard. This seemed to have the opposite effect because rather than engaging and energising people in the change process, it led to anxiety, resistance and a sense of imposition.

We can understand this situation as an emerging pattern or dynamic, rather than as a failing of leadership. There were anxious leaders pushing hard for change and anxious followers feeling they were not living up to their leaders' expectations and not being committed to changing in the way they were expected to change. As the day progressed, a sense of stuck-ness became apparent. The underlying emotional tone was one of frustration, fear and anxiety. Whilst no simple answers emerged by the end of the day, those present became more aware of the complexity of leadership around the transformation, their emotional involvement in the change process and the dynamics that were emerging between leaders and followers. This opened up the possibility for them to act differently in their attempts to facilitate and support change across the business.

The demands on leaders during transitions

Leaders consistently overemphasise their ability to manage change and the degree of time it takes for people to work through change processes. This often leaves them feeling frustrated or disappointed. If they are unable to process their disappointment and reflect on events, they can collapse either into blaming themselves or others for the failure to live up to their illusions about what is possible.

As we have seen, the process of transformation generates considerable anxiety and psychic distress for those affected. When uncertainty and risks are high, it is human nature to look for authority figures and believe that someone is in control. This invites people to project all sorts of feelings and emotions on leaders who are unconsciously used by them to help them to manage their anxieties. They may be subjected to all manner of unrealistic hopes and expectations regarding their capacity to know what to do. During periods of ambiguity and uncertainty, leaders may be expected to keep us safe, protect us and to give certainty. Alternatively, they may be attacked, criticised and blamed for the organisation's ills and problems because they have failed to control events.

For many leaders, particularly those in symbolically important roles such as the CEO or heads of business units, these projections can be so strong that they do not feel that people see them as a 'real' person rather than some kind of demi-god. The sense of inner distress and confusion that leaders often experience can often be seen as a reflection of the emotional turmoil that is being experienced in the organisation. I recall during the upheavals and changes at the business school that I was often left feeling a whole host of conflicting emotions, which at one level I knew did not fully belong to me; yet in the intensity of a meeting or interaction, I found it hard to separate from and not act on these emotions.

To lead in today's environment is to experience anxiety. The leader who does not experience some level of anxiety in the face of uncertainty is likely to be operating in a position of grandiose super-confidence or have their head in the sand. In my coaching work with leaders, I get to witness first hand their vulnerabilities and anxieties in the face of these demands. To be the subject of others' unrealistic and unconscious expectations creates doubts and psychic pressure. Leaders need to face their doubts if they are stay in contact with 'reality' and learn from experience. However, this necessitates a willingness to question oneself and to tolerate ambiguity and not knowing, as well as others' anxiety. When leaders defend themselves against such anxieties, they act as if they do not need to learn.

> *I worked with an organisation that was in a state of crisis. The organisation had been formed through a series of mergers between a number of smaller organisations several years previously. These changes did not, however, have wide support. This had resulted in opposition to the integration, low morale and poor engagement. A new chief executive had been recently appointed. He had clearly created a strong impact and positive impression during the appointments process. Word had got out that he was astute, engaging and insightful. I heard comments from employees along the lines of 'everything is going to change when they are appointed'. The mood in the organisation shifted to a sense of anticipation and optimism about how he would resolve the crisis and change the culture. A short time after he started in the role, he confided in me that he felt under enormous pressure because of the expectations that everyone seemed to hold about how he would change the culture. The chairman had asked him repeatedly for updates and the other members of the executive had all tabled their ideas of what they wanted him to do. The expectations of what he could achieve seemed hopelessly optimistic, despite his undoubted talents and presence. In our conversation, I could see the visible signs of strain in his face and doubts about whether he could remain on the pedestal he felt he was standing on.*

Containing anxiety

During periods of disruption and uncertainty, leaders need to contain the anxieties of their followers (Day & Power, 2009). This is the capacity to receive their unprocessed emotions and to transform them into some understanding of what they are experiencing so that their feelings and emotions can be thought about and understood (Bion, 1967). This involves accepting, tolerating and understanding the intensity of their emotional responses, particularly when they are experiencing the intense emotional response associated with loss, grief and mourning. To do this requires an awareness that people need to be given time and space to work through their reactions and a capacity to receive, hold and not act out others' projections.

To acknowledge uncertainty and to accept that we cannot anticipate what will happen next is a scary prospect for most people. Throughout this book I have explored how human beings try to maximise certainty, order and stability. If uncertainty is too threatening for us, then we deploy all sorts of mental, emotional and perceptual distortions to reduce our anxiety, such as denial, avoidance, simplifying the situation etc. Leaders, in uncertain and ambiguous contexts, need to enable people to learn from experience, not to be fearful of the unknown and to be able to connect across important differences (Krantz, 1998). Gordon Lawrence (2000) talked of the 'politics of salvation' or the 'politics of revelation' to highlight that alternative responses exist. 'The politics of salvation' centres on 'giving solutions' to people and not letting them take their own authority to create their life situations for themselves (Lawrence, 2000). In contrast, he saw 'the politics of revelation' as creating the conditions for people and systems to discover and transform the situation for themselves.

The 19th-century poet John Keats coined the term 'negative capability' to describe when a person 'is capable of being in uncertainties, mysteries, doubts, without any irritable reaching after fact and reason'. Wilfred Bion (1967) further developed the concept of negative capability to describe an ability to tolerate the pain and confusion of not knowing and not revert to imposing ready-made or omnipotent certainties upon an ambiguous or emotionally challenging situation. To come back to Kierkegaard (2015), in a state of anxiety, we face a choice to sit with it or avoid the discomfort of not knowing. Tolerating not knowing creates the possibility of new insight and learning. This requires a tolerance of ambiguity, a willingness to be outside of one's zone of familiarity and moving towards anxiety (rather than away from it). Mistakes are an inevitable part of discovery and exploration. To act into uncertainty, leaders need to adoption a position of *mature action* or relative potency (Lapierre, 1998), accepting both their own limits and the situation as it is. This is a capacity to hold on to a belief in their potency and capacity to shape a situation without believing they have omnipotent control over it or are helpless and impotent. In other words, a degree of humility is required on the part of leaders. It is better to acknowledge that we do not know what the future brings and to adjust accordingly, than to hold on to false illusions of certainty, knowledge and control.

'The politics of salvation' is a regressive response. It is a move away from uncertainty and anxiety by creating an illusion of certainty. A group attempts to preserve certainty and the status quo by avoiding or denying events that are taking place in the world. A leader may operate on the basis of a fantasy of omnipotence, believing they can exercise total control over the situation (Lapierre, 1998). In this position, they collude with and mobilise their followers to create simple solutions to complex problems. They may negate alternative points of view or opinions that threaten their own. Excessive planning and perfectionism can also be an attempt to create an illusion of control. In its more powerful forms, we see a wish for 'strong' authoritarian leaders who provide certainty and mobile scapegoats to be receptacles of people's projections of anger and hostility. Rather than containing people's anger and frustration, they redirect it towards others who are seen to be the objects of threat to the group.

When people feel anxious, they need reliable and dependable authority figures who act consistently and with their anxieties in mind. When leaders are unable to contain their own anxieties, they become inconsistent and erratic in their behaviour or unpredictable. This can manifest itself as an abdication of responsibility or an over-involvement in the work of others. This adds to the levels of uncertainty that people experience and the likelihood of neurotic defences and regressive responses.

When anxieties are high, the capacity of leaders to contain anxieties becomes more important that their technical knowledge or intellect. An individual's capacity to be a reliable and dependable authority figures reflects their attachment style. Leaders with a secure attachment style have a basic trust in the world and are more able to tolerate uncertainty, their own anxiety and that of others. They feel secure in their relationships, have high self-esteem and self-confidence. This helps them to contain followers as they are less likely to panic or over-react to events. In contrast, leaders with an ambivalent attachment style tend to have anxieties around rejection and are wary in relationships. They are more easily hurt and distressed when they experience tensions in relationships and feel greater anxiety during endings or periods of change. They are less able to regulate theirs and others' emotional responses under stress and are more prone to strong emotional reactions. If leaders have an avoidant attachment style, they evade intimate and close relationships and dampen their emotional responses to situations. They are more cautious in forming relationships, preferring to maintain distant relationships. As a consequence, their followers are likely to experience them to be distant, transactional and emotionally unavailable. This can leave them feeling they have been abandoned and left to fend for themselves.

Unreliable authority also arises because of the speed with which leaders move in some organisations, fuelled by constant reorganisations. In one civil service department with which I worked over an 18-month period, the head of the department changed twice and most of the executive team were either on interim assignments or on temporary promotion. My impression was that the leaders were reluctant to invest emotionally in their teams and their teams did not authorise them to lead because they were assuming, perhaps unconsciously, that they should not get too attached. The result was a relatively low trust and transactional climate, which made change very difficult.

When the consulting unit and the executive education departments of the business school were integrated together, I took on the leadership role of the organisation development and change department, one of three new departments. I look back on this experience as one of the most painful and challenging of my career. I think it would be fair to say that the decision to undertake the restructuring had little support amongst those affected. A high level of uncertainty and disagreement also existed around the reasons the changes were necessary and the roles of the new departments. This situation was compounded by a decision to co-locate the new teams in the same offices with little time to plan or prepare for the move. This all made for a highly emotional, uncertain and fraught situation.

In my role as a leader, I faced not only the challenge of helping the newly formed team I now managed to process the changes, including their frustrations and losses, but also my own. I sat on a new management team for the faculty, which was both trying to work out and agree how the new structure needed to function and how we were going to work together. Over this period of ambiguity, confusion and uncertainty, I tried to make myself available to people, to listen and to try to think with my team and my peers about how to help the new structure to function. This was proving to be very difficult because of the multiple and competing assumptions around roles, responsibilities and decision making, allied with fears around losses of identity, status and power.

I found the hardest aspect of this work was listening to and acknowledging frustrations, anger and disagreements around the changes whilst at times feeling lost myself and unsure of what I could do. The changes had left everyone confused around roles, boundaries and authority, which created a collective sense of impotence. Behind this confusion lay anger and resentment around how the reorganisation had been handled. As the changes unfolded, I struggled at times to deal with my doubts about my leadership and my own sense of powerlessness, behind which lay my own omnipotent fantasies of how the situation could be resolved. An immense amount of noise and discussion arose around what needed to be sorted out, which acted as a distraction from the actual work that needed to be delivered. I often felt pulled between old loyalties and the need to take up my role in the new structure.

As time progressed and we started to settle down, as a team we were able to acknowledge the impact of the changes of us, what we had lost and to organise ourselves. In the midst of such turmoil, I found it hard to judge whether what I did was effective or not. This is perhaps one of the challenges of leading during disruption. The uncertainty and unusualness of the situation meant I had to constantly judge the efficacy of my actions. Was it helpful to challenge a point of view or let it go? Did what I say or do support learning or provoke defensiveness in others? Was it better to try to get the new structure to work as best as we could or to argue that it was a mistake and we needed to go back to first principles?

My answer to these questions changed over time and as events changed; as I oscillated between feelings of omnipotence, impotence and a realistic sense of what was possible and what was not. Looking back now, I can see that in my moments of helplessness I was too challenging and confronting, caught up in my anxieties and the anxieties of those whom I felt I represented.

Sensemaking and meaning making

Uncertainty and ambiguity necessitate both sense-giving and sensemaking with others. Leadership is a process of mutual influence in which leaders and followers attempt to understand and define situations and discern what action they need to take. To make sense is to see connections and continuity between the past, present and future and to try to understand the 'total' situation – not just isolated events. Leaders need to help people to think holistically, to see interdependencies and to make connections between different patterns and events.

Leaders play an active role in constructing and framing situations. Through the process of sense-giving, they frame the central issues or challenges for the organisation and, in doing so, attempt to legitimise and justify the actions that they see are necessary. A 'frame' organises people's perceptions, giving meaning to a situation in which they are acting (Vansina & Vansina, 2008). For example, the 'War on Terror' or 'Brexit' are frames that have shaped how people have made sense of particular situations and events. For instance, defining situations as a 'crisis', 'turnaround' or 'transformation' are rhetorical devices that are used by leaders to mobilise particular responses and support from different actors. The framing and narratives that are used will appeal to different interest groups and articulate particular strategic debates, frames of reference and ideologies. The process of sensemaking is therefore contested and political in nature.

For a leader to gain followership, they need to tap into what matters to people and what they care about both now and in the future. This involves a capacity to intuit and sense what will mobilise a group of people and a capacity to appeal to a higher purpose – an ideal. Their framing of a situation can help people to see continuity with the past and generate hope for the future. This involves the creation of a coherent narrative around events, changes and opportunities that helps the flow of action to become intelligible. Those affected by changes need to understand why they are important, what they will mean in practice and how they are likely to be affected. The use of language and metaphor can paint an attractive and compelling picture of the future, or leave people feeling threatened and fearful. A generative image of the future, for instance, can enable people to imagine new possibilities beyond the prevailing social order (Bushe & Storch, 2015).

Hosting conversations and facilitating dialogue

A metaphor is emerging of leaders as convenors (Block, 2009; Brown & Isaacs, 2005) or hosts of conversations (Wheatley & Frieze, 2011) and the creators of transitional space. To convene is to invite people together to have conversations that would not otherwise happen or help people have a different conversation to the one they habitually have with each other. Leaders are able to legitimise investing time in reflexive conversations rather than getting caught up in the frantic and obsessive focus on speed and performance. Through dialogue a group is able to explore different perspectives and to become more aware of their deeper assumptions. This requires the group to be open to difference and able to listen to different accounts and points of view. Leaders can help create these conditions by modelling a willingness to listen and hear others without the need to impose their beliefs or assumptions.

I worked with a global corporation that had embarked on the transformation of its finance function. A considerable amount of time, energy and resources were invested in designing and planning a new operating model. The project, however, was stalled because the leadership team was unable to agree on several fundamental principles and the underlying conflicts were not being addressed. At a very simple level, the leadership team were unable to have a candid and direct conversation about what was necessary and what they were willing to give up and lose to enable the change. The vice president was unwilling to confront his team and explore the conflict, preferring to stand back from the disagreement and delegate it to the transformation team to resolve.

After about six months, during which the level of frustrations had increased dramatically, the head of the transformation programme was able to convince the leadership team that they needed to meet more regularly to explore their different needs and points of view. A weekly meeting was put in the diary and this created the space for dialogue. Over time, the leadership team deepened its understanding of their different perspectives and trust started to develop. This enabled sufficient common ground to emerge between them for the underlying conflicts to be constructively resolved.

Leadership gestures and symbolic acts

Leadership is a cultural phenomenon and the behaviour of leaders is highly symbolic. As Clifford Geertz (1973) observed: 'Acts are the said of social discourse'. Leaders create meaning through what they do and say. Acts of leadership are enactments of cultural paradigms and are interpreted according to this dominant paradigm (Alvesson, 2013). These acts can interrupt established patterns, which symbolically communicates an intent to change or reinforce established patterns.

Adrian McLean distinguishes high and low-profile symbols in organisations (McLean, 2013) – see Table 12.1. High-profile symbols are the grand, crafted and public gestures such as speeches, logos and public statements. Low-profile symbols are the everyday, informal and mundane gestures that powerfully convey meaning. These are the seemingly insignificant, spontaneous and everyday acts and utterances. They include who speaks to whom, seating arrangements, who gets invited to a meeting and who does not, what gets attention and what does not, and physical symbols such as the layout of an office. High-profile symbols are the carefully crafted images and grand gestures. These are open to manipulation, coordination and careful crafting. Senior managers use high-profile symbols, such as logos, mission statements or public statements, to communicate specific meanings and messages to different audiences.

It is the low-profile symbols that convey the deeper meaning of events, behaviours and changes in organisations. Our interpretation of situations is

Table 12.1 A comparison of high- and low-profile symbols

High-profile symbols	Low-profile symbols
Speeches, mission statements, logos, codes of conduct, formal artefacts (buildings, furnishing and fabric), launches, ceremonies, rituals, celebrations, branding, publicity...	Spontaneous, mundane, unrehearsed, everyday actions and statements... seemingly insignificant acts and utterances
	Might include: preferred expressions, parking arrangements, status symbols etc.
	Encoded in background artefacts, signs, space, policies, procedures, slide presentations...

(McLean, 2013)

shaped by these seemingly insignificant gestures of everyday life, and not just the highly visible symbols. This might include someone's tone of voice, hand gestures, choice of language, avoidance of particular topics or responses to our ideas, and so on. Low-profile symbols have high currency (McLean, 2013). When there is a mismatch between high- and low-profile symbols (i.e. what is said is not backed up by what is done), then people lose trust and become cynical about the intentions of leaders. Leaders need to ensure therefore that high- and low-profile symbols complement each other. It is what leaders do during period of change, not what they say, that makes a difference (Rowland & Higgs, 2008).

The implication for leaders is to be aware of the patterns of interaction that persist across the organisation and how their acts, gestures and language reinforce or disturb existing paradigms, assumptions and patterns. How leaders engage with people is symbolically more significant than what they say in public or at high-profile events. This requires leaders to notice their involvement with others as they engage in doing something with them (Stacey, 2012). They can only do this if they are aware of how their gestures are expressions of existing patterns of meaning. Leadership of change thus necessitates the exercising of reflection both in-action and on-action (Schon, 1983).

Ethics of leadership

Throughout this book, I have explored the radical and fundamental changes that are taking place in organisations and the disruption that this presents for organisations, their employees and the communities of which they are embedded. The magnitude and consequences of these changes presents ongoing ethical dilemmas to leaders. The short-term financial interests of corporations frequently have long-term consequences for different stakeholders, society and the environment. New technologies such as artificial intelligence offer tangible benefits yet have potentially detrimental consequences for people and society. A computer algorithm can depersonalise relationships, by separating the decision maker from those who are affected, and hiding biases and prejudices from public scrutiny. The closing of a production site or a retail outlet can be legitimised behind market pressures, yet it has consequences for employees and local communities. The economic crisis of 2008 demonstrates what can happen when decisions are made on a systemic basis without due concern for those who might eventually be affected.

Leadership is about acting on behalf of the collective good, rather than on behalf of the few or a narrow range of stakeholders (Burnes, Hughes, & By, 2018). It is an ethical process (Burnes et al., 2018). Leadership during periods of change should involve exploring different choices with stakeholder groups to understand their implications. This process of social deliberation is critical if people are to question their aims and the consequences of their behaviour. Our ethics are, however, a reflection of what we do in practice when confronted with dilemmas and difficult choices.

Moral and ethical questions, however, generate both conscious and unconscious anxieties for leaders. If they are unable or unwilling to bear the weight of responsibility that comes with their role, then we find a disavowal of people's feelings, needs or suffering. In a rapidly challenging world, our values are also questioned, challenged and changed. Leadership in today's world and the future requires a critical consciousness and an awareness of the potential and actual consequences of one's decisions and courses of action.

Conclusion

Leadership is an act that is on behalf of the collective and its needs. It is effective when it mobilises a group's creativity, energy and passion to pursue a set of aims that are 'in the common good'. When the future is uncertain, leaders need to critically reflect on their actions, who they represent and whose interests they are acting on. This itself is uncertain and rarely clear when the future of an organisation is challenged or at risk. It requires judgement as to what is ethical, necessary and possible.

When people are anxious, confused and unsure of how to respond to a situation, they look to leaders for answers or direction. Those in positions of authority and responsibility face a choice to rescue people from their anxieties or to help them to find their own authority and solutions. The role of leadership under these conditions is to facilitate mature and critical reflection on the goals of the organisation and how people are working together to achieve them. This requires leaders to be able to tolerate their own anxieties and those of their followers and to take of the role of sense-givers and sense-makers.

Works cited

Alvesson, M. (2013). *Understanding organizational culture* (2nd ed.). London, England: Sage.
Alvesson, M., & Jonsson, A. (2016). The bumpy road to exercising leadership: Fragmentation in meaning and practice. *Leadership*, 1–18.

Barrett, F. (2012). *Yes to the mess: Surprising leadership lessons from Jazz*. Boston, MA: Harvard Business Review Press.

Bion, W. (1967). Notes on memory and desire. *The Psychoanalytic Forum*, 2(3), 272–273.

Block, P. (2009). *Community: The structure of belonging*. San Francisco, CA: Berrett-Koehler.

Brown, J., & Isaacs, D. (2005). *The World Café: Shaping our futures through conversations that matter*. San Francisco, CA: Berrett-Koehler.

Burnes, B., Hughes, M., & By, R. T. (2018). Reimagining organisational change leadership. *Leadership*, 14(2), 141–158.

Bushe, G., & Storch, J. (2015). Generative image: Sourcing novelty. In G. R. Bushe, & R. J. Marshak (Eds.), *Dialogic organization development: The theory and practice of transformational change*. San Francisco, CA: Berrett-Koehler.

Day, A., & Power, K. (2009). Developing leaders for a world of uncertainty, complexity and ambiguity. *The Ashridge Journal*, Winter 2009–2010, 20–25.

Flinn, K. (2018). *Leadership development: A complexity approach*. London, England: Routledge.

Geertz, C. (1973). *The interpretation of cultures*. New York, NY: Basic Books.

Haslam, S. A., Reicher, S. D., & Platow, M. J. (2011). *The new psychology of leadership: Identity, influence and power*. New York, NY: Psychology Press.

Keats, J. ([1817] 2014). *Selected letters* (J. Barnard, Ed.). London, England: Penguin Classics.

Krantz, J. (1998). Anxiety and the new order. In E. B. Klein, F. Gabelnick, & P. Herr (Eds.), *The psychodynamics of leadership* (pp. 77–108). Madison, CT: Psychosocial Press.

Lapierre, L. (1998). Mourning, potency, and power in management. *Human Resource Management*, 28(2), 177–189.

Lawrence, G. (2000). *Tongued with fire: Groups in experience*. London, England: Karnac Books.

McLean, A. (2013). *Leadership & cultural webs in organisations: Weavers' tales*. Bingley, England: Emerald.

Rowland, D., & Higgs, M. (2008). *Sustaining change: Leadership that works*. Chichester, England: John Wiley & Sons.

Schon, D. (1983). *The reflective practitioner*. New York, NY: Basic Books.

Stacey, R. (2012). *Tools and techniques of leadership and management: Meeting the challenge of complexity*. London, England; New York, NY: Routledge.

Vansina, L. S., & Vansina-Cobbaert, M.-J. (2008). *Psychodynamics for consultants and managers*. Oxford, England: Wiley-Blackwell.

Wheatley, M., & Frieze, D. (2011). Leadership in the age of complexity: From hero to host. *Resurgence Magazine*, Winter. Retrieved from http://margaretwheatley.com/wp-content/uploads/2014/12/Leadership-in-Age-of-Complexity.pdf

Zaleznik, A. (1991). Leading and managing: Understanding the difference. In M. F. Vries (Ed.), *Organizations on the couch: Clinical perspectives on organizational behavior and change* (pp. 97–119). San Francisco, CA.: The Jossey-Bass Management Series.

13 Concluding thoughts

The growing challenges facing humanity and organisations highlight our collective dependence on each other. The future of the planet and its ecology, our capacity to cope with globalisation and our ability to leverage the potential of new technologies require collective, creative and humane responses. We cannot solve the problems with which we are confronted on our own. Equally, what worked in the past is not working today and will not work in the future. The health of the planet, our communities and our psychology calls for us to question what we value, what we are doing and how we organise ourselves. We need to understand 'our worlds' very differently because for most of humankind, its character and complexity has changed fundamentally and is overwhelming our capacity to cope. Human survival necessitates the creation of new social institutions based on 'the primacy of symbiotic and collaborative, as compared with individualist and competitive, *relations*' (Trist, 1997, p. i). This requires both personal and social transformation (ibid.).

In a complex, uncertain and turbulent world, we are confronted with a choice to pull together or pull apart. Swim together or sink together. Those organisations that will survive and thrive in such contexts will need to create the conditions that encourage people to collaborate and work together to meet the ongoing demands on them and remain relevant. They will need to mobilise the collective resources, abilities and creativity of people to achieve common goals that add social value. This will necessitate organisational forms that support decentralised decision making, self-managed and flexible project teams and the exercising of personal authority. Such organisations will have to be based on cultures of trust, common values and a shared purpose for employees to be willing to be dependent on each other, be willing to take risks and to experience the vulnerability that comes with exercising personal responsibility.

For many organisations, their rapidly changing contexts necessitate some form of transformation of purpose and/or form. This needs to be a creative and social process; however, as I have tried to convey, it is far from straightforward. Each organisation has, to a degree, to work out for itself how it needs to adapt to its environment. In an environment of constant change, organisational forms cannot be static and we need to think more about the process of organising and how people learn to improvise, experiment and adapt together. This requires the active participation of employees in co-creating new ways of working and mechanisms for sharing insights and ideas across organisational networks.

Such transformations involve a paradigm shift, a reconfiguration of relationships and a change in identities. This dislocates the established structures of meaning, creates a crisis of identity and disrupts social relations. At an existential level, our whole being, sense of existence and purpose are challenged. This is deeply unsettling and disorientating, and throws us into anxiety. We experience loss, both individually and collectively, which needs to be mourned and worked through. Change of this magnitude and complexity can, however, be growth promoting and self-actualising, as it involves stepping outside of one's comfort zone and into a zone of anxiety (May, 1977). Whether this happens rests on people's ability to tolerate anxiety. If we are to face to the 'realities' of what is happening, rather than avoiding events or seeking to hold on to the past, we need to tolerate not knowing and uncertainty. Instead of attempting to create order, transformational change requires us to embrace disorder and the unfamiliar. However, when the emotional and intellectual demands of this challenge exceed our capacity to cope, we regress to primitive defences. We try to hold on to or idealise the past, deny and avoid the realities of our situation, blame or scapegoat others, resort to simplistic solutions or look for authoritarian leaders who promise fictitious certainties and solutions. This inhibits and limits our capacity to learn from experience and to respond creatively to events.

Change of this degree demands a recognition of and compassion for the loss that people are experiencing. Those affected need space, time and social support to work through their grief. We do not readily give up the known and the familiar. To create the conditions that enable change to emerge, organisations need to work out how to contain these anxieties, fears and doubts. In the past, stable social structures and hierarchies provided containment. In more fluid and unstable organisations, containment has to be created by creating temporary social spaces that facilitate communication and connection. Those leading changes need to recognise the needs of people during periods of disruption and invest in the maintenance, development and repair of human relations. The containment of anxiety requires leaders who have the emotional maturity and confidence to tolerate not knowing and to help people process intense and conflicting emotions.

More than anything, turbulence and uncertainty calls for organisations (and each of us) to adopt a humanistic philosophy that values human dignity and believes in the capacity of people to grow and take responsibility for their lives. As humans, we are at our most creative, imaginative and adaptive when our needs for belonging, self-direction and meaning are fulfilled. We are, however, observing an erosion of humanness in organisations (Vansina, 2013), which is affecting both organisations' adaptive capacity and the well-being of employees. More than ever, we need compassion for and an understanding of when anxieties, fears and insecurities are driving our's and others' behaviour. When we experience that others have our best interests at heart, trust us and believe in our potential, then we are more likely to see the unknown as an opportunity for exploration, discovery and the expression of our creative potential rather than a threat. We would do well do hold in mind that organisation transformation and change is at heart a social and participatory process, intertwined with technological developments and economic dynamics, and which cannot be engineered, designed or imposed by those who hold power.

Works cited

May, R. (1977). *The meaning of anxiety* (Revised ed.). New York, NY: Norton.

Trist, E. (1997). Introduction. In E. Trist, F. Emery, & H. Murray, *The social engagement of social science: A Tavistock anthology. Vol III: The socio-ecological perspective*. Philadelphia, PA: University of Pennsylvania.

Vansina, L. (2013). *Humaness in organisations: A psychodynamic contribution*. London, England: Karnac.

Index